D1642370

Smith & Nephew
in the Health Care Industry

Smith & Nephew in the Health Care Industry

James Foreman-Peck

Fellow, St Antony's College
Oxford, UK

Edward Elgar

Published by
Edward Elgar Publishing Limited
Gower House
Croft Road
Aldershot
Hants GU11 3HR
England

Edward Elgar Publishing Company
Old Post Road
Brookfield
Vermont 05036
USA

British Library Cataloguing in Publication Data
Foreman-Peck, James
    Smith & Nephew in the Health Care
    Industry
    I. Title
    338.76161510941

Library of Congress Cataloguing in Publication Data
Foreman-Peck, James.
        Smith & Nephew in the health care industry/James Foreman-Peck.
        p.   cm.
        Includes bibliographical references and index.
        1. Smith & Nephew Medical.   2. Pharmacy–Great Britain–History.
    I. Title.   II. Title: Smith & Nephew in the health care industry.
        [DNLM: 1. Smith & Nephew Medical.   2. Pharmacy–History–Great
    Britain.   QV 11 FA1 F7s 1995]
    RS68.S65F67   1995
    338.7'616151'0941—dc20
    DNLM/DLC
    for Library of Congress   94–21252
                                                                            CIP

ISBN 185898 085 2

Printed in Great Britain at the University Press, Cambridge

Contents

markets – R & D and in-house new products – Organization, management and personnel – Regulation and the environment – Conclusion

Plates

Tables and figures

TABLES

FIGURES

Acknowledgements

This project began when I was Professor of Economic History at the University of Hull, seeking closer links between the University and local business. I should like to thank past and present officers and employees of Smith & Nephew, both in Britain and overseas, and in particular, John Robinson, Alan Fryer and Peter Nind, for their help in writing this history. Dr Martin Barth kindly supplied some fascinating insights from Lohmann's archives and Alan Berton made available material about the history of Arthur Berton. Louisa Dallmeyer, Melanie Phelps and June Bogie all provided valuable research assistance at various times. A number of scholars generously commented on draft chapters or gave me essential information. Without implicating them in remaining shortcomings, I am grateful to J. Armstrong, P. Bartrip, J. Bellamy, I.G. Bulkley, T.A.B. Corley, L. Hannah, D. Jeremy, G. Jones, S.M. O'Neill, J. Tomlinson and R.B. Weir for their support.

1. The pharmacy business in Hull, 1856–96

In 1856 when Thomas James Smith opened his small shop in a medium sized town on the east coast of England, Britain was the 'workshop of the world'. British industrial achievements had been fully demonstrated at the Great Exhibition of 1851. More recently the Crimean War gave Florence Nightingale the opportunity to expose the terrible inadequacies of medical treatment during that conflict. Nonetheless, the theory and practice of medicine were already intensively studied.[1] Just before the mid-century anaesthesia was introduced and by the end of the 1860s antisepsis began to reduce the horrendous levels of post-operative mortality. Popular interest in advances such as these, and in science more generally, was widespread, and, as an early member of the Chemical and Geological Societies, T.J. Smith was in the forefront. Like many other Victorians he was equally concerned with wider theological and metaphysical issues, yet still found time to devote himself to local government and to charities.

In part because of these multifarious concerns, throughout the remainder of the nineteenth century T.J. Smith's business, initially selling medical supplies, remained small. Yet he was in an industry with great potential for growth. The company style and the industry tradition were to draw upon the expertise of the medical profession in hospitals by maintaining close personal relationships with customers. Ascertaining what the medical profession thought their work required and persuading them of the advantages of new products gave the business a strong orientation towards the user, rather than towards the producer. The market, rather than technology, drove Smith's company and those of his competitors.

Smith's business survival was supported by the economic advantages of location in mid-nineteenth century Hull. The town was Britain's third largest port, after London and Liverpool, concentrating on trade with Germany and Scandinavia. For freight, water transport to and from London and the South was convenient. Railway communications were poorer, but they did not inhibit T.J. from undertaking a gruelling schedule of commercial travelling, after he specialized in the wholesale branch of his trade in 1858.

1

FAMILY BACKGROUND

T.J. was the eldest of four children born in 1827 to Horatio Nelson Smith and his wife Jane. His brother, George Frederick, came next in 1832, and Amelia Ann, the only daughter, followed in 1839. The fourth child was a son, Edward, who eventually went to live in Sydney, Australia. Of the three who stayed in the UK George Frederick was the only one to marry; Thomas and Amelia remained single and in later years lived together in Hornsea.

T.J. Smith's father was sufficiently financially secure that in 1860 he could lend Thomas £500 to buy new premises. The family moved several times; Thomas was born in Whitfield (Northumberland), Amelia in Iron Acton (a Gloucestershire village)[2] and when Thomas moved to Hull in 1856 he did so from Grantham, Lincolnshire, where he had been apprenticed to a dispensing chemist or pharmacist. George Smith married a Miss Harding who bore three children. Their sons, in order of age, were Thomas Brooks and Horatio Nelson; their only daughter was named Annie (see Figure 1.1).

Both Thomas and George founded businesses and Thomas's nephew was the younger son of George, Horatio Nelson Smith. The origins of George's company are not clear but the firm was formally incorporated as G.F. Smith and Son (London) Ltd in 1904, when the official objective was to acquire and take over the business of paper merchants and agents previously carried on by George Frederick Smith and Thomas Brooks Smith. George and his son had been trading in Manchester, then in Newcastle in 1893, moved briefly to Nottingham, and finally settled in Hull in 1896, the year when H.N. was taken into T.J.'s Hull company. Despite the reference to London in George's business name, he shared premises with H.N. in the early days.

The business activities of the succeeding generation in the two firms, represented by Thomas Brooks Smith and Horatio Nelson Smith, show that both had an eye for the main chance. Horatio Nelson, or Nelson as he preferred to be called, was able to see the potential applications of a product. He also possessed a knack of securing patent rights and contracts for such products on favourable terms, as the history of Elastoplast and Cellona in Chapter 4 bears witness. Thomas Brooks managed at least one comparable business transaction, although perhaps more by luck than judgement (see Chapter 4, note 4).

PHARMACY AND PHARMACISTS IN THE NINETEENTH CENTURY

When T.J. Smith trained for the profession, pharmacy had only recently emerged as a separate body from the traditional, hierarchical, tripartite organization of

Figure 1.1   The Smith family tree

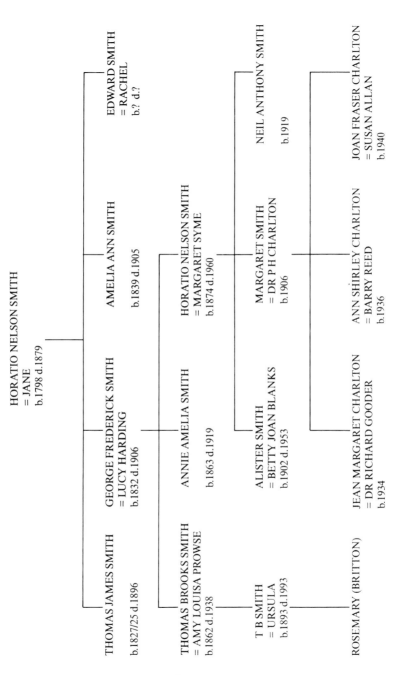

HORATIO NELSON SMITH
= JANE
b.1798 d.1879

THOMAS JAMES SMITH

b.1827/25 d.1896

GEORGE FREDERICK SMITH
= LUCY HARDING
b.1832 d.1906

AMELIA ANN SMITH

b.1839 d.1905

EDWARD SMITH
= RACHEL
b.? d.?

THOMAS BROOKS SMITH
= AMY LOUISA PROWSE
b.1862 d.1938

ANNIE AMELIA SMITH

b.1863 d.1919

HORATIO NELSON SMITH
= MARGARET SYME
b.1874 d.1960

T B SMITH
= URSULA
b.1893 d.1993

ALISTER SMITH
= BETTY JOAN BLANKS
b.1902 d.1953

MARGARET SMITH
= DR P H CHARLTON
b.1906

NEIL ANTHONY SMITH

b.1919

ROSEMARY (BRITTON)

JEAN MARGARET CHARLTON
= DR RICHARD GOODER
b.1934

ANN SHIRLEY CHARLTON
= BARRY REED
b.1936

JOAN FRASER CHARLTON
= SUSAN ALLAN
b.1940

3

Figure 1.2   Origins of the Pharmaceutical Society

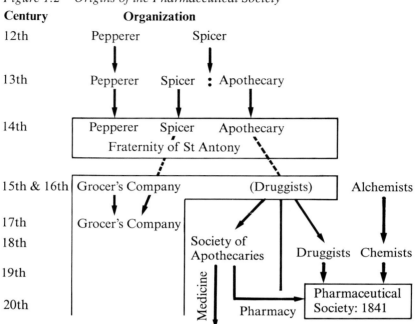

Century   Organization

Source: F.M.L. Poynter, *Evolution of Pharmacy in Britain*, London: Pitman, 1965.

the medical practitioners (physicians, surgeons, apothecaries). The Royal Pharmaceutical Society of Great Britain was formed in 1841. Many apothecaries became more interested in medicine than in pharmacy, leaving retail chemists and druggists to supply drugs (see Figure 1.2). However the formation of the society was a response to the potential restrictions of Benjamin Hawe's Medical Reform Bill proposed in 1841, whereby apothecaries attempted to stop pharmacists dispensing. Formed for protectionist purposes, the society gradually became a professional association, placing emphasis increasingly on science, education and the elevation of the profession. In order to achieve these goals the Society set its first examinations in February 1844, in accordance with a by-law made after the incorporation of the society by Royal Charter in 1843. The by-law required 'all persons, except those who were in business on their own account before the date of the charter, to pass an examination prior to admission [to the Society]'. (See Matthews 1962, pp. 120–25; Holloway 1987, pp. 129–58; Trease 1964, p. 191.)

    The examinations were both written and practical, and examinees could acquire their training by several routes. The society ran its own School of

Pharmacy in London from 1842 and in 1844 this became the first school in Britain to supplement chemical and pharmaceutical lectures with practical instruction in its own laboratory. There were several other private schools which students could attend; otherwise candidates were preferred by apprenticeship. As well as passing examinations, the Society required that associates be either the proprietor of a pharmacy or at least 'a superintendent engaged in the confidential management of the business of others' if they were to be admitted to membership. T.J. Smith supplemented his early practical pharmaceutical knowledge acquired while apprenticed in Grantham, Lincolnshire, with theoretical expertise gained by attending University College London between 1854 and 1855 (where both Lord Lister and Dr Gamgee, innovators in antisepsis and surgical dressings, studied).[3] The minute books of the Council of the Royal Pharmaceutical Society record T.J. Smith as having passed the Minor Examination in June 1855. In August he became the twelfth person to pass the Major Examination, enabling him to become a member of the society. On 6 February 1856, T.J. was formally elected as a member and six months later he bought a shop at 61 Whitefriargate, Hull, as a going concern, from his friend Mr (later Alderman) John L. Seaton, who had moved to Hull in 1847 from London.[4]

T.J. Smith was at least on corresponding terms with the founder of the Pharmaceutical Society.[5] A letter from Jacob Bell (of John Bell & Co., Oxford Street, Member of Parliament and a patron of the arts), to T.J. Smith in 1856, answered a query about cod liver oil, in which Smith was to specialize within a couple of years.

Jacob Bell wrote:

> With regard to the analysis of the oil I think there is a good field for further experiment. I believe it is the general opinion of those who have paid attention to the subject that the efficacy of cod liver oil does not depend on any medicinal agent ... but on the nutritive properties of the oil and its ready assimilation into the system. Where it agrees with the stomach it is easily digested and seems to act as a 'fuel' in the animal economy ... As you are investigating the subject the result of your experiments in the form of a paper for one of our Pharmaceutical meetings would be acceptable in October or whenever ready.

T.J. apparently never took Jacob Bell up on his offer.

As the demand for urban health care grew during the nineteenth century, the number of chemists and druggists rose correspondingly. From between 20 and 30 in Hull during 1820 they grew to 51 by the late 1830s, and to 122 in the census of 1841 (though some of this number were still at the apprenticeship stage). By the 1861 census, there were almost 200 Hull chemists and druggists. Nottingham, where Jesse Boot began his empire, boasted only 47 in 1853 and 82 in 1874.[6] New or increasingly popular products, such as sugar-coated pills, could no longer most easily be manufactured at the back of the shop on demand, but were more efficiently made in factories. Consequently many pharmacists like T.J. Smith, Allen & Hanbury and Southalls directed their efforts away from retailing and towards production. Capital requirements were still no barrier to entering manufacturing and as professionally trained pharmacists, they knew what the market wanted. They also possessed the technical expertise both to manufacture and to control and monitor quality, potentially a matter of life or death in pharmacy.

Today the chief role of the pharmacist is to make up prescriptions provided for patients by doctors but in the second half of the nineteenth century matters were very different. Until the National Health Insurance Act of 1911, perhaps 90 per cent of doctors were still compounding and dispensing their own prescriptions.[7] Most medicaments did not require prescriptions and visiting the doctor was an expense which many could not afford. The pharmacist was therefore often a family's first port of call for medical treatment, especially since traditional rural remedies were far less available in the rapidly expanding towns. Medical practitioners sometimes took aggressive action over what they regarded as this infringement of their prerogative (Chapman, 1973, pp. 28, 41). Members of the Pharmaceutical Society too were defensive of their privileges of dispensing poisons and using the title of pharmacist secured by the 1868 Act. A decision of 1879 weakened their position and enhanced the strength of price-cutters and heavy advertisers, like Jesse Boot, who merely employed pharmacists. As a founder member of the Hull branch of the Pharmaceutical Society (by its second year consisting of 20 full members and 12 associates) it was clear on whose side T.J.'s sympathies lay (Bellamy 1968).

The proliferation of trade associations of pharmacists in Hull gives some indication of the motive for T.J.'s concentration on importing, processing and wholesaling, rather than retailing; competition was intense and new entrants many. As well as pursuing educational objectives, the associations made frequent but ultimately ineffectual attempts to control this competition. A Hull branch of the United Society of Chemists and Druggists was established in 1863, followed and perhaps replaced by the Hull Chemists' Association in 1868. From 1869 this association provided a subsidized education for trainee pharmacists – 26 pharmaceutical evenings were arranged, overseen by a lecturer from Hull Medical School (1831–69). The association also compiled a uniform price list. Of a total of 122 chemists, 68 agreed to the list. Membership of the Hull Chemists' Association peaked in the mid-1870s and then declined as the Chemists' and Druggists' Trade Association became prominent. This second organization was formed to protect the interests of the retail chemists who were being undercut by grocers and general stores selling proprietary medicines. Small retail chemists were also losing their dispensing business to the stores run by Boots in the Midlands, Lewis & Burroughs and Parkes in London, Day's and Timothy White's in the south and Taylor's and Inman's in the north of England. The Chemists' and Druggists' Trade Association was wound up in 1887, to be replaced nine years later by the Proprietary Articles Trade Association, similarly aiming to establish uniform prices, reasonable profits and better combination of retailers.

COD LIVER OIL AS A MEDICINE

T.J. Smith began business as a general retail chemist, but commercial pressures and his interest in cod liver oil soon encouraged him to become predominantly a wholesaler, supplying hospitals and dispensaries. An order of December 1857 shows wholesale business in bandages, absorbent white wool,[8] lint, tow,[9] belladonna plaster[10] and adhesive plaster. Although there is no mention of cod liver oil here, T.J. was dealing in it well before the oil was officially recognized in the 1864 British Pharmacopoeia. In a recommendation dated 21 November 1859 a house surgeon of the Lincoln County Hospital wrote:

> Mr T.J. Smith of Hull has supplied this hospital with cod liver oil for the last two and a half years, which both in quality and price has given me satisfaction.[11]

T.J. bought two cottages, 10 and 11 North Church Street, and converted them into a warehouse in 1860 with £500 borrowed from his father.[12] In the summer of the same year he visited Norway to buy cod liver oil. As there was no regular passenger service to the Lofoten Islands from Bergen, the Norwegian government allowed him to travel on one of their gunboats. Cod liver oil became an increasingly important part of the business and from 1861 T.J. described himself as 'a wholesale druggist and cod liver oil merchant'. An appreciation of the place of cod liver oil in mid-nineteenth century medicine is helpful to understanding his specialization.

Cod liver oil is first recorded as used by the medical profession in Britain during 1772 at Manchester Infirmary, by Drs Kay and Darby (Reed 1988). Apparently by chance, they found that when taken internally cod liver oil ameliorated the pain and immobility associated with chronic rheumatism. In 1782 Darby wrote:

> For several years after I came to the infirmary, I observed that many poor patients, who were received into the infirmary for the chronic rheumatism, after several weeks' trial of a variety of remedies, were discharged with little or no relief... About ten years since, an accidental circumstance discovered to us a remedy, which has been used with the greatest success, for the above complaint, but is

very little known in any county, except Lancashire; it is the cod, or ling liver oil. (Quoted in Cripps 1927.)

The efficacy of cod liver oil was but slowly recognized in the UK although conceded by the German medical profession from the early nineteenth century. Cod liver oil came to the attention of British doctors in 1841 through the publication of Dr John Bennett's 'Treatise on the Oleum Jecoris Aselli'(Bennett had spent some time studying in continental Europe). Henceforth the oil was adopted as a treatment for two common scourges of the time, rickets and consumption. In 1849 Dr Blausius Williams, while working at the Brompton Hospital for Consumption, collected details of the efficacy of cod liver oil in 542 cases of confirmed phthisis (a general term covering tuberculosis of the lung) in all age groups – a marked improvement in weight was found in 63 per cent of cases.[13] The contemporary appeal of cod liver oil can be appreciated when it is realized that in 1851–60 deaths from pulmonary tuberculosis among women around 30 ran at 450 per 100 000. By 1901 this had fallen to almost one-third of the mid-century level (PEP, 1937 p. 283). In 1865 cod liver oil was confidently recommended by the famous French clinician Trousseau as the 'well known and perfect cure for rickets'. (Quoted in Reed 1988.)

With the benefit of modern medical knowledge, the efficacy of cod liver oil in cases of rickets and consumption may be attributed principally to the high content of Vitamins A and D. In the case of rickets, a deficiency of Vitamin D makes the body unable to utilize calcium salts that are of fundamental importance in healthy bone formation. In both the prevention and treatment of consumption, now known as tuberculosis, environmental factors play a crucial role, but in the treatment of tuberculosis it is now believed essential to maintain a high intake of Vitamin D, and to a lesser extent, of Vitamin A.

Vitamins had not been identified in the second half of the nineteenth century. It was observation of the success of past treatment rather than theory that initiated the first administration of cod liver oil to patients. Not until 1918 did Sir Edward Mellenby prove the anti-rachitic activity of cod liver oil and a few years later Elmer McCollum identified the anti-rachitic factor as Vitamin D (Sneader 1985, pp. 242–4).

A major drawback of cod liver oil was the taste. Nowadays cod liver oil is therefore commonly taken in capsule form. The modern product in any case bears no comparison to that of the mid-nineteenth century, when the oil was deep golden brown in colour, with a strong and extremely unpleasant fishy flavour. Some London outpatients found the oil so unpleasant that they preferred to burn it in oil lamps instead. There was clearly a large market for a better-tasting product. T.J. Smith sought a means of supplying these potential customers. At the time cod liver oil was generally shipped from Newfoundland, although available elsewhere. During his 1860 visit to Norway, T.J. bought 750 gallons of cod liver oil and obtained contracts for further supplies, becoming the first Englishman to do so. Norwegian oil fulfilled the market's requirements; it tasted better than the traditional Newfoundland oil, with the added advantage of being cheaper. T.J. had been paying 4s. 9d. per gallon in London, whereas the Norwegian oil cost 3s. 6d., a price reduction of more than one quarter.

MARKETS AND MARKETING

With this stimulus T.J.'s business expanded; his ledgers show that in the same year, 1860, he secured many new contracts with large hospitals, especially those of London. Orders in these early years were sent to London and the south of England by sea, by way of Princes Dock. A year later, Thomas decided that the shop in Whitefriargate was too small and sought larger premises. He took over a house, shop and outbuildings at 10 North Churchside, at a rent of £18 a year.[14] In 1880 he bought the freehold for this site with a loan of £500 from his father, Horatio Nelson Smith, and shortly afterwards the premises next door were also acquired for the storage and refining of the oil.

A ledger covering the years from 1874 to 1888 shows more than 360 separate customer accounts, plus some pages of sundry others.[15] T.J. clearly served a national market; entries can be found for such geographically dispersed locations as Aberdeen, Truro, Yarmouth, Liverpool, Mold in Wales, Ventnor on the Isle of Wight and Dublin. There is also an entry for an early continental European customer – E.H. & D. Cordes, of Hamburg; outside Europe Viscountess Strangford placed an order for the Cairo Victoria Hospital in 1883.[16] Many of the accounts had been opened before the dates found in the ledger, since there are frequent transfers into this ledger from earlier ones. The total sales on some accounts are over £100 for the year of 1874, while two accounts, those of the Great Ormond Street Hospital and Brompton Hospital, both of London, exceed £300 (£301 10s. 4d. and £350 3s. 11d. respectively). During these years T.J. had on his books 117 hospitals (gross sales to hospitals for 1874 were £3 355 4s. 11d.), 53 chemists, wholesale chemists, druggists and dispensaries, 17 'photographic artists', and 39 Hull customers. Among other purchasers were Poor Law Unions and Guardians, asylums, convalescent homes, orphanages, grocers, printers, an 'Establishment for Gentlewomen, London', a bookseller, a currier, a cooper, an organ builder, a cabinet maker and one fishmonger! The cod liver oil was supplied in returnable containers and accounts were credited on return. By far the greatest proportion of business was in cod liver oil, but T.J. was also selling a wide variety of other products.

Testimonials[17] written at about the time of the move to North Churchside provide some evidence as to the regard in which T.J.'s cod liver oil was held. On 3 January 1861, William H. Short, resident apothecary of the Charing Cross Hospital, wrote:

> I have great pleasure in giving my testimony as to the purity of the Cod Liver Oil supplied by Mr T.J. Smith of Hull, finding it quite as efficacious as those oils for which we have been paying a much higher price – I can speak as to its being free from any nauseous taste, from personal experience.

Similarly, J.H. Colley, house surgeon at Yarmouth Royal Hospital, wrote on 7 March 1861:

> I am anxious to bear testimony to the great efficacy of Mr T.J. Smith's Cod Liver Oil and cannot too highly recommend it to all hospitals as being the best and most palatable I ever met with.

Later the same year J. Reeve Shorts MRCS, LLA Lond., resident surgeon of the Royal South Hampshire Infirmary, Southampton, wrote:

> I have much pleasure in offering my opinion as to the quality of the Cod Liver Oil supplied by Mr T.J. Smith of Hull. I consider it to be the best Cod Liver Oil in every respect that this Infirmary has ever consumed. The patients all say it agrees remarkably well with their stomachs. I believe it to be quite equal and even superior to Cod Liver Oil that formerly we paid three times the price for. I have taken it myself and thus personally can speak of its good effect. Mr T.J. Smith supplies this Institution with about eighty gallons per annum.

A similar testimonial of May 1861 from Reinhardt and Sons of 76 Briggate, Leeds, shows that he was also supplying retailers:

> We have been supplied for some time with Cod Liver Oil by Mr T.J. Smith of Hull to our entire satisfaction. We purchase his best quality, and never have a complaint.

Where some medicaments were concerned testimonies were completely fictitious, but in T.J. Smith's case they were undoubtedly genuine, as were the sentiments they conveyed. That T.J. Smith really did supply an excellent product was demonstrated in 1883 at the International Fisheries Exhibition in London. He won a gold medal for his oil, the only British supplier to do so.

Collecting testimonials was only one way in which chemists and druggists could provide information for potential customers in order to encourage sales; another was the use of brand names. Branding of patent medicines took several distinct forms. Medicines were often advertised as being developed by a member of the medical profession, such as Dr Williams's Pink Pills for

Pale People (Corley 1987). Whether association with a member of the medical profession was claimed or not, another common selling device was to use an adjective suggesting purity, goodness, value or some similar virtue. Smith only took this course after it was suggested to him by a doctor, as late as March 1880. Mr Reginald Thompson, a member of the medical staff at the Brompton Hospital, London, had been corresponding with T.J. Smith since 3 May 1876 on the subject of cod liver oil.[18] In his first letter he asked numerous questions as to the differences between Norwegian and Newfoundland oil and on what they depended, which oil T.J. had most demand for, and on whether certain oil was brown due to the poor quality of the liver in its manufacturing. T.J. visited him in London and lent him some books on the matter. In March 1880 Reginald Thompson suggested a brand name for the proprietary marketing of T.J.'s cod liver oil.

> You would I doubt not have a very good sale for your best oil specially bottled and sent out with a registered title – perhaps Paragon would do... A pure tasteless inexpensive oil is a desideratum and I think your best oil will serve every purpose.

Smith took his advice and Paragon Cod Liver Oil sold well into the twentieth century.

T.J.'s Norwegian cod liver oil possessed two advantages over that from Newfoundland. First, the closer proximity to Britain of Norway as compared with Newfoundland meant that supplies were fresher, enhancing the comparative flavour of the oil, and reducing the price by economizing on transport costs. Second, the Norwegians had developed a process by which the stearine (the fat in its solid form) could be removed from the oil, yielding a purer, clearer product. These facts explain the success and extension of T.J. Smith's business in the early years. They do not explain his later success at the International Fisheries Exhibition; by 1883 both the novel source and manufacturing technique were exploited by many others.

Ernest Cripps (1927) claims that the earliest manufacture of cod liver oil took place at Allen & Hanbury's Plough Court pharmacy.

> The livers were bought at Billingsgate Market and were boiled down during the night in copper pans over charcoal fires. Two of the staff would spend most of the night over the preparation, the livers being stirred till pulped and the oil strained out through flannel. The method of storing the oil was in large earthen Florence jars; an ordinary dinner plate covered the mouth and was secured to it by plaster of Paris.

As the popularity of cod liver oil increased, the Plough Court pharmacy had neither the space nor the facilities for making the required quantity of oil. In 1860, the same year as T.J. Smith secured contracts in Norway, a representative of Allen & Hanbury was sent out to Newfoundland to set up a factory for production of the oil, which was then shipped to England and refined. This was an unfortunate decision for the company for 'only four years later, in 1864, medical opinion pronounced...the oil from cod caught in Norwegian waters to be of better quality than that from the Newfoundland fisheries'. Such evidence suggests that T.J. was well ahead of his contemporaries. Allen & Hanbury are said to have been 'quick...to keep abreast of the best knowledge of the day [for they] set up the first factory [in Norway]' as soon as medical opinions were known (Cripps 1927). In adopting Norwegian oil, T.J. Smith was four years ahead of them.

There were several subsequent ways in which the taste and appearance of cod liver oil were improved. The most important were the blending of different oils, and using the action of sunlight on the blended product. T.J. employed both practices with the help of his foreman, James Reed. The interior of the premises of 10 and 11 North Churchside was lined with tanks of varying capacity from 100 to 500 gallons. When blended, the oil was put on a flat roof adjoining the premises in one-and-a-half gallon bottles to be bleached by the sun, a process which also enhanced the taste.

Although he was first in the British market to exploit Norwegian cod liver oil, T.J. did not reap the greater part of the rewards. Longer established and bigger competitors were able to bring down costs and control quality by establishing plants in Norway where the cod was caught. Southalls of Birmingham, ironically later to be merged with Smith & Nephew, had become an early multinational in 1879, with a (seasonal) factory north of the Arctic circle, and Allen & Hanbury preceded them in 1864. By the beginning of the century, rising costs in Norway shifted both plants to the North of Scotland. Hull nonetheless retained a foothold in the business.

Why T.J. Smith favoured Norwegian oil so much earlier than others must be explained by his location in Hull. He began trading in Hull before he imported Norwegian oil and the subsequent establishment of a regular shipping service between Hull and Norway enhanced information flows and lowered transport costs relative to those of competitors elsewhere.

LOCATION

When T.J. Smith first set up shop, Hull was a small but growing industrial centre and port. In 1851 population reached 84 690, rising to 150 924 in 1881. Over the 30-year period this represents an increase of more than three-quarters or an annual average growth of 1.9 per cent. A rather lower growth in housing between 1831 and 1861 was achieved, the number of dwellings rising by about two-thirds, from 12 000 to over 20 000.

A small town, Hull was one of England's largest ports, with the consequence that most business activity was based directly or indirectly on seaborne trade. Large employing industries in Hull were shipping, ship building, oil milling, plant manufacture, fishing and cotton manufacture. However business tended to remain small in scale; there were 41 shipping firms in Hull in 1878, but of these only five owned more than six ships.[19] Like Smith & Nephew, some were destined eventually to grow large. In 1840 Isaac Reckitt established the company that has become Reckitt and Colman. Joseph Rank, a flour miller, began business on his own account in Hull in 1875; his firm is now known as Rank Hovis (Bellamy 1966).

Hull was well placed for overseas trade with Northern Europe which, although advantageous in many respects, also suffered drawbacks as well – employment tended to be seasonal due to the freezing of the Baltic in winter, and the port suffered severe disruption during European wars. Import figures show the predominant trade pattern. In 1860, 554 000 tonnes out of a total tonnage of 711 000 came from Northern European ports. More foreign than British tonnage arrived from several countries, notably Norway, Sweden, Denmark and Germany. In 1858 the shipping firm of T. Wilson and Sons scheduled the first regular weekly sailings to Scandinavia – to Christiansund, Christiana (Oslo) and Gothenburg. As suggested above, the date of this development is important for the present study since T.J. Smith used the service for his oil imports within two years of its inception. The service to and from Hamburg was more comprehensive, leaving four times a week, on Tuesday, Wednesday, Friday and Saturday. The German connection was also to prove decisive in his company's future. Similarly there was an intracountry service to London on Wednesdays and Saturdays.[20] Coastal water transport freight volumes at the beginning of the twentieth century were large in comparison with railways, and T.J. took full advantage of Hull's shipping facilities.[21]

Hull was served by a comprehensive inland waterway network. Goods could be shipped up the Trent to Nottinghamshire and Staffordshire, through the Aire and Calder navigation system to Sheffield and Leeds, and up the Ouse to York. For rail transport Hull was not ideally positioned – the town was 35 miles from York, the nearest station on the main London to North East railway. July 1840 saw the opening of track linking Hull to the West Riding, via Selby to Leeds.[22] Hull's rival on the other side of the Humber estuary, Grimsby, was far better served by railways – a line direct to Peterborough and London was opened in 1850. A rural line between Hull and Hornsea was opened in 1864, which within two years had merged with the North Eastern Railway. (See Gillett and MacMahon 1989, p. 308; ch. 21 generally; *Victoria History* 1969, pp. 394–5.) T.J. Smith lived in Hessle during the early years of his business, but later moved to Hornsea with his sister Amelia when the construction of the railway line made feasible travelling to work in Hull from Hornsea.

Hull's medical community, too small to support T.J.'s business on its own, was nonetheless distinguished. The Hull and East Riding School of Medicine in Kingston Square opened in 1832 and was closed down in July 1869. It was one of the earliest provincial schools, being preceded by those of Manchester (1824), Birmingham (1825), Sheffield (1828) and Leeds (1831), but itself antedating those of Bristol (1833) and Newcastle, Liverpool and York (1834). The certificates of the Hull school were recognized by the Royal College of Surgeons, and in his presidential address at the 1850 meeting in Hull of the Provincial Medical and Surgical Association (now the BMA), Dr F. Horner paid it the following compliment: 'Nor should I omit the medical school; the best test of its efficacy is that its pupils have invariably passed their examinations in London with the highest credit and ability'. (Quoted in Rolleston 1933.) A Hull Medical Society was established in 1888.

That Hull should have remained a viable production centre for Smith & Nephew for so long owes less to the persistence of these institutional and intellectual assets than to a combination of relatively cheap land, a suitable labour force and tolerable accessibility. But for T.J. Smith, the founder of a new small business, the cultural environment *was* a matter of importance.

T.J. SMITH'S INTELLECTUAL AND PHILANTHROPIC ACTIVITIES

T.J. was a Fellow of both the Chemical Society (from 1856) and the Geological Society. Whether a branch of the Chemical Society existed in Hull is not known, but a local Geological Society was founded in 1888. In 1896, the year of T.J.'s death, the society had 60 members and provided winter lectures and summer excursions. There was also a Literary and Philosophical Society in Hull, which attained 400 members. Judging by his interests T.J. would have belonged to this society. One of the few surviving pieces he wrote was an 1860 address to a school in the village of Tealby, Lincolnshire, entitled 'Work and Rest'. An example of the style is:

> Language is imperfect no more so where the term common is employed. Light, dark and life are all common yet almost miraculous…Work is also common and antedates the fall of man. God makes available the fruits of creation for men to use by labour. Human work is woven into the texture of our earth. Man is a tool user by nature.[23]

Further evidence of his concerns may be gleaned from another talk of his in 1875.

Last Saturday evening a large audience were gathered together in the Albion day-school to hear Mr Councillor T.J. Smith give some account of a visit to Bavaria to witness the 'Passion Play of Ober Ammergau'... Copious extracts were given, and comments made on the incidents of the play, the question of Pilate 'What is truth?' being forcibly dwelt upon.[24]

T.J. was proud of his learning. He required his daybooks to be headed with the dates in Latin. He was also keen to save money. Instead of buying ruled account books he purchased plain paper and had it bound by a local book binder.

In 1875 T.J. became a local government councillor, at first representing the Lowgate ward and later Queens ward, after a boundary rearrangement. He remained a councillor until 1882, only to resume these responsibilities in 1885, retaining a seat until 1892.[25] While serving on the council he was a member of numerous committees and subcommittees. T.J. served regularly on the Finance Committee, the Parliamentary Bills Committee, the Grammar School Committee, the Coal Committee and the Sanitary Committee. His place on the Parliamentary Bills Committee, showing an interest in the political environment, may be linked to his membership of the East Yorkshire Conservative Association.

A natural development from his interest in medicine and social welfare was his membership of the Sanitary Committee. From 1876 public health and housing was the responsibility of the Hull Corporation, which was then faced with two major problems. First, the ever-growing population, exacerbated by Hull being a main immigration port, put a strain on housing. Second, Hull's large and expanding overseas trade meant that the risk of epidemics from abroad was high. Sanitary improvement was accelerated by two crises: high mortality from infantile diarrhoea from the 1870s through to the first decade of this century; and the scarlet fever epidemic during the second half of 1882 which killed 689 people. (See *Victoria History* 1969, vol. 1, pp. 265–6; Gillett and MacMahon 1989, pp. 376, 286–9, 380.) During the crisis years of 1878 and 1879 T.J. was honorary secretary to the Mansion House Relief Fund Committee.[26] He also served the Hull Chamber of Commerce for many years as honorary secretary and honorary treasurer, and for two years as president (1879–80). He jointly founded the Hull branch of the Hospital Sunday Collections in 1873 (a means of voluntarily financing hospitals). From 1876 T.J. was joint honorary secretary of the Charity Organization Society and was, in the words of a local newspaper of the day, 'ever a useful worker in all charitable undertakings and institutions in the Town'. It should be recognized, however, that in his commitment of time to local government and charities, T.J. Smith was certainly not a unique nineteenth century businessman. Among many others, Sir Thomas Barclay, discussed in Chapter 2, was similarly active.[27]

CONCLUSION

After a protracted illness, T.J. Smith died in 1896. The business then employed a manager/commercial traveller William Bousfield, the oil foreman James Reed, and the 35-year-old 'lad', Alfred Mowforth.[28] James Reed was a friend of the family by then. G.F. Smith and H.N. set him up in business at 9 Churchside by 1905 as a tobacconist in recognition that T.J. wanted Reed's contribution appreciated.[29] Nine months before his death T.J. invited his nephew Horatio Nelson Smith to join his firm. Soon afterwards H.N. became a partner.

T.J. Smith's enterprise was sufficient to provide him with a living, but not much more. Without his nephew's entrepreneurship, the twentieth century would have heard little of his business. T.J. decided to make his contribution to the community through charity and political administration, as well as through business. His choice was to keep the business small.

The younger, unqualified, Jesse Boot offers a striking contrast. His mother's shop was still described as a medical botanist in 1870 but, beginning manufacture of a small number of patent medicines only in 1885, by 1893 Boot owned 33 retail chemist outlets and 92 in the year of T.J.'s death (Chapman 1973, pp. 61–2, 77). The potential was there for a larger enterprise in Hull, but not one based primarily on cod liver oil, as was T.J.'s.

NOTES

1. Florence Nightingale (1820–1910), widely regarded as the founder of modern nursing, was born in Florence to wealthy parents. By 1844 she was clear that her vocation was to nurse, and first gained experience in Germany. She successfully reorganized a small Harley Street hospital in 1853 and the next year sailed to the Crimea with 38 nurses to work in military hospitals. There her nightly rounds gained her the title of 'the lady with the lamp'. Her voluminous *Notes on Matters Affecting the Health, Efficiency and Hospital Administration of the British Army* was published in 1858. She founded her Nightingale Nursing School at St Thomas's Hospital, London, in 1860.
2. See UK *Census of Population 1881*.
3. The evidence is a 1960 memo from H.N. Smith in the Smith & Nephew Archives referring to a certificate of University College London lent to the University of Hull for an exhibition. H.N. died in 1960 and the certificate itself is presumably held by his family. T.J. will not have formally studied for his Pharmaceutical Society exams there because the University of London had declined to teach for them. The Society's School of Pharmacy was almost next door to University College in Bloomsbury. See Matthews (1962), p. 159.
4. *Hull Times*, 14 February 1903. Seaton did not move out of Hull or pharmacy; he had become interested in oil refinery and set up a business at Bankside which continues today. See Bellamy (1968).
5. On Jacob Bell see Holloway (1991), chap. 1.
6. See Bellamy (1968). Holloway (1991), p. 36 presents a table of the growth of pharmacists in selected towns, excluding Hull and Birmingham, to 1850.
7. 'Outside cities and towns, the pharmacist rarely saw a prescription unless he or she had an

arrangement with a Friendly Society or a doctor's club.' *Pharmaceutical Journal*, Supplement, 27 April 1991, p. 13.

8. Probably what is now called cotton wool.
9. A form of jute that is very hygroscopic, absorbing up to 25 per cent of moisture, that was used as a dressing for wounds.
10. Belladonna is the juice of the deadly nightshade and its active ingredient is atropine. Plaster of belladonna is used in the treatment of muscular rheumatism and may be applied to the breasts to arrest the formation of milk in threatened abscess. It is doubtful that the belladonna in plaster is of any real therapeutic value.
11. Smith & Nephew Archives, Hull.
12. Notes prepared by L. Sherwood Selle, 20 December 1954, based on T.J. Smith's letters to John Seaton.
13. Dubos and Dubos (1953), pp. 139–40. The authors point out that it was still used in TB cases as a vitamin and dietary supplement at the time of writing and that it was a matter for conjecture whether the cruder oil then used contained some additional as yet unidentified beneficial substance.
14. Contract in Smith & Nephew Archives, Hull.
15. Compiled by June Bogie.
16. Emily Strangford, author of *Egyptian Sepulchres and Syrian Shrines* (1860) and a pamphlet *Hospital Training for Ladies*, was a nursing reformer. She went to Cairo in 1882 under the aegis of the Order of St John to organize a hospital for British officers and the soldiers of the Egyptian Khedive. See Summers (1987), pp. 48–9.
17. Smith & Nephew Archives, Hull.
18. Smith & Nephew Archives, Hull.
19. *Victoria History: A History of Yorkshire East Riding*, Oxford University Press (1969), vol. 1 p. 227. The exceptions were the large cotton mills but the first had closed by 1878.
20. *Victoria History*, p. 220; *White's General and Commercial Directory of Hull and District*, William White (1882).
21. See Armstrong (1987). The despatch book of 1894 shows that by this time most goods went by rail, although Grimsby and East Anglia were served by steamer.
22. See Bellamy (1971), pp. 23,31,42. In 1869 the Hull–Doncaster line was opened and in 1885 the Hull–Barnsley link.
23. The talk shows the extraordinary breadth of T.J.'s interests, ranging over geology, geography, history, agriculture and science. He was addressing (or expecting to address) primarily agricultural workers. The chances are that, like the Southalls in Chapter 2, he was interested in the Adult School movement.
24. See 'Saturday Evenings for the People', *Hull News*, 7 August 1875.
25. Obituary, Eastern Morning News, 5 October 1896; Obituary, *Pharmaceutical Journal*, 17 October 1896, p. 356; (Hull) *Daily Mail*, 7 October 1896, p 4; *Chemist and Druggist*, 10 October 1896, p. 566.
26. See *Pharmaceutical Journal*, 17 October 1896, p. 356.
27. More generally see Nenadic (1991). Gillett and MacMahon (1989; p. 378) have harsh words to say about the probity of some Hull businessmen.
28. See 'Meeting HN', *Sanaco News*, 1, pt 1 (1954), p. 17.
29. Letters from Amelia Smith to J. Reed 1896, 1900, from H.N. in 1898 on purchase of 9 North Church Side by auction, memorandum of agreement 1905. Reed had sold patent medicines from 9 Church Side until 1889 when his licence was transferred to 199 Regent Street, Hull. In possession of S. Reed.

2. Nineteenth century origins: family enterprise in Birmingham and Lancashire

Even before T.J. Smith first opened for business, other enterprises, later to join Smith & Nephew, were already trading. Their traditions modified the company style, shifting management goals and methods of problem solving. Unlike businesses in countries that began industrializing later, Smith & Nephew operated in markets where the growth of demand was slower and where a large number of relatively small firms was already well established. Expansion in the later twentieth century therefore required that many of these enterprises cease independent operation if economies of scale in production and marketing were to be reaped. Rather than force them out of business, Smith & Nephew absorbed them into a structure that preserved some of their distinctiveness but made them viable in a manner quite impossible had they not been integrated into the group. Lancashire textiles were to find new directions in health care through Smith & Nephew and Southalls of Birmingham eventually spearheaded Smith & Nephew's consumer products.

Almost everywhere in the first half of the nineteenth century businesses were family enterprises even when they outgrew the home where they so often started. Not only were top managerial positions passed down from father to son but so were jobs on the shop floor. Family-provided capital ensured continuing family control. Even when more money was needed for investment than the family was able to supply, generally they continued to hold a controlling interest. This 'personal capitalism' was willing to admit other, non-family, managerial talent. Smith & Nephew's nineteenth century forebears show how other families could be absorbed into the hereditary management organization, sometimes with and sometimes without acquiring an interest in the firm's capital.

How well 'personal capitalism' served the British economy continues to be hotly debated. Lancashire, until the First World War, dominated the world textile industry and the industrial structure of small, increasingly highly specialized family-run enterprises went unquestioned. In Birmingham, the emergence of German superiority in pharmaceuticals and inorganic and fine chemicals from the last quarter of the nineteenth century was readily apparent. There the need for new approaches to industry was felt, but not found, until after the Second World War.

BIRMINGHAM: GENTLEMEN AND PLAYERS

Family enterprise had seemed particularly appropriate in the previous century for the mushrooming small metal workshops and houses of Birmingham and the Black Country, where nails, locks, files and such-like were forged with tools no more sophisticated than anvils, hammers and vices.

Rapid population growth and rising incomes in the nineteenth century created a far stronger demand for medical supplies in Birmingham than in Hull. The already long established Quaker family of Southall was therefore able to found their Birmingham business in 1820, earlier than T.J. Smith's, and to grow faster.

A now common impression of the evolution of the British economy over the last century and a half or more is that businessmen have been anxious to become 'gentleman' and cease to be 'players', e.g. Coleman (1973). The behaviour of the owners and managers of the Birmingham company of Southalls before 1914 suggests that being a 'gentleman' entailed a deep and practical concern for the wider social, professional and scientific environment within which their company traded. Though they built up a profitable company, profits were not their sole interest. The Southalls and the Barclays to different degrees, like T.J. Smith, were aware that business was only a means to an end. In principle being a professional businessman 'player' did not preclude exercising a practical 'gentlemanly' concern for the less well-off members of society. But since time is scarce, the likelihood is that a desire to maintain family managerial control as well could constrain the growth of the firm.

The firm of Southalls began when Thomas Southall, a chemist and druggist from Leominster, Hereford, moved to Birmingham and opened a small single-fronted shop at 17 Bull Street in 1820 (Southall 1957, p. 25). Trading was at first unsatisfactory but his brother William, also a chemist, joined him a year later and the business soon began to flourish, helped by the Quaker reputation for honesty and integrity. By 1835 the single-fronted shop window at Bull Street had been doubled (John Cadbury, the chocolate maker, into whose family the Southalls were to marry many years later, began trading just up the road). Thomas Southall had been apprenticed to John Bell of Oxford Street, London. (The Quaker John Bell, 1774–1849, was Jacob Bell's father – see Chapter 1.) With his brother William he did much to forward the incorporation of the Pharmaceutical Society in 1841.[1]

The next generation of Southalls entered the business in 1851 in the person of William junior (see the family tree of Figure 2.1), and trade was suffi-

Figure 2.1   The Southall family tree

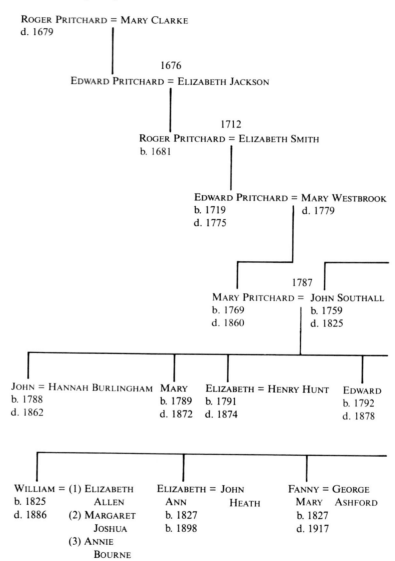

ROGER PRITCHARD = MARY CLARKE
d. 1679

1676
EDWARD PRITCHARD = ELIZABETH JACKSON

1712
ROGER PRITCHARD = ELIZABETH SMITH
b. 1681

EDWARD PRITCHARD = MARY WESTBROOK
b. 1719   d. 1779
d. 1775

1787
MARY PRITCHARD = JOHN SOUTHALL
b. 1769   b. 1759
d. 1860   d. 1825

JOHN = HANNAH BURLINGHAM   MARY   ELIZABETH = HENRY HUNT   EDWARD
b. 1788   b. 1789   b. 1791   b. 1792
d. 1862   d. 1872   d. 1874   d. 1878

WILLIAM = (1) ELIZABETH   ELIZABETH = JOHN   FANNY = GEORGE
b. 1825   ALLEN   ANN   HEATH   MARY   ASHFORD
d. 1886   (2) MARGARET   b. 1827   b. 1827
               JOSHUA   b. 1898   d. 1917
           (3) ANNIE
               BOURNE

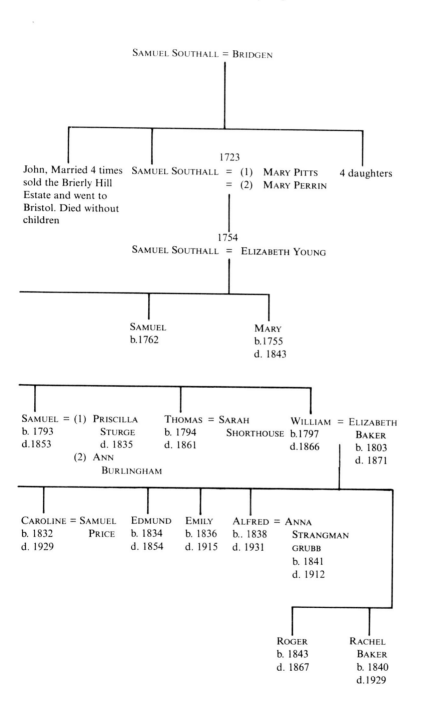

SAMUEL SOUTHALL = BRIDGEN

John, Married 4 times sold the Brierly Hill Estate and went to Bristol. Died without children

1723
SAMUEL SOUTHALL = (1) MARY PITTS
= (2) MARY PERRIN

4 daughters

1754
SAMUEL SOUTHALL = ELIZABETH YOUNG

SAMUEL
b.1762

MARY
b.1755
d. 1843

SAMUEL = (1) PRISCILLA
b. 1793   STURGE
d.1853   d. 1835
         (2) ANN
           BURLINGHAM

THOMAS = SARAH
b. 1794   SHORTHOUSE
d. 1861

WILLIAM = ELIZABETH
b.1797   BAKER
d.1866   b. 1803
          d. 1871

CAROLINE = SAMUEL
b. 1832   PRICE
d. 1929

EDMUND
b. 1834
d. 1854

EMILY
b. 1836
d. 1915

ALFRED = ANNA
b.. 1838   STRANGMAN
d. 1931   GRUBB
          b. 1841
          d. 1912

ROGER
b. 1843
d. 1867

RACHEL
BAKER
b. 1840
d.1929

ciently buoyant that a George Dymond was allowed to join them in 1856. In 1864 the Corporation of Birmingham Directory lists 'Southall, Son and Dymond, Wholesale Druggists and Chemists, 3 Coachyard, Bull Street, *and* 17 Bull Street'.

Long before the 1868 Pharmacy Act, Southalls had been concerned with standardization of compounds, and in 1869 introduced student sets of *Materia Medica*, a handbook treating the more important of the animal and vegetable drugs used in medicine, including the whole of those contained in the British Pharmacopoeia (the official classification of drugs and medicines). It was therefore appropriate that William junior should become President of the Pharmaceutical Society of Great Britain in 1879–80. In the same year he was President of the Birmingham Natural History and Microscopical Society. William junior combined erudition and religious standing with his leadership of professional bodies. He was a Fellow of the Linnaean Society[2], an examiner for the Pharmaceutical Society and was twice President of the Friends' Reading Society.

William junior's younger brother, Alfred, was apprenticed to the family business from the age of 17. Alfred Southall was a member of the 1865 Pharmaceutical Conference, becoming a member of the Pharmaceutical Council in 1886. Throughout his life he upheld the family Quaker tradition and at the age of 63, in 1901, Alfred retired from active business so as to throw himself more fully into temperance, religious and social work. He had already been teaching at the Adult School at Severn Street since 1855, influenced by a strong sense of duty rather than by a belief that he was a good teacher.[3]

As an encouragement to temperance, Alfred opened the first coffee house in Birmingham in 1876. He kept extremely fit even in old age; during his ninety-second year Alfred's diary recorded him cycling a total of 457 miles. His sons Alfred, William and Gilbert became directors of the family concern in due course, as did yet another William Southall, grandson of the founder William. William junior, the son of the founder, had a son Wilfred who joined the firm in 1884, becoming a director five years later (see Figure 2.1). Like Alfred, but a generation later, he too was drawn into Adult School teaching at Severn Street.

Undoubtedly the most prominent managerial influence on the company in this period was Sir Thomas William Barclay. Born in 1839, he was apprenticed to John Morson in Newcastle-upon-Tyne.[4] Thomas joined Southalls as a commercial traveller in 1861 because of his salesmanship talents. Seven years later, after the deaths of the founders in 1861 and in 1866, he became a partner in Southalls. He was accepted as a pharmaceutical chemist in 1871 and became president of the local chemists' association in 1874 and 1875. At a meeting about unfair prosecutions under the Sale of Food and Drugs Act,

Thomas was instrumental in the formation of the Chemists' and Druggists' Trade Association. He also represented British pharmacists at the International Congress of 1881.

Like T.J. Smith, Thomas Barclay took a close and active interest in local educational, political and economic affairs. He served on King's Norton School Board between 1875 and 1882. Between 1885 and 1894 he was a member of the Birmingham City Council (serving on the Water Committee) and was one of the pioneers of the scheme for bringing water from the Elan Valley in Wales to Birmingham, which was opened by King Edward VII in 1903. His lecture on the subject was published in 1888 and was elaborated in successive editions of his *The Future Water Supply of Birmingham*, the third of which was published in 1898.[5] Sir Thomas was also a Justice of the Peace for Warwickshire and Birmingham. He was a prominent Methodist, organizing a large-scale commemoration of the John Wesley bicentenary in 1903.[6] In 1908 he was knighted, sharing the distinction with another North-Eastern chemist, Joseph Swann, inventor of the electric light bulb.

Thomas Barclay's family also gained representation on the Board of Southalls. His eldest son, John, had joined the company in 1892 when he was 26 years old. John held a Bachelor of Science degree and was a lecturer in Materia Medica and Pharmacy at Mason University College, soon after absorbed by Birmingham University. Editor of Southalls' *Organic Materia Medica*, he died in a Swiss walking accident in 1903. Thomas Barclay junior, a qualified surveyor, second son of Thomas Barclay senior, joined the company with Alfred, William and Gilbert Southall in 1896. He was also on the Board and became the second chairman of the company on the death of his father in 1921.

PRODUCTS

Just as T.J. Smith was to do a generation later, the Southall brothers began as retailers, but they soon turned to the manufacture of drugs and chemicals. Minimum efficient rates of production generally supplied more than individual retailers could sell, providing an incentive to develop sales to other pharmacists. Southalls produced potassium iodide on a considerable scale by 1838, for company policy was to manufacture any chemical or galenical (a medicament in which several, usually herbal, remedies were mixed) which they needed but found impossible to buy in the right quality. Potassium iodide was widely employed as a remedy for syphilis, to lessen the secretion of milk and to absorb the products of inflammation. It was an expectorant and used in the treatment of lead poisoning. The problem with potassium iodide was that impurities were liable to poison the patient. Concerned to avoid association with any such misadventure, Southalls therefore manufactured the compound themselves. As a Quaker firm, Southalls inherited a reputation for fair dealing and a refusal to sell adulterated products. But they were tolerant of other religious practices, being happy to supply Cardinal Newman with a special kind of incense for the oratory at Edgbaston.

Between 1865 and 1875 Southalls extended their interests to cotton goods, surgical dressings and sanitary towels. Stimulated by demand during the American Civil War, oakum dressings (made from shredded old rope) found favour with a number of surgeons, who recommended Southalls as the suppliers (Bishop 1959, p. 58; Miall 1931, p. 138).

In the development of their dressing trade, Southalls worked closely with Dr Sampson Gamgee (1828–86) of Birmingham and Robinsons of Chesterfield. Gamgee was experimenting with cotton wool dressings in the late 1870s. When Southalls introduced him to Robinsons, the upshot was the Gamgee Tissue of 1880 made on machinery designed and manufactured by William Robinson and sold through Southalls (Elliott 1964, pp. 55–6; Bishop 1959, p. 76).

The decision to manufacture sanitary towels was no doubt influenced by the similarity of basic materials needed for surgical dressings. In the 1870s the secrecy and taboos surrounding this product made it a bold move, though one in keeping with the nineteenth century trend to commercialize previously home-made products. In 1880 the company was granted the first sanitary towel patent based on an idea from Dr Sampson Gamgee. Marketing the towels through drapers' shops was at first difficult. Drapers have now disappeared from retailing through competition from chain and department stores but until the 1960s these shops specialized in those items which women were expected to buy, not just rolls of cloth and curtains but hats, cheaper underwear and sanitary towels.

Thomas Barclay senior remarked in 1880, 'the squeamishness of the draper to stock the goods seems to be obstinately insuperable'. But a decade later drapers had overcome their inhibitions and did display 'Southalls' Specialities' as well as 'imitations from the US, Europe and the Colonies'.[7] Among the British imitators were Robinsons of Chesterfield, who began manufacture in 1886 using machinery and a method devised by William Robinson. William transferred rights in manufacture and sale of similar sanitary towels in the US to Southall Bros & Barclay in the same year in exchange for royalties.

The area needed to run the business then extended behind the shop at 17 Bull Street and along Dalton Street. Expanding dressing and towel manufacture put greater pressure on the available space. With sales booming, an additional workshop was built for towel production along the Lower Priory building line. This was finally fronted by an office block in about 1885. Laboratory accommodation was extended in 1871 to allow the company chemist to undertake technical analysis. Two years later Southalls introduced machinery for the manufacture of pills in bulk. In association with Professor Gamgee, Southalls began production of absorbent cotton wool and antiseptic surgical dressings.

In the last two decades of the century, the firm became extraordinarily eclectic. It supplied 300 000 gallons of artificial sea water for the aquarium at Aston in 1880 and in 1885 opened a scientific department for the supply of chemical and photographic materials. Analysis and research took up more time and more space and the equipment needed continual improvement. Original research and the assay of all drugs and chemicals in use were carried on to the extent that, by the turn of the century, 7 000 independent analyses were performed annually; the number had risen to more than 8 000 by 1910. From 1893 this work was described in Southalls *Annual Laboratory Reports* which were distributed among the profession worldwide.

Between 1865 and 1890 the partnership was mainly directed by Thomas Barclay senior and Alfred Southall (younger son of William the founder member). This period shows the greatest progress in the nineteenth century as the firm pioneered production, advertising and marketing of the first genuine sanitary towel, with associated security and protective garments; introduced basic surgical dressings; extended the factory to fill all the available grounds in Bull Street, along Dalton Street and along the south side of Lower Priory; and became large manufacturers of drugs and chemicals. Separate buildings on the site included laboratory and analytical premises, drug mills, pill factory, printing department, sanitary specialities, table waters, offices and wholesale counters.

In the shop each assistant was in charge of a special section of counter space and bottles on the shelves behind. He had small hand-scales, measure glasses, pestles, mortars, his own till and wore a white apron. The chemist would round pills or spread plasters while the customer sat opposite making what comment he saw fit. Prescriptions still could occasionally include dried cockroaches and cobwebs. In addition to making up prescriptions, Southalls pharmacists were expected to supply a variety of advice and assistance. Once a Southalls customer entered the shop in great distress, clutching his face and unable to speak. A perceptive senior leant over the counter and wrenched the man's dislocated jaw back into place (Southall 1957, pp. 26–8).

The company was well aware of the contribution of general advertising to sales. At the 1886 *conversazione* of the British Association at Bagley Hall, Southalls' ancient alchemist shop and laboratory 'At the Sign of the Crocodile' attracted enormous attention and gained a great deal of publicity for the firm.[8]

After the medical press had drawn attention to impurities in drinking water, a department for producing a series of table waters (made with distilled water only) was built in 1890. As a member of the Water Committee of the Birmingham City Council from 1885 to 1894, Sir Thomas was particularly concerned to avoid the consequences of contaminated drinking water, both in the short term with his bottled water, and in the long term, with his scheme for an improved public water supply.

T.J. Smith's business was too small to secure control and quality of Norwegian cod liver oil by integrating backwards but Southalls could improve competitiveness with this strategy. Southalls became a multinational company in 1879 by building a factory at Balstadt in the Lofoten Islands, off the Norwegian coast, for the manufacture of cod liver oil. The venture was to ensure a product which met Southalls' standard of purity, removed indigestible fats which tended to solidify in cold weather, and which they could guarantee as being made only from the livers of true cod. Guided by the same desire to guarantee pure products, Southalls also made castor oil and olive oil.

As Smith & Nephew withdrew from the cod liver oil business, Southalls' A1 cod liver oil sales boomed. When Thomas Barclay visited the Norwegian factory in the spring of 1902, there were 500 boats at the fishing station (compared with perhaps 2 000 in the whole district). The fishermen lived communally for the season in rented huts. About 40 000 persons worked in the area earning around £9 a head or 150 krona for the season. Southalls claimed the cods' livers but their roes were exported to the South of France, backbones and heads were used for manure and the remainder was sold as klipfish or stokfish to Catholic countries. Official rules limited the number of days on which fishing was allowed, to prevent depletion of stocks, but even so within the decade Southalls was obliged to shift operations to Buckie near Aberdeen. Competition from British firms, especially Allen & Hanbury, and a bad 1910 season in Norway precipitated the move.[9]

Sir Thomas Barclay was particularly concerned that the company by 1914 was becoming restricted to one product, sanitary towels, which made them vulnerable. He wrote to his son,

> We all remember that for many years we have often mourned over the fact that the business was largely dependent upon one speciality, which if anything happened in regard to it, would, with the enormous amount of capital in the business in the way of buildings, and plant etc., be ruinous because it was the Towels, and Towels alone which was the key to the success of the whole position. This, of course, we only breathe to each other in confidence, but has always been to me a sort of nightmare...

Sir Thomas's proposal was to market a competitor to the German product 'Sanatogen' – 'Vitafer' a concentrated food or nerve tonic. Developed by Southalls' chemist E.W. Mann, Vitafer allegedly tasted better than Sanatogen.

There would be a strong and regular demand for such a product, Sir Thomas maintained, and it would therefore be safe and profitable. Another Birmingham chemist and druggist, Alfred Bird (1811–78), had introduced a best-selling custard powder. James Crossley Eno (1820–1915) made large sums from his 'Fruit Salts' (Matthews 1962, p. 238). Two years earlier the German Dr Beiersdorf had brought out 'Nivea Creme' (though Sir Thomas did not show he was aware of this product which was to be acquired by his corporate descendants). Why should not Southall & Barclay achieve a similar success? Thomas junior objected that the advertising necessary to launch the product properly and to compete effectively with 'Sanatogen' would be enormous and the money would be better devoted to developing existing lines. He was overruled and a contract was negotiated to ensure a large and regular supply of separated milk ingredient.[10] But the launch date was not propitious and no more was heard of the product after the war.

GERMAN COMPETITION AND COOPERATION

As a prominent chemist, Sir Thomas was very conscious of the advantage that the German industry had achieved by the first decade of the twentieth century. He pointed out how much quicker the Germans were at exploiting radium (quoting Sir Frederick Treves of 'Elephant Man' fame) even though they were obliged to use ore from Cornwall. According to Sir Thomas, the nub of the problem was the lack of state aid to British universities, in marked contrast to the position in Germany. Development of an adequate British technological base was hindered by poor university funding.[11]

This concern for British industrial development did not prevent Sir Thomas cooperating with a German-led chemical cartel when his company's interests were served. Relatively high fixed costs of chemical production and low variable costs rendered price competition potentially ruinous, for competitors would cut prices as low as variable costs in the short run if necessary to maintain their market share. Avoiding this eventuality gave chemical firms a common interest in establishing durable market controls. In 1907 Southalls & Barclays joined the long established Iodine Preparations Combine to ensure an adequate supply of iodine. The purpose of the group was 'to share in the sale of iodine preparations in the same proportion as they took from the combinations in 1887/8'; the quantity of iodine worked determined the participating companies' sales quotas. Southalls' quota was fixed at 21 cwt per annum. The combination in Britain was organized by Leisler Bock in Glasgow, and in marked contrast to the US where such agreements were illegal, there was no need to be underhand about the organization. Though the rule books were confidential, they were printed and circulated among members.

The 1898 version of the agreement listed four Berlin companies, two in Milan and Waldhof, one each in Paris, Darmstadt and Dresden, and George Atkinson of London, the British Chemical Company of Glasgow, Howard & Sons of Stratford and T. Morson & Sons of London. Cohesion of the cartel was ensured by the requirement that each member deposit £1 000 in promissory notes. If the member broke a rule then some of the notes were forfeited.[12]

A more parasitical and less symbiotic relation with German industry emerged with the introduction of new bleaching technology in 1911. German companies undertook the expense of developing new equipment which Southalls could then copy and avoid development costs. Thomas junior reported that the new £280 vacuum kier (a vat in which cloth is boiled for bleaching) from Germany was a great success. Costs could be cut by passing the design on to British firms. Jacksons of Bolton undertook to make a comparable kier and supply it with a guarantee for only £188.[13] For relatively simple products there was little to be lost and something to be gained from adopting such a follower role. But in the pharmaceutical and medical devices sector in which Southalls were based, simplicity was becoming less common and the advantages of a continuing, systematic, large-scale industrial research programme were becoming more apparent.

When the historical roots of British relative economic decline since 1945 are sought, it is typically to these years, the period 1870–1914, that critics turn.[14] They point to a lack of interest and ability in new technology and entrepreneurial inertia. In particular they focus their attack on electrical engineering and organic and pharmaceutical chemicals, pointing to the German strength in these industries of the future. At first Britain held an advantage in the newer chemicals by virtue of her position as the world's greatest trader. During the mid-nineteenth century she was able to get privileged access to exotic substances from different parts of the globe that could form the basis of novel pharmaceutical preparations. Then in 1856 Perkin discovered the first aniline dye, initiating in Britain the world organic chemicals industry. Yet 20 years later the business had almost entirely migrated to Germany. Almost fifty companies entered the infant German pharmaceutical industry between 1870 and 1900. Bayer and BASF played key roles (see Haber 1971, p. 17). Bayer made a major breakthrough in organic chemistry when in 1878 they established that synthesis of indigo was viable (although nearly two decades were to elapse before commercial production could begin). BASF spent more than £1 million on development work, and in so doing took out 152 patents (see Reed 1992, p. 115). The established British chemical industry concentrated what research they undertook on alkaloids. The foremost research-oriented company in the British industry in these years was Burroughs Wellcome, founded in 1880 by two Americans of those names. Their Physiological Research Laboratories were opened in 1894, followed two years later by their Chemical Research Laboratories (Burroughs Wellcome 1980; Turner 1980).

What the Southalls & Barclays story suggests is that there was no lack of entrepreneurial vigour in the pharmaceutical industry. Profits were maintained by seeking what the market wanted and was prepared to pay for immediately. As William Lever (whose company, Lever Bros, became Unilever in 1929 after his death) and others demonstrated for soap, and Jesse Boot, Wellcome, Beecham and many others showed for patent medicines, in Britain this did not typically require investment in advanced technology but in advertising.[15] Britain's early urbanization created a mass market for basic consumer products not so obvious in nineteenth century Germany.

When the German dyestuffs industry demonstrated that profitable pharmaceuticals could be made from their technology, British firms aimed to copy them fairly quickly. But long established family firms were unwilling to change their organizations radically enough to accommodate the scientific research that was apparent in Germany and so rarely introduced new products in a market where trial and error was less and less appropriate. The traditionalist firm of May & Baker continued to maintain a technological base that was primarily a 'recipe book' of secrets (Slinn 1984, pp. 42–3). In fact the military requirements of self-sufficiency during the First World War intervened and accelerated the imitation and catching-up process. Southalls then began to manufacture salicylic acid, the best known medical use of which was in the German company Bayer's Aspirin, and Burroughs Wellcome took up the production of another German pharmaceutical discovery, Salvarsan.

Before 1914, although as we have seen Sir Thomas was anxious to diversify, he directed his attention to low technology consumer products, rather than to high technology producer goods. Organic and fine chemicals was only a small sector and different countries could be expected to develop different specialisms (Pollard 1989). Nonetheless it was an industry in which Britain lost a clear lead and the reason seems to be that the lack of a research culture blinded management to possibilities in this new field (Richardson 1968). They were therefore unwilling to devote the resources to research necessary to keep their company abreast of developments that could eventually prove profitable. That advance had to wait until after 1945. Equally it must be recognized that *at that time* humble items using low technology, may have conferred more benefit on society than technologically advanced pharmaceuticals.

Meanwhile, even before the outbreak of war, some of the widespread British hostility to Germany probably reflected a resentment at the German ability to make technical advances that enhanced their industrial competitiveness in a few sectors at British expense. But it was a reality that companies had to recognize. In 1914 Sir Thomas noted that antagonism towards the Germans could benefit the sales of a British Sanatogen substitute and in 1933 John Cochrane at Smith & Nephew reminded directors: 'Much has been said to our detriment on account of the German connections of Elastoplast'[16] (see chapter 4).

GOING PUBLIC: NEW CAPITAL FOR EXPANSION

If they neglected some new technology, Southall & Barclay did not ignore profits and growth. On 29 June 1898, Southall Bros & Barclay Ltd presented a prospectus to the public and a subscription list opened for the sale of 46 667 £1 preference shares. The prospectus described the principal activities thus:[17]

The business ... is now carried on in various departments as follows:-

Wholesale Chemists and Druggists	) Lower
	) Priory,
Druggists Sundriesmen and Druggists Shop Fitters	) Birm.
Pharmaceutical and Analytical Chemists	Bull St
Manufacturing Chemists and Drug Grinders	)
	) Dalton
Manufacturers of Surgical Dressings and	) Street,
Sanitary Appliances	) Birm.
	)
Manufacturers of Distilled Table Waters	)
Manufacturers of and Dealers in Scientific and	) Broad St,
Chemical Apparatus	) Birm.
Manufacturers of Cod Liver Oil	Balstad, Norway.

Outside capital was needed primarily to buy four acres of land at Saltley Common, Birmingham, and to build and equip factories on the site. Potential subscribers were told that sales in 1897 were higher than in any previous year and that rising net profits were more than sufficient to pay three times the dividends on all the preference shares being issued, which included 23 333 taken by the existing owners of the firm.[18] Property, equipment and stocks, exclusive of goodwill, were valued at £84 640 19s. 3d. The current issue of capital totalled £150 000, £80 000 in ordinary shares, none of which were offered to the public. Only the ordinary shares, held by the Southall and Barclay families, carried full voting rights. The expansion was the beginning of Southall Bros & Barclay as a public limited company, but still under family control. Over the next half century the business was to grow steadily on the Saltley site; by 1949 the Saltley Works occupied about eleven acres and employed 2 000 people.

At the turn of the century management efforts were concentrated on this site. Previously the dressings and towels made at Bull Street were almost certainly from finished cotton and gauzes bought in bulk, probably from Lancashire mills. Saltley was to be the new producer of cotton wool from raw materials, and gauze from the yarn stage. Machinery was needed for bleaching and carding cotton wool as well as looms for weaving and plant for bleaching the gauze and bandage cloth. It was then generally held that Lancashire expertise and the damp Lancashire climate were essential for this work. But this bold management decision proved right and Saltley flourished.

In the first two decades of the twentieth century, still well before the discovery of antibiotics, the demand for medicated dressings was at its most intense. With the experience in manufacturing drugs and chemicals now joined to the manufacture of dressings, Southalls was well placed to satisfy this demand. Surgical lint was the main medium used in the antiseptic treatment of wounds. It was a heavy cloth on which a nap was raised before impregnation with antiseptic and, in either plain or medicated form, was secured by bandage to give an external protection to wounds.

Southalls expanded by acquiring the use of Charford Mill, Bromsgrove. Weaving was one of the oldest industries in Bromsgrove, which was famous for its linen, woollen and cloth manufacture as long ago as the fifteenth century. Charford Mill has deeds dating from 1778 when it was used for corn grinding. In 1802 part of the mill was leased to a worsted manufacturer who made his wool in one section while corn grinding continued in another. William Garnett Taylor, then a patent pure lint manufacturer, bought the entire property in 1874. Mr Taylor died in 1895 and Charford Mill was leased to Southall Bros & Barclay Ltd in 1900 for 21 years. As sales of dressings and towels doubled between 1908 and 1913, not only was the new acquisition fully employed but mill extensions were needed.

LANCASHIRE COTTON

Southalls preference for supplying its own textile needs would not have concerned Lancashire before 1914 though perhaps it should. The world's first industrial revolution of the late eighteenth and early nineteenth century is typically located amidst the hills and fast-flowing streams and rivers of Lancashire. There a great number of cotton mills sprang up, operating the most advanced technology of the time. Many such mills eventually became

part of Smith & Nephew and earlier were company suppliers. By the outbreak of the First World War textiles alone accounted for one-quarter of
British exports. Extraordinary advances in productivity achieved by factory
machinery in this industry allowed Lancashire to conquer markets round the
world in the nineteenth century but also encouraged complacency in the face
of rising foreign competition. In 1911 the remark to a manufacturer that the
number of Japanese spindles was growing prompted the following response:

> My lad never again let anybody in Lancashire hear you talk this childish stuff
> about foreign competition. It's right enough for Londoners and such like, but it
> puts a born Lancashire man to shame as an ignoramus. It's just twaddle.

The manufacturer then went on to justify this position by the climate, Lancashire skills and brains and by the number of spindles in Oldham being greater
than in the rest of the world put together (Bowker 1928, p. 23).

Volume cotton textile production at very low cost was achieved towards
the end of the nineteenth century by great specialization in different functions
or stages of production and marketing including:

- cotton buying and grading
- shipping
- warehousing
- spinning
- doubling
- weaving
- dyeing
- bleaching
- printing
- finishing
- yarn and cloth agenting
- wholesaling

Three typical Lancashire families specializing primarily in spinning and weaving were the Whiteheads, the Tunstills and the Ecroyds. Though their business dynasties disappeared long ago, they contributed buildings, management and expertise to the present Smith & Nephew group. David Whitehead
& Sons is linked to Smith & Nephew through the management team that left
in 1947 to join Glen Mills and in due course provided a chief executive and
deputy chairman as well as other senior management for the Smith & Nephew
group. Like Southalls the company's prosperity depended upon the cooperation of successive generations of not just one family but two. The Whitehead
brothers began the textile firm of David Whitehead in 1815 in the Rossendale

valley. Soon they shifted from water to steam power in Rawtenstall. They built the first Methodist church in the town, and founded the first day school, savings bank and the first Provident Trust. David was keenly interested in political reform and entertained the radical MPs Richard Cobden and John Bright at his home. Together they discussed how to repeal the Corn Laws and the formation of the first cooperative store that opened in Rochdale. A day school for employees was introduced in 1839.

David died in 1865 and was succeeded by his son Thomas Hoyle, who lacked his father's drive. Harry Whitehead in turn followed his father as chief shareholder and manager. Together with Samuel Whittaker he took over Broadclough Mill, Bacup in 1888. Whittaker's son became general manager at the age of 25 in 1900, having successfully managed the Bacup mill. His son, George, in turn, joined the firm in 1921.

The physical structure of the principal Smith & Nephew mill in 1990 can be traced to the Tunstills. In about 1834 Henry Tunstill of Brierfield House founded Henry Tunstill & Sons, which on his death in 1854 changed its name to Tunstill Brothers. The company was incorporated in 1904 under the name Brierfield Mills Ltd with Harry Tunstill as sole proprietor. At the time the company consisted of two stone built, fireproof spinning mills, one for weft which contained 50 108 spindles, and the other for twist, containing 41 148 spindles and three weaving sheds with 2 205 looms. In addition there was warehouse accommodation, 62 good cottages and building land. In 1907 a new weaving shed of 608 looms was added. This was the building into which the greater part of Smith & Nephew textile work was to be collected from 1957.

In 1940 Smith & Nephew bought Lomeshaye Mill from Nelson Corporation to use as a shadow factory for the Hull plant. The earlier owners, the Ecroyd family, had moved their business to Lomeshaye more than a century and a half before in 1780. Their business occupied a three-storey building in which was installed spinning machinery powered by the nearby river. Wool combing and dyeing was also carried out on the premises, but weaving continued to be done by cottage handlooms. Half a century later cottage workers were displaced, and weaving looms were installed alongside the combing, spinning and dyeing machinery in the mill. At the same time the village of Lomeshaye began to grow as the Ecroyd family built cottages to house their workers. The Ecroyds' enlightened thinking is demonstrated by their establishment of educational classes, discussion groups and a library for the employees.

Some 30 miles from Lomeshaye Mill, the well known Co-op shop originated in a consumers' cooperative formed in the town of Rochdale in 1844. Workers in the Nelson area decided to form a similar cooperative 16 years later in 1860 when the success of the Rochdale experiment was obvious.

The first meeting was held with the help and encouragement of Mr Ecroyd, who made available the weft room at Lomeshaye Mill. By this date the cottages in which the Ecroyd family housed their workers could boast gas lighting and a cold water supply. The Ecroyds had even installed gas street lighting in the village, when the adjacent town of Nelson generally lacked such facilities. In 1882 land and buildings were provided about three-quarters of a mile from the mill for the use of the workpeople of the town. The development included a coffee tavern, reading rooms and lecture rooms, where talks on travel, literature, science and politics were given.[19] Like their counterparts in Birmingham and Hull, these early small, innovative, Lancashire employers clearly concerned themselves not just with profits but with the well-being of their workforce, the area in which they lived and with wider national issues. Indeed, because access to water power required their mills to be so often far from towns or any facilities, they were frequently obliged to provide more for their workforces than those businesses in urban areas.

CONCLUSION

Smith & Nephew's most obvious legacy from these nineteenth century traditions by the end of the 1950s was the plants in Birmingham and Lancashire, but more important were the cultures of integrity in pharmacy, of innovation and drive in textiles and, in both, wider social concerns. These traditions were transmitted by personnel from Birmingham and Lancashire rising to all levels in Smith & Nephew up to chief executive and chairman from the late 1950s. That most firms disappeared or remained small may be explained by the vagaries of personal capitalism which kept the management and information pool small, although not so limited as has sometimes been claimed. The cost of 'an early start' was the creation of industrial and firm structures less appropriate to the technological and market possibilities of 1914 than they had been in 1850. Particularly obvious in organic chemicals and pharmaceuticals, similar problems were to emerge in textiles in the interwar years. The other side of the coin was a belief that management carried social obligations wider than those merely to their firms.[20]

NOTES

1. See T.B. Powell and J.N. Hillman *The History of Southalls (Birmingham) Ltd 1820-1957*, unpublished ms, n.d; *Chemist and Druggist*, 28 July 1906; *British and Colonial Druggist*, 29 June 1906. The company was therefore a beneficiary of the increasing reliance of

medical men on pharmacopoeia: standardization at the expense of drugs compounded by apothecaries (Liebenau 1987).
2. A society of botanists and zoologists founded in London in 1788.
3. Some of his diary sentiments will have been echoed by many professional teachers before and since.

31.5.1857 'Went to First Day School in good time and had Mr Baker's class which is composed of unruly boys, and I hope that I shall not be obliged to take it for my own, but I nevertheless got on better than 1st day before.'
22.1.1860 'Began the day badly: up late and did not pray much for help at school, therefore managed rather poorly, was not half in earnest in either meetings.'
1.1.1861 'I gave each of the boys a small tract entitled "The Untravelled Journey–Thoughts for the New Year" but had not the courage to speak much to them about the New Year.'
8.4.1862 'This evening had my first Day Scholars to tea–they were rather difficult to manage.'
14.12.1863 'I had 12 boys at school yesterday and with your help I hope I did my duty in teaching them, but it is hard work. I often think I am not adapted for a teacher, but yet feel that it is my duty. I do not visit my boys as I should. I find it so difficult to talk to their fathers and mothers, who always will do the talking instead of the sons, but I have sometimes had pleasant visits.' Wilfred Moss, *Alfred Southall (of Birmingham) 1838-1931: A Memoir*, Leominster, for private circulation 1931
4. Newcastle-upon-Tyne was the centre of the chemical industry in the 1860s, as demonstrated by the early formation of the Newcastle Chemical Society in 1868, well before the founding of the Society of Public Analysts and Other Analytical Chemists in 1874 and the Institute of Chemistry of Great Britain and Ireland in 1877.
5. Birmingham Central Library, Local History section. This is a very detailed and comprehensive account of the scheme, described at the time as the greatest of its kind ever attempted in Britain.
6. *Pharmaceutical Journal*, 14 November 1908; *Daily Mail*, 2 July 1903.
7. Porteous 1965 p. 160; *Warehouseman and Drapers' Trade Journal*, 19 April 1890, p. 349.
8. W. Heal, *Ye Historie off ye Ancient Alchemiysts Laboratorie* (1886), Birmingham Central Library Local History section.
9. *Daily Gazette*, 26 April 1902; *Daily Post*, 26 April 1902; Tweedale (1990), p. 78; Minutes of a Meeting of Southall and Barclay Directors 23 January 1911.
10. Sir Thomas Barclay to Thomas Barclay junior, 13 January 1914, and associated correspondence, Smith & Nephew/Southalls, Birmingham.
11. *Birmingham Mail*, 9 March 1910. Discovered by Madame Curie in 1902, radium compounds emitted a great deal of radioactive energy and induced chemical action, such as releasing hydrogen and oxygen when suspended in water. Moreover radium preparations destroyed skin and tissues, cured some skin diseases and influenced the nervous system.
12. Minute 10, December 1907; Leisler Bock Co to Southalls & Barclays 1907; The Iodine Preparations Combination, *Agreement for the Constituting and Regulating the Iodine Preparations Combination*, Glasgow, 1898 and 1911.
13. Thomas Barclay junior to Sir Thomas Barclay, 20 September 1911, Smith & Nephew/Southall Birmingham (S&N/S).
14. For example Barnett (1986), Wiener (1981).
15. Wilson (1954), vol. 1, pp. 38–44. Lever seems to have been influenced by American practice. See also Chapman (1973), chaps 2–3.
16. Sir Thomas Barclay to Thomas Barclay junior, 13 January 1914, p. 2, Smith & Nephew/Southalls; J. Cochrane, *Preliminary Report on EMSA Radium Plaster*, 5 January 1933, Smith & Nephew Archives, Hull.
17. Southall Bros & Barclay Ltd Prospectus 1898, S & N/S.
18. The largest number the vendors could take with a view to obtaining a settlement on the Birmingham Stock Exchange.

19. G. Whittaker, 'A Handful of Shale', unpublished ms, 1979; I. Laycock 'Lomeshaye Mill–Nelson', unpublished ms, 1988?; *Brierfield Mills Ltd 1904–1925*, 1925?

20. Even this though may not have been entirely beneficial, in so far as owner-managers' social welfare activities remained amateurish and under-resourced.

3. The development of the health care market, 1850–1939

A full appraisal of the originally pharmacy-based, nineteenth century health care businesses requires an understanding of the social, technical and intellectual context which gave rise to the demand for health care they faced and which allowed it to be met. When T.J. Smith first opened for business, more than half of England's people lived in towns. Despite rapid population growth, living standards rose slowly but persistently, maintaining British purchasing power above that even of the United States until nearly the end of the century. This increasing affluence created an expanding urban demand for health care that was no longer satisfied primarily by the traditional remedies of rural folk medicine. The medical profession, the state of scientific and technical knowledge, and broader political and cultural factors then translated this need for medical services into a demand for health care products from businesses. How well the health care market matched demands and capacities must be judged by the state of health of society.

INTERRELATIONSHIPS IN THE HEALTH CARE MARKET

Figure 3.1 shows some of the interrelationships. War (bottom right) is obviously the most radical and direct influence on the health of combatants but there are two less obvious types of causation; contagion and learning. Most Crimean war fatalities were caused by disease rather than enemy action. The Crimean War, the American Civil War and the Franco–Prussian War all prompted some improvements in medical treatment. Orthopaedics was initially 'the surgery of war'. Some progress was only temporary, as with the introduction of fracture clinics during the First World War. A second influence unrelated to health care is that of living standards broadly described (the top right of Figure 3.1), now thought to have explained the later-nineteenth century fall in TB death rates. Greater purchasing power alone does not guarantee better health, for that depends on how the money is spent. The use of opium to calm infants and generally in patent medicines, and rising alcohol and tobacco consumption, might be expected to have had adverse effects on health in the nineteenth century. Consumption of spirits per head of

Figure 3.1   The health care market

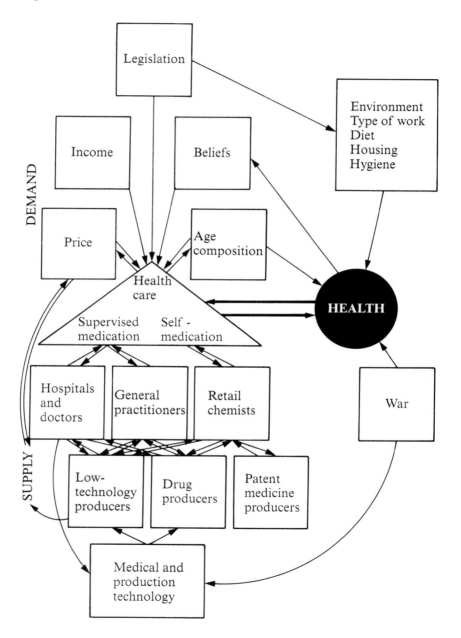

population stood at 3.1 litres (100 per cent alcohol equivalent) in the UK at the end of the nineteenth century, compared with 1.7 litres in 1985/6. Beer consumption fell from 259 pints per head to 191 over the same period.[1]

As the triangular block in the middle of the figure shows, health care may be divided into supervised provision and self-medication. The division between the two, and the volume of resources devoted to both, has been influenced by the demand side which, in turn, has depended upon the factors represented in the top left of Figure 3.1. Among the most important was legislation for national health insurance in 1911 and earlier public health acts. On the supply side, patent or proprietary medicines for self-medication were offered by apothecaries, pharmacists and retail chemists. Physicians, surgeons and nurses in hospitals or general practice supplied the other component of health care. Behind them both are the health care companies, the producers of sugared pills, of high technology drugs and of low technology wound dressings. They in turn depend upon the state of medical technology and scientific knowledge (bottom left). Both businesses and practitioners contribute to these fundamental determinants of the effectiveness of health care. In what follows, developments in each of the major components of Figure 3.1 are examined. The first stage in the analysis is the definition and measurement of health.

HEALTH

Health is the state of being bodily and mentally vigorous, and free from disease. Although a continuous decline in health leads first to sickness and ultimately to death, many, perhaps most, people get by without being fully healthy, as the Peckham experiment in the 1930s showed. Of 1 666 individuals in 500 families attending the Health Centre, only 144 individuals and 17 babies were free of any diagnosable disorder. And even those few did not necessarily fulfil the requirements of the definition of health, for not all ailments could be diagnosed then, or now. For a nation, attaining a healthy state is even more difficult than for an individual, first because health status varies considerably between individuals, and second because 'health' itself is not recorded. Levels of health have to be estimated from data that happens to be available, in particular figures for mortality and sickness rates. Data on absence from work through sickness are available in Friendly Society records. These show how sickness rose with age in the nineteenth century (Table 3.1) from an average of generally less than one week a year at age 20 to between one and two weeks a year at age 40 and over three weeks by the age of 60. Heights have been employed as an index of nineteenth century living standards, including health states, on the grounds that taller people are better

Table 3.1   Number of weeks of sickness a year by age recorded by certain Friendly Societies, 1824–1903

Age	Highland Society 1824	C. Ansell 1835	Ancient Order of Foresters 1873	Manchester Unity 1903
20	0.575	0.776	0.845	0.901
30	0.621	0.861	0.906	0.957
40	0.758	1.111	1.272	1.449
50	1.361	1.701	1.953	2.384
60	2.346	3.292	3.871	5.198
70	10.701	11.793	10.371	14.617

nourished and healthier. (Riley 1989; Floud et el. 1990; PEP 1937). Some data are liable to underestimate ill-health for good social reasons. TB was a notifiable disease in the years between the world wars but the costs in potential loss of job and difficulties with insurance certainly encouraged underregistration of all but the most serious cases.

From 1850 to 1939 mortality declined and life expectancy increased. Over the first 30 years of the twentieth century death rates in the age range 30–40 fell by 40 per cent. Tuberculosis deaths after 30 and broncho-pneumonia in late middle age were reduced. Illnesses were not typically causes of death. One-third of all cases treated by doctors (GPs) were the common cold and its developments (pneumonia and influenza) but these accounted for only one-twelfth of all deaths.

Increased life expectancy exposed individuals to more episodes of ill-health over his or her lifetime. Both the risk of death and the chances of ill-health were increased by previous bouts of ill-health because the body was debilitated. Consequently, as an individual aged, he or she became more vulnerable to a range of possible causes of death or illness (nearly half of the deaths attributable to the common cold and its developments were at ages above 70 in the interwar years). In short, a decline in mortality led to more aggregate ill-health; more years of life were experienced in which each sickness episode increased the risk of future ill-health.[2]

These changes came about because of rising living standards, a reduction in the virulence of, and susceptibility to, epidemic diseases, greater medical knowledge, and improved health care techniques and availability. The average age of the population rose and the most important cause of death changed from acute infectious disease to chronic degenerative disease. Cholera and

typhoid almost disappeared but TB remained a major killer. A smaller proportion of the population died at each age but the quantity of sickness,
especially protracted sickness, increased at each age. The greatest fall in
mortality occurred in younger age groups: by about 60 per cent in the ages 1–5
in the period 1900–30. Falling mortality, increased life expectancy and the
tendency for average heights to rise suggest that health conditions were improving, but sickness rates indicate that health itself was not. The demand for
health care therefore grew for this reason as well as because of rising incomes.

The distribution of income strongly influenced the extent and type of ill-
health and the effective demand for health care. The very rich in the nineteenth century often ate and drank excessively, which boosted their demand
for remedies such as anti-bilious pills.[3] In typical northern towns in 1930, a
high proportion of working-class wards had infant mortality rates of 100–150
per 1 000, while in the middle-class suburbs rates were around 40. Among
Tyneside families in 1933 with incomes of 10 shillings per head per week or
less, in one district 53 per cent, and in another 34 per cent, of households
contained at least one member with TB. Those most in need of health care
were those least able to afford it (Webster 1984).

HEALTH CARE OUTPUT DATA

To know what was afforded, some measures of health care commercial
industry output are required. Unfortunately sources of such data during the
years 1850–1939 are typically of limited coverage and dubious reliability.
Receipts from the patent medicine stamp duty are available from 1800 and
numbers of licensed medicine vendors from 1865. From these it is possible to
estimate total expenditure on patent medicines. Some attempts have been
made to compute consumers' expenditure on all health care in the early
twentieth century. The final figures have the disadvantage for our purposes
that they exclude spending by hospitals. Prest and Adams (1954) use patent
medicine figures to obtain estimates of spending of £2.9m in 1907, £3.25m in
1913 and £6.0m in 1924 (see also Stone and Rowe 1966). But for the
interwar years stamp duty receipts show a downward trend, most probably
reflecting increasing tax avoidance. The 1937 *Report of the Select Committee
on Stamp Duty* notes that instead of the actual figure of £0.75m, the full yield
in 1937 should have been £3.3m, approximately equivalent to a turnover of
£16–20m. The *Censuses of Production* provide value and volume figures for
drugs and medical appliances. These have been used with an official estimate
of £42.7m at retail prices for 1935 to get a first approximation of £10.5m in
1907, and £29.5m in 1924, including hospital expenditure on drugs. Final
figures of £12m and £30m exclude hospital expenditure and add in an allow-

ance for the greater importance of dispensing by chemists in the early years.
Intervening years were interpolated and extrapolated from patent medicine
duty figures. Estimated drug and appliance expenditure then rises from £9.9m
in 1900 to £12.8m in 1912, little more than 0.5 per cent of national income in
both years (Figure 3.2). The overall price index for the group rises over these
years by 3.5 per cent and the quantity index rises by 10 per cent, implying a
rather slow Edwardian average annual growth rate of health care.

An estimate of health care spending for the years between the world wars
concludes from household budgets of 1937–39 that expenditure on drugs and
appliances totalled £22–23m. Adding on hospital expenditure raises the figure to £33.9m (net of dental supplies and spectacles), about 0.75 per cent of
national income. As expected the proportion of national income spent on
health care had risen with increasing affluence since the Edwardian period.

Figure 3.2   Health care expenditure, 1900–39

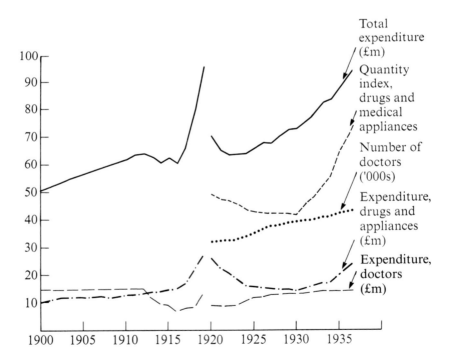

Surprisingly, the pharmaceutical drug quantity index drifts downwards from 1920 to 1930 and then doubles by 1938. The price index falls sharply in the 1920s and then remains fairly stable in the 1930s. Although the method of calculation may conflate quantity increases with quality improvements, the 1930s on any interpretation looks like a period of rapid supply improvements in health care products. Comparable changes do not occur in nursing and hospital services or in the supply of doctors, dentists and opticians.

DEMAND

Turning to the reasons behind these trends, we first distinguish the demand for health care. Obviously people wanted to be healthy but their success in achieving this goal depended upon how much health care they could demand, the importance they attached to other activities, how much they needed and how effective the available health care was. Consultation with both orthodox and unorthodox providers of health care reflected demand for a certain level of health, while diet, fitness, living conditions and personal habits influenced the need. Cod liver oil, antiseptic dressings, and various forms of sanitary protection were all in demand because they were believed to be effective in a socially acceptable manner. More objective characteristics also influenced demand: the age composition of the population, the level and distribution of income, and the role of government and health care professionals. The very young and the very old have disproportionately large needs for health care. State support for health insurance achieves a stronger demand for health care and a more equitable distribution of health care resources. Such schemes reduced the price, broadly interpreted, that the average employee had to pay for health care by introducing compulsory payments. But beliefs were among the fundamental determinants of health care demand.

The most influential source of health care information in the middle of the nineteenth century was the family or local community. Beliefs were passed down by word of mouth from generation to generation. As unwritten tales, legends and proverbs took the form of folklore, so health care attitudes were embodied in folk medicine. Traditional folk medicine consisted typically of the administration of herbal remedies and fruits and vegetables that were thought to have healing powers. Honey, alcohol, willow bark and sphagnum moss are all traditional treatments that modern medical science now concedes are efficacious, respectively as an aid to wound healing, an antiseptic, an analgesic and a hygroscopic wound dressing.[4] Industrialization that led to increased urbanization broke down the folk medicine tradition. Young people moved to urban areas in search of work, and in doing so their traditional source of health care information was cut off. Even if health care beliefs were transferred by immigrants to urban areas, the often uncommon ingredients of medicaments were much less available.

At the beginning of this period, consultation with doctors was restricted to the wealthy élites who could afford their services, which in any case were of dubious value. A limited amount of medical attention could be gained by the less affluent from Friendly Society benefits, through Poor Law institutions and the growing number of hospitals for the sick (but their high mortality made such institutions places of last resort – Peterson 1978, p. 201).

From 1913 National Health Insurance spread medical services more widely. But in the middle of the nineteenth century for most people there was little intermediation by health care professionals. Consumers or patients were dependent upon their own beliefs and those of other people, or groups (such as 'bone-setters' at the beginning of our period) thought to have greater knowledge of health care issues than the rest of the population.

After 1850 a general rise in consumers' disposable incomes boosted demand for patent medicines (Corley 1987, pp. 111–29; Chapman 1974, pp. 11–30; Bartrip 1990, pp. 179–84). Towards the end of the century the industry was employing perhaps 19 000 in 1 000 different businesses. Patent medicines may be defined as those bearing proprietary names protected by trade marks, which are intended primarily for self-medication. At one extreme they shade into foods, such as Nathan's dried milk 'Glaxo' (introduced in 1906), and at the other extreme into cosmetics, like Dr Beiersdorf's 'Nivea Creme' of 1912. Sales and output of such goods increased faster than living standards and population, suggesting that medication was a priority item of working-class budgets.

Information on the perceived effectiveness of patent medicines was spread primarily by word of mouth communication between potential consumers, and between consumers and retail chemists or druggists. There were several alternative ways to promote products on a large scale. In the second half of the nineteenth century literacy among ordinary people increased, and as a result the market for basic reading matter grew. Evidence is seen in the large sales of low-priced health care manuals such as Buchan's *Domestic Medicine*, Wesley's *Primitive Physick* and Cox's *Companion to Family Medicine Chests* (Brown 1980, p. 312). But, more important for patent medicine sales was the wider circulation and increase in sales of tabloid newspapers. Newspapers provided a means of reaching a wider audience through advertisements. Most patent medicines were sold through emerging retail outlets and selling prices were conventionally fixed. Competition took place on a non-price basis, the most important being through advertising and distributor goodwill, though Jesse Boot offers a striking exception (Chapman 1974; Corley 1987, p. 115). Thomas Holloway, a producer and merchant of pills and ointments, spent £50 000 on publicity in 1883, when his profits would have been approximately the same; his annual turnover for that year is estimated at around the £230 000 mark. In 1884 Thomas Beecham's expenditure on advertising was £22 000, by 1891 this figure had increased to £120 000. As a consequence his turnover rose at an annual rate of more than 22 per cent in the 1880s, reaching £174 000 in 1890. Thereafter growth slowed to an annual average of 1.6 per cent until 1913.[5] Whether any particular patent medicine was more effective than its rivals was often doubtful but branding created the possibility of attracting a wide market through consumer loyalty.

The medical profession objected to the sale of most patent 'secret remedies' ostensibly because they were at best a waste of money and at worst, as for many of those included ingredients such as opium and cocaine, harmful to health. Patent medicines were excluded from the Pharmacy Act of 1868 and from the Sale of Food and Drugs Act of 1875. The British Medical Association and the *British Medical Journal* may have had a hidden agenda in their campaigns against patent medicines as well: to protect their monopoly of medical practice. As an encouragement to the provision of genuine information, from 1904 medicines which stated their ingredients were relieved of the patent medicine tax. Attempts were made to clean up the industry's advertising claims during the interwar years, when patent medicines had acquired rather a bad name.[6]

Demand for health care was moulded by law as well as by the beliefs of the mass of the population. Some legislation, like the Public Health Acts of 1848, 1858–59, 1866, 1872, 1875 and 1913, when effective created a healthier environment and therefore reduced the need for health care. Other legislation, by boosting the effective demand for health care, also contributed to health improvement. An Act of 1853 made vaccination of infants against smallpox compulsory but provided no enforcement machinery. In 1867 Poor Law Boards of Guardians were empowered to enforce infant vaccination. Effectiveness of vaccination was revealed by the high smallpox death rate in the French Army of 1870, for whom there was no compulsory vaccination, compared with the German forces, for whom vaccination was obligatory. The efforts of the British public vaccinator helped to lower smallpox death rates from 1871. The last British epidemic of smallpox occurred in 1934.

Other legislation raised the effective demand for health care with less compulsion on the subjects: the 1897 Workmen's Compensation Act, the basic first aid provisions enforced under the Factory Act of 1924, and National Health Insurance under the 1911 Act. This last scheme provided for the insurance on a compulsory contributory basis of all employed males and females between the ages of 16 and 70. Sickness benefit ran for 26 weeks and could then be followed by disablement benefit if necessary. Medical benefit consisting of medical attendance, treatment and medicine as would normally be provided by a general practitioner was also available, as was maternity benefit. Medical benefits were administered by newly created insurance committees in each county and county borough from 1913. The British Medical Association objected very strongly to the Act but eventually acquiesced when most of their concerns about representation and payment were met. More than half of the population remained outside the scheme, whose impact was not really felt in normal times until after the First World War (Braithwaite 1957; PEP 1937; Eder 1982; Orr and Orr 1938; Harris 1946; Bartrip 1985).

One of the principal concerns behind the 1911 Act was national efficiency. Public opinion had been shocked by the large proportion of young volunteers for the Boer War who were found to be unfit for military service; 11 out of 12 East Enders were rejected in 1900. The great rival, Germany, had passed health insurance legislation in 1883 and accident insurance the following year. It is no coincidence, in view of the boost such legislation gave to health care demand, that the German health care industry was so advanced by the first decade of the twentieth century.

By the end of the 1930s Britain began to catch up in this respect also. Nineteen million people were covered by national health insurance in 1936. Their benefits were financed jointly by their own payments, by their employers and by the government. Sickness benefit payment cost nearly twice as much as medical benefits but did focus administrators' minds on treatments that would reduce the period off work. Expenditure on prescriptions per head of population differed radically between areas, with Manchester and Salford at the top of the league and Oxford at the bottom. The variation was generally attributed to the differing incidence of ill-health between the towns. GPs' prescription expenses were checked occasionally for extravagance. Expenditure by both approved Friendly Societies and insurance committees of National Health Insurance funds was audited by Treasury appointees. Dependants of insured persons, mainly wives and children, were excluded from benefits, as were small traders and other self-employed.

About £7m was paid out annually in 450 000 compensation cases under Workmen's Compensation legislation. This expense encouraged greater commercial interest in rapid and effective health care treatment. H.N. Smith cashed in on concern with compensation payments by organizing a dinner on the *Scythia* in Liverpool harbour and later on the *Majestic* at Southampton, to demonstrate the cost-effectiveness of Smith & Nephew's plaster bandage 'Cellona'. On each dinner table sat one insurance representative, one business person and one doctor. The demand for Cellona rose strongly.

SUPPLY

Health care output grew not only because of the expansion of demand but because supply also increased. Three distinct components each contributed: medical knowledge, medical professionals and health care businesses. The years 1850–1939 saw the growth of scientifically based medical knowledge largely created by medical professionals. Health care firms in Britain for most of the time only responded to the demands of medical researchers and practitioners, although they also played a role in diffusing innovations. Pharmaceutical chemistry began to make a substantial impact on medical practice in the later part of the period.

Medical Knowledge

The foundations of modern medical knowledge were laid by the European research community around the middle of the nineteenth century independently of health care businesses (Cartwright 1972, pp. 131–51; Youngson 1978). The practical results were anaesthetics and the understanding of antisepsis. A number of helpful medical appliances antedated these breakthroughs: Laennec invented the stethoscope in 1816 and Joseph Lister's father made important contributions to the microscope. Anaesthesia was first successfully used in 1846. The importance of the innovation was quickly recognized: not only was the patient freed from pain but the time in which the surgeon had to operate was therefore greatly increased. Joseph Lister (1827–1912) collected statistics on death rates in cases of surgical amputations in hospitals where he had worked between 1864 and 1866, arriving at the figure of 45 per cent. Seeking an explanation for the sepsis and fevers that had carried off so many of his patients he alighted on the work of Louis Pasteur. Pasteur (1822–95), a chemist primarily concerned with fermentation, announced his discovery of the action of micro-organisms in 1864; between 1878 and 1881 both he and Robert Koch, working independently, proved that a specific germ caused a specific disease. Pasteur combated micro-organisms by heat sterilization (pasteurization). Lister's achievement was his experiments with chemical antiseptics, from which he eventually chose carbolic acid, recently employed to disinfect sewage at Carlisle. He began to operate under a carbolic spray, radically reducing infection and mortality. His 1867 paper in the *Lancet*, 'On the Antiseptic Principle in the Practice of Surgery', announced his discovery. As Listerian doctrine was gradually accepted, helped by horrendous mortality in the Franco–Prussian War, the scope for surgery increased and the risk associated with operations was greatly reduced. The most important advances in uses of bandages and dressings were a direct result of Lister's discovery that airborne bacteria were a source of infection in the operating room. Before Lister's discovery, the post-operative mortality rate was as high as 90 per cent in some hospitals; patients who recovered did so in spite of, rather than because of treatment.[7] Within 35 years medical practice was transformed, aided by such simple but effective products as rubber gloves and gauze face masks (1897). William Halsted at Johns Hopkins Hospital Baltimore was an innovator in 1889–90 when he asked Goodyear Rubber Co. to make him rubber gloves for surgery (Bishop 1960, p. 173).

Medical advances accelerated towards the end of the century. Diphtheria antitoxin, developed at the Koch Institute, Berlin and funded by Hoechst, was announced in 1890, and lowered the death rate from diphtheria in London fever hospitals from 63 per cent in 1894 to 12 per cent in 1910. Rontgen or X Rays (discovered in 1895) were quickly recognized as of utmost importance in surgery and treatment of fractures. German pre-eminence in organic chemistry spilled over into medical science. One of the first synthesizing achievements of the young science of organic chemistry applied to medicine at the turn of the century was salycylic acid, a derivative of willow bark which gave health care Bayer's Aspirin in 1899. Salvarsan, the first effective antisyphilitic remedy, was discovered by Paul Ehrlich (supported by the German firm Hoechst) in 1909. Salvarsan was the first 'magic bullet' – a chemical that would attack the disease and not the patient. Some bacterial diseases are the result of toxins produced by bacteria. The body naturally manufactures antitoxins. Vaccination, unlike magic bullets, is a small amount of toxin that encourages the body to react by producing antitoxins.

Antisepsis practice was forced to advance during the First World War. Infection on the Western Front was a particularly acute problem because the ground was so contaminated with waste products and human remains. Eusol (Edinburgh University Solution), a solution of chlorinated lime and boric acid in water, became widely used to combat general sepsis and gas gangrene (Lawrence and Payne 1984, p. 18).

By the end of the First World War other industrial nations were rapidly narrowing the German lead in pharmaceuticals and related chemistry, a process made easier by confiscation and the German economy's postwar difficulties. In 1918 vitamin theory was formulated. The Canadian extraction of insulin in 1922 provided a treatment for diabetes, the manufacture of which was quickly taken up by the long-established firm of Allen & Hanbury (Bliss 1982; Tweedale 1990, pp. 128–30). Sir Alexander Fleming discovered in 1929 an antibacterial substance that he named penicillin (although it was only after Howard Florey and Ernst Chain at Oxford resumed work between 1938 and 1943 that the drug was put to use). The first sulpha drug 'Prontosil' was demonstrated in 1935 at IG Farben but it was the British-based May & Baker (founded almost a century earlier at Battersea in 1839 and then owned by the French Poulenc Frères) that synthesized the powerful sulphapyridine, 'M & B 693' in 1937.[8]

During the late 1930s the cumulative effects of previous pharmaceutical discoveries revolutionized the efficacy of medical care. The incidence of infectious disease was radically reduced by innovative preventative techniques and new methods of treatment. Immunization against many common childhood infections became possible and if infections did develop, they could be treated through the use of sulpha drugs and (from the early 1940s) antibiotics. TB remained unconquered until after the Second World War, though.

For one non-infectious disease of increasing importance, cancer, X ray diagnosis and deep therapy appeared promising. The Radium Trust and the Radium Commission were established to develop and control such therapy. But in 1936 only a small proportion of those who might have benefited were receiving the treatment (Webster 1984).

Medical Professionals

Each of the three principal professional groups supplying health care became increasingly organized around the mid-century. Pharmacists, the source from which so many pharmaceutical and health care manufacturers originated, were weakly regulated by the Pharmacy Act of 1852.[9] This legislation restricted membership of the society to those who had taken the exams and established a register of qualified persons. The Act protected use of titles denoting a qualified pharmacist but did not regulate the sale of poisons. That waited until 1868.

Far more restrictive was the professionalization of the doctors. Under the Medical Act of 1858 the General Medical Council became responsible for keeping the Medical Register of those who had qualified as practitioners. The council supervised, monitored and made recommendations about medical examinations and provided for the publication of the British Pharmacopoeia. No medical certificates required under the 1858 or subsequent Acts were valid unless given by a registered practitioner.

Surgeons and physicians were no longer permitted to cooperate with unqualified practitioners. This restrictive practice created some difficulties with 'bone-setters'. In striking contrast to mainstream medical practice, the bone-setter's technique was based on massage and manipulation. The secrets of this traditional craft were passed down the generations within families, at least one of which made the transition to professional doctor. The Thomas family's bone-setting began with Evan (died 1814). Evan Thomas II (1804–84) became a full time practitioner in Liverpool. He gave his five sons medical education and used them as a 'cover' for his own practice. One of his sons, Hugh Owen (1834–91), a student of James Syme (1799–1870), Professor of Surgery at Edinburgh, found this intolerable and separated from his

father in 1859. Thomas was effectively the founder of the Liverpool ortho-
paedic tradition, transmitted through his student Robert Jones (1857–1933).
Jones conducted the first X ray diagnosis in the UK in 1896 and emphasized
manipulation and splintage as treatments for most fractures. During the First
World War he became director of orthopaedics and instigated the British
Orthopaedic Association in 1918 (Le Vay 1990, pp. 76–9).

Nursing did not establish entry barriers such as applied to doctors. The
problem at the mid-century was rather to train a profession. Although Florence Nightingale had attracted the publicity, as she recognized, reform was
initiated by the Anglican Nursing Sisterhoods of which St John's House was
the earliest and most influential. The first steps in a nurse training programme
were taken by Sister Mary Jones in 1857. From 1856 St John's took full
responsibility for nursing at Kings College Hospital. The Nightingale School
at St Thomas's Hospital opened in 1860 only because an extension of the St
John's training would have had to have been restricted to members of the
Church of England (Cook 1913; Cartwright 1972, pp. 155–6; Baly 1986).

The 1850s were a decade for founding new hospitals as well as consolidat-
ing medical professions. Voluntary hospitals were few in number and would
not admit children or the chronic sick. By 1861 there were 66 specialist
hospitals in London compared with 12 at the beginning of the century. Between 1851 and 1853 four small children's hospitals were opened. The Royal
Hospital for Incurables in Putney dates from 1854. The Royal National
Orthopaedic Hospital, with which Smith & Nephew were to have close
contacts in the future, was founded in 1856 as the Spinal Hospital for the
Cure of Deformities, in London (Cartwright 1972, p. 158; Le Vay 1990, p.
127). Church collections for the upkeep of voluntary hospitals were consoli-
dated in the Hospital Sunday Fund in 1873 (T.J. Smith was a joint founder of
the Hull branch). The following year the Saturday Fund administered by
Working Men's Clubs was introduced. Workmen soon claimed the right to
hospital treatment in return for their payments. Poor Law infirmaries, later
often acquired by local authorities, supplemented this ramshackle provision.

Health Care Businesses

British retail pharmacists, who traditionally supplied many of the products
used by the hospitals and health care professionals, in the eighteenth and
nineteenth centuries integrated backwards to production, often of proprietary
foods and medicines. They emphasized and derived their competitive edge
from marketing. Allen & Hanbury of London, Southalls of Birmingham,
Boots of Nottingham and T.J. Smith of Hull are covered by this generaliza-
tion. Once scientific technology became indispensable, they imported the
expertise in the form of new products, as far as possible. Smith & Nephew

acquired Elastoplast and Cellona/Gypsona from Germany. Only after 1945 or later did research laboratories become widespread and indigenous technology develop. In this sense Britain was a technological latecomer where the health care business was concerned.

There is a danger of overemphasizing the legacy of an 'early start' and neglecting the beginnings of recovery in the interwar years (Robson 1988). Burroughs Wellcome and Evans Sons Lescher & Webb both established pharmaceutical research departments before the First World War. Burroughs Wellcome ceased to be importers of American products because of the stamp duty, setting up a factory first at Wandsworth, and moving in 1889 to Dartford. Like other British companies they supplied laxatives, tonics and cod liver oil. But they did so by presenting them as 'compressed medicines'. More unusual was Henry Wellcome's commitment to research which gave rise to the volume production of diphtheria antiserum from 1894. Distinguished research into diphtheria vaccines continued to flow from the Wellcome Laboratories between the world wars. The director of the Physiological Research Laboratory from 1906–14, Sir Henry Dale, won the Nobel prize in 1936 (Burroughs Wellcome 1980).

May & Baker, the chemists, licensed drugs such as Sulphonal from the German pharmaceutical company Bayer. They were too small to produce the range of drugs that Bayer managed with their 27 chemists and 1 000 employees. May & Baker, like many other British chemical firms, grew up before the chemical revolution took hold and found adopting new ways difficult. But they did maintain close contacts with metallurgy and chemistry professors at Kings College London, which gave rise to a number of new processes and products in the 1880s. In the interwar years when May & Baker had built up a research department, access to hospital research facilities proved invaluable. M & B 693 was tested at the Middlesex Hospital on the pathologist's mice with pneumococcal infection. In 1939 May & Baker cooperated with the London School of Tropical Medicine to set up a laboratory for testing antimalarial compounds (Slinn 1984).

ICI, formed in 1926 from four chemical companies, became the giant of the British industry but was somewhat diffident about pharmaceuticals. ICI pursued a technology-driven research strategy from 1926. The invention of 87 new products including pharmaceuticals in the Dyestuffs Group between 1933 and 1935 and polyethylene in the Alkali Group's research laboratory in 1935 is evidence of its success. At the date of the formation of ICI, unlike the great German rival IG Farben, there were no pharmaceutical interests in the four merging companies. That seems to have created a long-lasting structural problem, preventing ICI from gaining a position in pharmaceuticals comparable with that held in other chemical firms. Pharmaceutical sales rose from £4 000 in 1928 to a mere £13 000 in 1935. ICI deliberately avoided taking

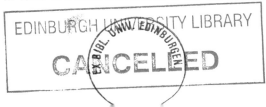

licences or buying information, uniquely preferring to build up pharmaceutical expertise on their own (Reader 1975, p. 200).

When Glaxo was still a dairy products firm, their chemist visited E.V. McCollum at Johns Hopkins Hospital Baltimore while at a Washington dairy conference in 1923 and was convinced that there were two distinct vitamins, A and D, in cod liver oil. By the next year Glaxo was marketing its first medical product, phials of Vitamin D extracted from fish liver oil. Glaxo's research programme expanded during the 1930s but total outlays on long-term research were less than £5 000 a year before the Second World War. A panel of external scientific consultants advised on research directions and most projects were undertaken in cooperation with the Lister Institute or the National Institute of Medical Research (Jephcott 1969; Tweedale 1990, p. 120; Davenport-Hines and Shinn 1992, p. 86).

By the outbreak of the Second World War, Beecham's, the successful Victorian pill-makers, was also on the verge of acquiring a research base under Philip Hill. On the way the company's first pharmaceutical product, Beecham's Powders, was developed, and sold from 1926. Hill endowed the Beecham laboratory at the Royal Northern Hospital in London in 1937 so as to test his products more rigorously. And then he acquired a valuable laboratory when he bought Macleans.[10]

Within the present Smith & Nephew Group generalizations about the separation of business from research practitioners do not entirely stand up either, even for the nineteenth century. Dr Gamgee worked with Southalls and with Robinsons to produce new dressings in the 1870s.[11] One of the Southall & Barclay company directors, John Barclay, was a pharmaceutical lecturer at a college later absorbed by the University of Birmingham. Although most of the company's analytical activities were routine, it did conduct research into new products before 1914. The difference from the German pattern was that the search for profits in the British market, before national medical insurance, directed attention to products such as nerve tonics, with a mass demand, unlike pharmaceutical preparations for specific ailments. Southalls itself was not small, in part because it was diversified across health care more broadly defined than pharmaceuticals, although it did rely on German imports of commodities such as iodine.

In the interwar years state funds began to trickle into medical research through the Medical Research Council (MRC) (£195 000 in 1937–38), probably exceeding those invested by health care businesses. The MRC had been founded as an adjunct to the new health service, so demonstrating the pervasive effect on health care industry demand exercised by a less fragmented health service. Private and charitable funds had earlier been tapped by such organizations as the Imperial Cancer Research Fund (1902).

Early production techniques in health care firms were simple but effective. John Garnett Taylor's patent (no. 12859) for an improved lint-making machine in 1849 (the Latin document is still held by the Smith & Nephew group) improved the supply of medical dressings. Each machine did the work of six women homeworkers but the total number of persons engaged in lint production increased. Lint was originally made by scraping the surface of linen obtained from the inner woody portion of the stem of the flax plant. Taylor's machine used a treadle to bring down a knife on the cloth so as to raise a pile. In addition to Taylor's company, Southalls, Newsome's and Robinson & Sons of Chesterfield (Porteous 1965, passim; Elliott 1964; Bishop 1959, p. 56) were interested in medical dressings in general and lint manufacture in particular when demand expanded as a consequence of the Crimean War in 1854. Charles Newsome of Oldham bought grey cloth from Benjamin Lees and linted it. In 1859 Newsome's were taken over by Lees but the name continued for more than a century. Smith & Nephew maintained close and cooperative relations with Robinsons for much of the company's lifetime. When the demand for dressings fell after the war, Robinsons bought out other manufacturers in the belief that lint would come into general use by the medical profession. The hunch paid off and as demand grew, Robinsons became the first firm to make lint entirely out of cotton as opposed to the usual cotton/linen mix.

The 1850s also saw a number of other useful health care manufacturing advances. Machines for spreading plaster were invented and the modern syringe was designed. Pulverizers and evaporators came into use in manufacturing pharmaceuticals (Matthews 1962, pp. 303, 320).

Robinsons began experiments in earnest to produce cotton wadding with the same absorbent qualities as wool in 1877, but experienced considerable difficulties. Research was probably initiated after the chance discovery in 1871 that layers of finely carded raw cotton would filter out germs, preventing their entry to a wound. In 1883 the firm secured the right to manufacture the first absorbent cotton wool from a patent taken out by Dr Gamgee.

In 1878 Robinsons added bandages to their list of products. Early bandages were tightly woven, similar to rough sheeting, with very little flexibility or elasticity. Robinsons, mistakenly, sent out a quantity of very loosely woven cloth. When they contacted the hospital customer, to apologize and replace the cloth, doctors proclaimed the cloth was exactly what they had been looking for. Loose woven bandages then became the norm.

These developments in surgical dressings and bandages were more fundamental than may at first be realized. Although the products were not sterile, they were clean and well packaged. Previously bandages had been made from rags that were often unwashed and far from hygienic. Similarly the cotton previously used as dressings was often collected from the sweepings from the floors of the textile mills. Furthermore, surgeons operated in their street clothes and washing before operating was uncommon. Dr Gamgee is said to have been one of the first surgeons to wash invariably (Johnson and Johnson 1979, p. 3; Porteous 1965, p. 146).

After his successful experiments with antiseptic dressings, Lister followed Dr Gamgee's example and made contact with Robinsons (Porteous 1965, p. 161). In 1889, antiseptic dressings were produced on a large scale, making them available to all members of the medical profession. Robert Wood Johnson, founder of the American company of Johnson & Johnson, who had heard Lister speak on antisepsis, began to manufacture antiseptic dressings at a similar time to, if not before, the parallel developments at Robinsons. In 1890, Johnson & Johnson started to treat their dressings with dry heat in an attempt to produce not only an antiseptic product, but one that was sterile as well. Two years later, after an in-house bacteriological laboratory had been established, the company successfully produced a sterile product. The dressings were kept under aseptic conditions and were subject to repeated sterilization, first by dry heat and later by steam and pressure, throughout the production process.

Companies spread information about these products to health care professionals or to consumers by advertising and by employing travellers. In the case of patent medicines, advertising was aimed at the individual, and travellers were used to gain the goodwill of retail chemists. As markets extended the manufacturer of products was no longer able to visit clients himself. Salesmen were employed for specific areas of the country, simply to encourage the retailer to stock their product, through the offer of discounts and the provision of publicity material in the form of handbills and window displays. The United States between the world wars was similar to Britain in that consumers obtained less than 5 per cent of their medicines directly from doctors in 1929. Pharmacists still operated independently. Prescriptions were not needed to buy any non-narcotic drug and therefore less than 5 per cent of pharmaceutical advertising was aimed at doctors (Liebenau 1986, p. 91; Chapman 1974, p. 57; Corley 1987, p. 115; Temin 1980, pp. 46–7).

As the twentieth century progressed British pharmaceutical firms increasingly used travellers to sell to the medical profession. The function of travellers, or 'detail men', was not merely to sell; they performed an educative role as well. Company representatives needed considerable scientific knowledge and efficient means of communication in order to sell new products. Booklets, pamphlets and lectures all conveyed the corporate messages. Through advances in the photographic industry, more sophisticated methods were provided in the form of first slides, and then moving films. Similar methods of supplying information were used by producers of medical care products other than drugs; the sector of the industry that supplied bandages, surgical dressings and other basic but essential equipment. Accounts of Lister's work were circulated widely, and a large number of books and pamphlets were published. Two examples are of particular relevance to Smith & Nephew: Dr Gamgee's *On the Treatment of Wounds*, 1878, and Johnson & Johnson's *Modern Methods of Antiseptic Wound Treatment*, 1888.

CONCLUSION

By 1939 the cumulative impact of medical and scientific advances embodied by companies in practical manufacturing techniques, and put into use by an increasingly highly trained profession, was to transform the effectiveness of health care. The relative advantages of self-medication and professional medicine were more often tilted in favour of the second. Institutional and legislative changes made professional treatment more possible as did rising levels of income. State support for, and organization of, health insurance expanded the demand for health care products, giving an initial advantage to health care firms in Germany, where national health insurance was first introduced. By the interwar years, the period of Smith & Nephew's accelerating growth, this lead was rapidly eroded by firms in other developed countries. National health insurance contributed on the demand side to the rapid rise in British consumption of health care products during the 1930s, an increase in which Smith & Nephew participated from the side of supply.

NOTES

1. J.-C. Sournia, *A History of Alcoholism*, Oxford: Blackwell (1987).
2. The rising sickness rates shown in Table 3.1 as the nineteenth century passes is consistent with this position but, because the samples may not be comparable across societies at different dates, they do not prove the point. 'The healthier we are, the longer we live and the longer we live, the more likely we are to require the benefit from medical care.' (McKeown 1988). The very low sickness rates among the members of the Steam Engine Makers' trade union in 1835–46, averaging 2.5 per cent, with 75 per cent never off work sick, is also consistent. See Southall and Garrett (1991), pp. 231–52. But it is also consistent with a relaxation of rules as to when workers were allowed to go sick over the century, perhaps under trade union pressure. William Farr estimated one in 20 of the population were constantly disabled by illness in 1837; see McCulloch *A Statistical Account of the British Empire* (1837), vol. II, ch. 4. See also Whiteside (1987) pp. 228–46.
3. Turner (1952), p. 69 mentions Cockle's anti-bilious pills recommended by ten dukes and five marquises.
4. Willow bark contains salicylic acid, a key ingredient of Bayer's aspirin. On sphagnum moss and honey see Lawrence and Payne (1984).
5. Communication from T.A.B. Corley.
6. Lazell (1975), p. 14. Whatever the doctors' motives, the BMA criticisms of patent medicines, in *Secret Remedies* (1909) and *More Secret Remedies* (1912), together with the 1914 *Report of the Select Committee on Patent Medicines* (PP 1914 IX), provided devas-

tating ammunition against the patent medicine trade. For the United States market, see Young (1961). The *Journal of the American Medical Association* in 1900 defaulted on its pledge to exclude patent medicine advertising. Controls on the American pharmaceutical industry emerged earlier than in Britain following the wake of the 1938 Elixir Sulfonamide tragedy that killed more than 100 people. Under the 1938 Federal Food Drug and Cosmetic Act, 'unsafe' pharmaceutical products could not be marketed and instructions had to be provided for those that were sold.

7. Godlee (1917); Elliot (1964), p. 19; Johnson & Johnson (1979), p.2. Lister's father was a microscopist and naturalist, although he worked as a wine merchant. This background may have helped Joseph Lister accept Pasteur's doctrine. Lister studied at University College London, becoming an FRCS in 1852. He was Professor of Surgery in Glasgow from 1860 where he made his discoveries of asepsis. Lister returned to London as senior surgeon at Kings College. He was the first medical man to be given a peerage.

8. Gerard Domagk was awarded the Nobel prize in 1939 for his discovery of Prontosil. A J Ewins, May & Baker's chief chemist, was made an FRS for the discovery of sulphapyridine (M & B 693). The May & Baker chemist who actually synthesized the compound was Dr M.A. Phillips.

9. Jacob Bell had hoped to obtain for members of the Pharmaceutical Society the monopoly right to sell medicines, but Parliament was unsympathetic (Holloway 1991, p. 185).

10. T.A.B. Corley, 'The Beecham Group in the World's Pharmaceutical Industry 1914–1970', University of Reading, unpublished.

11. Joseph Samson Gamgee, the son of an Italian vet, himself qualified as a vet in 1849 before going on to study medicine at University College Hospital. He qualified as MRCS in 1854 and served in the Crimean War. From 1857 he was a surgeon at the Queen's Hospital in Birmingham (later Birmingham Accident Hospital). His 'Gamgee Tissue' is still in medical use.

4. Growth and diversification: Elastoplast, Gypsona and Lilia, 1896–1939

Fundamental changes in the character of T.J. Smith's business began with his death and his nephew's succession. The product range was extended and emphasis quickly shifted from cod liver oil to bandages and surgical dressings. Under H.N.'s management Smith & Nephew entered a period of unprecedented growth in employees, in the area covered by the premises, and in the number of plants, including overseas branches.

Three principal product lines, Elastoplast, Cellona/Gypsona and Lilia, provided the basis for the more than hundredfold growth of the company's capital in 30 years. Two of these three brands originated from Johannes Lohmann, a German with whom H.N. enjoyed a long and warm friendship.[1] Lohmann set up the production of surgical dressings for H.N. In return, most probably it was through H.N. Smith that Ernest Buckley in May 1904 introduced a new accounting scheme at Lohmann's firm Lüscher & Bömper.[2]

H.N.'S EARLY YEARS

Horatio Nelson Smith, named after his grandfather, was the third, rather late, child of George Frederick Smith and Lucy Harding. His elder brother, Thomas Brooks, had been born 12 years earlier, and his sister, the suffragette Annie Amelia, was 11 years older. Thomas Brooks entered his father's paper business, but when he was nine, H.N. was sent from Manchester to Hornsea to live with his uncle Thomas and his aunt, Amelia Ann. He was educated in Hornsea for four years and then attended the City of London School. A significant phase in his education for the development of Smith & Nephew was a year spent in Germany.

In 1890 at the age of 16 he started work for £12 a year with Fredrick Doble and Sons, of 20 Aldermanbury, London. The firm was a wholesale drapers and woollen manufacturers, with a subsidiary in Dewsbury, Yorkshire, making rugs and blankets.[3] H.N. worked for the business until January 1896, when on being refused a rise, he joined his uncle in Hull. The knowledge of textile manufacture he acquired was to prove invaluable.

H.N. at first shared Hull business premises with his father and brother, Thomas Brooks, who also shared an entrepreneurial streak with H.N.[4] H.N. cooperated with Brooks's firm until 1916 to the extent of undertaking business for them when visting the US.[5] Thomas Brooks was a director of T.J. Smith & Nephew Ltd when the company was registered under the Companies Act in 1907.[6] H.N. became a more successful entrepreneur than Brooks; Brooks left the paper business at the beginning of the 1920s and set up as an organizer of travel excursions.

H.N. was known for many qualities. He was variously described as 'the rudest man you have ever met', as having 'the most inquisitive and penetrating mind I had ever come across'.[7] He had something of the pirate about him, according to his long-time friend and collaborator, Johannes Lohmann, but that was more than compensated by his warmth and genuine concern for people, especially but not only those who worked for him.[8] He was uninterested in display for its own sake and had simple tastes. His colleagues noted his humour, his insatiable curiosity and his humanity.

There is no doubt that H.N.'s most important Hull business relationship was with Ernest Buckley, because of the financial expertise and control that Buckley provided as a director of Smith & Nephew from 1920. Buckley proved valuable to H.N. in 1907 when Smith & Nephew became a private limited company and had to submit to the (very minimal) legal requirements that status imposed. Smith & Nephew continued to benefit from Buckley's guidance for more than three decades.[9] Within two years of assuming control, on his twenty-fourth birthday, H.N. felt secure enough to marry, at a Baptist Chapel in Bromley, Margaret Syme, the daughter of a builder.[10]

When H.N. took over his uncle's firm the principal business was cod liver oil and a limited range of Robinsons bandages and dressings. End-of-year

Table 4.1   Value of end of year stocks at T.J. Smith & Nephew, 1896–1902

	Total			Cod liver oil			Dressings			Sundries		
	£	s	d	£	s	d	£	s	d	£	s	d
1896	690	9	4	514	12	11	67	1	9	108	14	8
1897	460	4	2	177	8	11	219	19	6	62	15	9
1898	486	7	7	173	4	0	210	13	8	102	9	11
1899	453	16	10	181	14	0	180	1	3	92	1	7
1900	765	6	8	166	10	0	426	15	8	172	1	0
1901	1155	16	3	123	8	0	610	7	0	422	1	3
1902	1220	1	8	179	4	7	687	6	10	353	10	3

Note: Sundries are mainly oils, such as turps, petroleum jelly and linseed meal.

stock figures show how quickly H.N. changed the direction of the business (Table 4.1).

In December 1896 cod liver oil stocks were three-quarters of the total. A year later they were little more than one-third. If stock levels reflected turnover between 1897 and 1902 H.N.'s business grew by 165 per cent or at an average rate of nearly 20 per cent per annum.

Employment expanded slightly less rapidly. In 1896 there had been three members of staff. At the end of the century the number employed in the firm reached five, with H.N. acting as his own travelling salesman. By 1906 the staff had risen to 12; when H.N. secured a contract with the Turkish War Office on the outbreak of the Turkish–Bulgarian War in 1911, this figure more than quadrupled to reach 54, and the annual turnover touched £40 000.[11] On the factory side there were about 12 men, jacks of all trades, stockmen, packers and one bandage machine operator plus one job, that was disliked by everybody: impregnation of Iodoform gauze. They all worked 11 hours on weekdays beginning at 7 a.m. and finishing at 1 p.m. on Saturday. Office staff, including H.N. Smith, signed in morning and afternoon. Some, again including H.N., worked until 10 or 11 in the evening.[12] Edwin Robinson, eventually to retire from the Smith & Nephew Board in 1961, joined H.N. in 1912 as buyer of printed matter and packaging material.[13] The following year, a chemist, Noel Akers, was hired.[14]

H.N. took over the small competitor Hull company of Lambert & Lambert just before the outbreak of the First World War. The pattern of absorbing top management of acquired companies which has been a characteristic of Smith & Nephew's growth had already begun when G.A. Lambert became H.N.'s sales manager.

THE IMPACT OF WAR AND DEPRESSION

With the outbreak of the First World War in 1914, the demand for bandages and surgical dressings escalated. Over the four years of the war, Smith & Nephew fulfilled contracts with the French government, the Belgian Army Medical Service, the Serb Army, the British and American Armies and the American Red Cross. The number of staff rose to 1 200 and the turnover for the four years exceeded £2.5m. H.N.'s passport shows how widely he travelled in search of these contracts, including the French military zone in his sweep. His directorship of Lambert & Lambert probably brought him into contact with Anglo-French Supplies, a company particularly concerned to act as middlemen in ambitious armament sales. Anglo-French introduced the French minister of ammunition to an offer of 4–5 million rifles and ammunition.[15] This association was the reason for opening H.N.'s Manchester factory

at Park Gate, Hollinwood, to supply bandoliers and other military equipment.[16] Edwin Robinson had been sent to Manchester in 1915 to open a
buying office. Together with H.N. he started the sewing factory that employed over 400 sewing machines by the Armistice.[17] H.N. also contracted
for very large quantities of surgical dressings for sale to the French government before he had the capacity to deliver. He approached the firm of Smith
& Forrest, weavers of Blackburn, and managed to carry out these contracts,
firmly establishing Smith & Nephew in the field of surgical dressings.[18]

Expansion required the securing of raw materials and therefore a mill was
bought near Rochdale to satisfy the company's need for cotton wool and lint.
The Wardle Cotton Company acquisition was one of the earlier cooperative
ventures of H.N. with Ernest Buckley. Buckley and James Smith of Blackburn
(also of Smith & Forrest above) established the Wardle Cotton Company to
supply military medical dressings from Rochdale in 1916.[19] Products were
sold both unbranded and under the trade mark 'Wardella'.[20] Buckley and
James Smith transferred all the shares in September 1919 to H.N. Smith and
Adam Brown, an employee of H.N. The following year Wardle was sold to
the Amalgamated Cotton Manufacturers' Trust. In 1924, despite the slump,
the company was still a profitable supplier of medical dressings, employing
over 200 people and 14 000 spindles. Wardle was an integrated concern but
Smith & Nephew itself did not become so fully integrated again until the
early 1950s.

Like so many firms geared to wartime production, Smith & Nephew en-
countered severe problems when the war finally ended; by October 1920 the
number of staff had shrunk to 183. However, the company's response, together with some fortuitous legislation, shaped the company's future and
enabled it to attain international stature. The first major entrepreneurial coup
was employing the enormous war surplus stocks of lint substitute at the
Manchester branch, centred around the Rochdale mill. These were made into
women's underwear which sold surprisingly well and provided the basis for
later clothing manufacture, under the brand names of 'Trimsona' and 'Land-
o-Nod'.

When the 1924 Factory Act made compulsory the keeping of first aid kits
on the premises for a wide range of industrial and commercial establishments, a market was created that Smith & Nephew were well equipped to
supply. At the same time the Board of Trade were required to ensure that
miners carried personal first aid kits at all times. Smith & Nephew provided
dressings of a standard size and tin containers were commissioned to hold the
dressings. Because of a failure of communication, the tins were made smaller
than the dressings. Smith & Nephew therefore quickly developed a technique
to compress their product; the resulting compressed bandage was used for
many years.

LILIA

Two years later, in 1926, Smith & Nephew produced a cellulose sanitary towel with the brand name 'Lilia'. In common with many innovations in the health care field this one also originated in Germany where necessity was the mother of invention. Paper-based soluble towels appear to have been introduced during the war as a consequence of the difficulties of getting cotton through the Allied blockade. Lohmann's company, Lüscher & Bömper, in 1916 acquired Hedwigsthal, a paper mill that still exists today. After the war Lohmann bought the mill himself and invited Smith & Nephew to take a half share.[21] They took up the offer in 1925, together with Alfred Meissner of Jülich.

Smith & Nephew's move into sanitary protection had originated with the purchase of a small Leicester manufacturing business, SASHENA ('Sanitary Absorbent Safe Hygienic Every Nurse Advocates') in 1912. Maternity pads had been made for hospital use by hand, the cotton wool filling being cut on a guillotine and encased in open gauze. Sanitary towels for general sale were imported free of duty before 1914 and retailed at 6d per packet of 12.[22]

As for Southalls earlier, Smith & Nephew's diversification made good sense because the materials needed for sanitary towel manufacture were similar to those used in the production of surgical dressings. More importantly the initiative was a response to a rapidly growing demand. The tertiary sector was expanding; education, nursing, clerical work and retailing provided jobs for women and freed them from 'the prison of domesticity' (Checkland, 1965, p. 400). Votes for women over 30 in 1918, and for those over 21 in 1929, symbolized their increasingly active role in society as a whole. As the proportion of women in the work force grew, the disposable sanitary towel must have been very welcome.

Lilia came under the Smith & Nephew banner through another of H.N.'s acquisitions, a company controlled by John McLaren. McLaren sold a cellulose towel, chiefly to factories, under the trade mark Lilia. He became sales director of SASHENA. Sam Lovatt, the production director, developed machines for producing cellulose towels using 37-ply cellulose bought in sheets from Robinson's of Chesterfield.[23] Rising demand for Lilia required the opening in Kentish Town of a factory supplying only London and the South, and in 1933, the acquisition of a factory in Failsworth.

Mass production of sanitary towels came to be the principal concern of Smith & Nephew's engineering capacity in the interwar years. From 1918 until 1924 hand-made cotton wool towels and cellulose towels were produced in Hull in small quantities, primarily for Woolworth's, under their brand name. Between 1924 and 1928 Smith & Nephew operated a plant making cotton wool at Platt Bridge, near Wigan, part of which was equipped with attachments for producing cotton wool in sliver form. This enabled the company to start semi-automatic production of cotton wool and cellulose towels on filling machines produced by Smith & Nephew engineers at Hull and using tubular gauze made by Hindle Warburton. During the 1930s the engineering department of Smith & Nephew saved the company buying American machines by themselves making equipment for round-ended Lilia towels.[24]

Towards the end of the end of the interwar period cultural evolution and product development brought more changes to this market. In 1935 Tampax introduced their tampon, and Smith & Nephew three years later initiated what the Board minutes refer to as 'the search for the perfect tampon'.[25] Not until 1954 though did this search culminate in the launching of the company's Lil-let brand.

ELASTOPLAST

Origins

Smith & Nephew's rights to Elastoplast originated with the Lohmann connection in which financial expertise and access to finance were exchanged for new products. Buckley was elected to the Lohmann's supervisory board in May 1931, probably for a four-year period. Lohmann invented an elastic type of cloth spread with an adhesive in 1924, known as 'Elastoplast'.[26] H.N. Smith took a keen interest in the developments and licence agreements were reached, but apparently not signed, in 1927.

The agreement of November 1930 assigned the rights to the British patent for the manufacture of novel adhesive bandages and the corresponding rights to the trade mark of 'Elastoplast' to Smith & Nephew. Smith & Nephew were also given the right to register the trade mark of Elastoplast and to manufacture, sell and distribute the product in all countries that were part of the British Empire.[27] Lüscher & Bömper, or Lohmann AG (the name was changed in 1929 and the document had been prepared before then) agreed not to take part in any of the above activities in any of these areas, and not to restrict or interfere with Smith & Nephew's business in any way. The British company was granted full rights to develop the product and to apply for patents. The condition for obtaining these rights was the payment of 2 per cent of the net proceeds of the sales made by Smith & Nephew to the German company as long as the patent was valid.[28] At the same time Johannes Lohmann also agreed to grant René Fisch manufacturing process rights for 'Elastoplaste', 'Elastocorn' and 'Elastofuron' for France and the French colonies on similar terms. On the strength of this licence Fisch established in 1931 a joint venture with Lohmann AG, Société Elasto, Mulhouse.[29]

By July 1931 financial difficulties associated with the world depression and economic crisis in Germany, and a prior dispute, forced Lohmann AG to sell the Elastoplast manufacturing rights and trademark to Beiersdorf AG. A new agreement was drawn up between Smith & Nephew and Beiersdorf less favourable to the first company. Smith & Nephew was not to impede Beiersdorf in Britain and the British Empire. The German company henceforth was allowed to manufacture and sell elastic plaster in these regions but not under the trade mark name of Elastoplast. In return Smith & Nephew was allowed to sell, though not to manufacture, elastic plaster outside the British Empire, but similarly not under the Elastoplast name. A price range for the product was to be agreed by the two companies to allow some pricing freedom while avoiding policies of undercutting. A further stipulation was that neither company should refer to the other in its advertising. The agreement also required that any difficulties should be settled in an amicable fashion, and that the two companies should enter into closer relations at a future date. René Fisch in France was in a similar position to Smith & Nephew.

H.N. granted the Beiersdorf subsidiary in Britain, at Welwyn Garden City, a non-exclusive licence to manufacture and sell Elastoplast surgical bandages in the UK in 1933, renewed in 1937.[30] With the outbreak of the Second World War, Beiersdorf UK was taken over by the Custodian of Enemy Property, and its name changed to Herts Pharmaceuticals; in 1951 this company was acquired by Smith & Nephew Associated Companies. Laboratoires Fisch are now also owned by Smith & Nephew and during the 1930s made pharmaceutical products and plaster of Paris bandages, as well as Elastoplast.

Manufacture

Elasticity was already incorporated in the cloth when it arrived in Hull; there is in fact no elastic as such woven into the fabric; flexibility is attained through a special twisting of some of the threads during the cloth's manufacture. The first port of call in Hull was the company-owned laundry in Bean Street. The cloth was washed in a machine to achieve shrinkage and then passed through a scutching (dressing by beating) process. Next lengths of the material were fed up and over a beam, which was positioned to allow the fabric to fall on to a pivoting metal plate. Girls were employed to swivel the plate so as to untangle the cloth, which was pulled out and then passed through an ironing process; it was then pleated and cut. The selvedges were used to make rugs.

After cutting, the material was moved to the Elastoplast Department in Neptune Street. The lengths of cloth were stretched over a long table, held at one end by an iron retention bar; a hand wheel extended the cloth, which was then retained by spiked boards. As the cloth was stretched, it passed under a spreader box full of the adhesive mass. There were six small machines that mixed the adhesive before spreading. As far as it is possible to tell, the cloth was cut at this stage, or just before, into 12 bandage widths. Girls transferred the spread bandages on to a circular frame (this looked like a scaled-down version of a Ferris wheel at a fair), which held approximately 144 bandages. The bandages were separated by long wooden sticks; the positioning of these sticks required great skill for the process ran at great speed, and there was some rivalry between workers as to who could work fastest.

Once loaded on to the frames the bandages were transferred to a drying room for two to three hours, after which they were spooled on to cores using a basic manually operated spooling machine. The girls employed during the spooling process were paid piece rates, so much for a gross (144) bandages. It was very hard work and in the 1930s they took home on average around 30 shillings (£1.50) a week.[31] This wage represented approximately half the average adult male wage in manufacturing, the figure for which stood at £2.95 in 1931.

Market and Marketing

The American company, Johnson & Johnson, had introduced Band-Aid at the beginning of the 1920s (Johnson & Johnson 1979), but there was no product on the market with the elasticity or adhesive qualities of Elastoplast. As with many innovative products, the need for Elastoplast was not self-evident at the time. The application of Elastoplast in first aid was obvious but it was more expensive than traditional forms of dressing. Elastoplast became established on the medical market through the friendship of H.N. with a surgeon at St Mary's Hospital, London, Arthur Dickson Wright, FRCS.[32] Dickson Wright was concerned with the treatment of leg ulcers and was attempting to revive compression as a means of treatment. H.N. was very keen on Bridge, playing regularly with Wright and others. After he had negotiated the agreement with Lohmann, H.N. took a sample of Elastoplast bandage along to one of his Bridge evenings and told his friends of his latest business venture. He passed the bandage over to Wright, asking if he could see any use for it in his work. Wright found that Elastoplast had all the properties he was looking for in treating leg ulcers, and asked for an immediate supply.

In his address to the Medical Society of London on 23 February 1931 entitled *The Treatment of Indolent Ulcer of the Leg,* Dickson Wright made a strong case for the use of Elastoplast or similar bandages (Dickson Wright 1931). He estimated the number of cases of indolent ulcers under treatment in Britain at the time of his article at one quarter of a million. (The total population of the United Kingdom was 46.87m in 1935.) Dickson Wright had managed to cure 41 cases of ulcer in which amputation had been advised, by a novel form of support for the limb as a means of combating the gravitational forces upon the circulatory system that caused ulcers.

> The support that I use is an *adhesive plaster of an elastic type;* the market is now flooded with different types and this in itself is an excellent sign. So far I have not changed from *the original Elastoplast bandage* which I have now used for over two years. The adhesive is applied directly to the skin, ulcer, and eczema, and extends from toes to knee and requires six metres of three inch bandage for the purpose. (Dickson Wright 1931, p. 459)

The fundamental principles of Dickson Wright's argument for the general adoption of his methods were:

> The treatment of a common chronic disease of the lower classes, like gravitational ulcer, must be simple so that any doctor can apply it because the disease is so common. It must also not be timeconsuming because to the doctor time is important. It must be ambulatory, if possible allowing the patient to work. It must not be painful or productive of great inconvenience to the patient, otherwise the treatment may not be followed and a relapse, if it occurs, will be regarded by the patient as a catastrophe and destroy all confidence. It must not involve any hospitalisation because there are not enough hospitals to go round. It must as far as possible be a permanent cure. And lastly it must be cheap. (Dickson Wright 1931, p. 458–9)

Dickson Wright gave two vital instructions (ibid., p. 460; see also Dickson Wright 1940). The first was that the patient should return for regular checkups, during which the bandages were changed and the accompanying varicose veins were treated. The second was that the patient should go back to work and take plenty of walking exercise. Before the elastic adhesive bandage the only way to treat these ulcers through neutralization of the effects of gravity on circulation was by confining the patient to bed for months, and sometimes years at a time. The freedom to work and walk during treatment that Elastoplast facilitated was revolutionary. The patient could earn a living and hospital expenditure was cut, thanks to the reduction in the number of beds occupied by ulcer patients. The average duration of treatment was also drastically reduced, as Wright pointed out in his address to the Medical Society (Dickson Wright 1931); he had cured an ulcer, that had afflicted a patient for 15 years, in seven weeks. 'The patient [in question] had been a regular hospital outpatient for twelve years and had had an Unna's paste dressing applied *three hundred* times at least.'[33] Similar evidence was published by A J Cokkinis:[34]

The early results of the sodium morrhuate and Elastoplast treatment are usually extremely satisfactory. The venous stagnation is relieved, the pain and oedema disappear, and the ulcer rapidly diminishes in size. This rapid improvement of the ulcer is sometimes astonishing. ...I find that in no less than 63 of my cases [out of 144], either rapid or very rapid initial diminution of the ulcer is recorded. ...Ten cases show an average rate of healing of over 2 sq. in. per week,...two actually giving a healing-rate of 3 1/2 sq. in. in a week! (Cokkinis 1933, p. 1171)

Cokkinis went on to announce an 80 per cent success rate; though less than Dickson Wright's, perhaps the results were more credible. After considering some minor disadvantages of the treatment, such as the frequent occurrence of eczema, Cokkinis stated:

'With the exception of Elastoplast itself, I have not found other forms of perma- nent support very successful... The advantages of the ambulatory method [thus achieved] overshadow its disadvantages. It is relatively inexpensive, gives early relief, heartens the patient...and above all saves the patient and the State much waste of time and money. (Cokkinis 1933, pp. 1171–2)

On economic, humanitarian and perhaps psychological grounds, the use of Elastoplast was a major advance in the treatment of a too common scourge.[35] Quantification of the contribution to society of Dickson Wright's use of Elastoplast requires comparing the cost of treatment using Elastoplast with the only effective alternative, bed-rest in hospital for one year. The following categories of costs should be taken into consideration: materials, medical supervision, hospital for the period of treatment, the loss of earnings of the patient and any of his or her family who assume a nursing role, and patient discomfort. Estimates of these costs have been ascertained from contempo- rary sources, and a very approximate calculation of the social gains from the new treatment are presented in Table 4.2.

The results obtained by Dickson Wright and Cokkinis proved the value of the Elastoplast bandage but the diffusion and acceptance of the results could have been a slow business. H.N. Smith was able and willing to employ imaginative and novel marketing techniques to speed up the process. Dickson Wright's findings first appeared in the *Clinical Journal*, and H.N., feeling that the news should not be restricted to the *Journal*'s readership, enquired as to the possibility of reprinting the article. To his dismay he found that reprints were restricted to a run of 500, so instead he had the entire issue reprinted, a total of 40 000 copies, which were circulated to members of the medical profession, one for every doctor in the country.

In April 1929, H.N. sent sample boxes containing about six different samples of Elastoplast, the standard bandage in various lengths and widths, and in dressing form designed for fingers, boils and so on, to strategically placed London doctors and surgeons, especially those in Harley Street. Two

Table 4.2   Potential cost reductions from the use of Elastoplast in the treatment of varicose ulcers, 1931

Traditional treatment	Elastoplast treatment
Hospital expenses and wages foregone per annum	Cost of Elastoplast 1s. per week Total cost of treatment £10 Wages foregone (2 weeks) £5
£280 per patient	£15 per patient

Total number of ulcer patients
250 000
Total cost of treating all patients

£280 × 250 000 = £70m (1.67% of 1931 national income)	£15 × 250 000 = £3.75m

Cost reduction = £66.25m

Source: calculated from Dickson-Wright (1931).

months later the first orders began to arrive, mainly from wholesale chemists, including Sangars in Hampstead Road.[36] At around the same time H.N. used another marketing ploy, donating Elastoplast dressings for the FA Cup Final.

More controversial was 'Phyllis', a rather realistic shop window model whose anatomy displayed the then 14 different types of Elastoplast. She attracted a great deal of interest at medical exhibitions in Manchester, Leeds and Dublin. Finally the excitement she created at the 1932 London Medical Congress persuaded the Congress President that she should be modestly covered and Phyllis therefore became redundant (Dagger 1971).

CELLONA/GYPSONA

In 1930 Smith & Nephew launched their plaster of Paris bandage, Cellona, later called Gypsona, from the Greek name for the mineral alabaster, 'gypsum'. The Romans used gypsum-based plaster on the walls of the Second Legion's barracks at Caerleon in Monmouthshire and in their coffins at York. Yet plaster of Paris was then forgotten in Britain until the later Middle Ages when it was imported, as the name suggests, from France. In the Harz mountains of Germany deposits of gypsum exceed 100-feet thickness but in England they are rarely greater than 15 feet. Particularly suitable for surgical bandages is Nottinghamshire gypsum, 99.8 per cent pure and very white. Gypsum is heated in a kiln and then ground to a powder to make plaster of Paris.

Egyptian self-setting bandages date from 1600 BC but neither they, nor their succesors in Europe, employed plaster of Paris. Bone-setters in eighteenth century England stiffened bandages with egg whites and wheat flour. By the end of that century Arab doctors were efficiently using plaster for severe compound fractures. The Dutch military surgeon Matthysen was responsible in 1852 for the predominant self-setting plaster bandage in Europe for more than half a century before 1930. This was the application of strips of coarse cotton cloth into which finely powdered plaster had been rubbed.[37]

Before the introduction of Cellona the making of these plaster of Paris bandages was (a messy) part of the probationer nurse's training in all general hospitals, and thus the selling of a proprietary bandage was not easy. Smith & Nephew's Cellona bandages were made with a specially woven cloth (Leno) impregnated with a high-quality, cellulose-compounded plaster. Cellona's strengths lay in the fact that it was uniform, easy to handle and, after being dipped in water, it set in two minutes. If used correctly, the bandage was much more comfortable for the patient, and its lightness shortened the treatment, saving time particularly on physiotherapy. However, it cost more than the traditionally prepared bandage which created the need for further innovative marketing. Casts of feet were made from the specially devised plaster and then bandaged with the new product, showing the strength and lightness of Cellona/Gypsona. Thousands were made and sent to hospitals in an attempt to gain customers, but cost continued to be a problem.

As an encouragement, Smith & Nephew offered large hospitals a three month supply of Cellona/Gypsona for the cost of the cloth and plaster they used in making their own. The superiority of Cellona/Gypsona was recognized and demand grew. The timing of the launch was fortuitous. The British Medical Association had ordered a report on the treatment of fractures, in response to increasing interest in the economic consequences of industrial accidents. In 1897 the Workmen's Compensation Act required employers to pay half the wages that an employee lost through job-related injuries; later legislation provided compensation for job-related illness as well. During the First World War the treatment of fractures was for the first time undertaken on a systematic basis, but after hostilities ceased, the clinics were disbanded and much of the expertise was lost.

During the 1920s industrial accidents cost approximately £12m a year in compensation paid by employers and loss of earnings by employees. Interest in reducing these costs may be seen in the basic first aid provisions enforced under the Factory Act of 1924. Accidents that caused permanent disability were of even greater concern to employers, insurance companies and trade unions alike, on both economic and humanitarian grounds. Since disability was often the result of broken or fractured bones, treatment of such injuries attracted increasing attention. A British Medical Association report was commissioned in the belief that through more careful treatment of fractures, better results could be achieved, and time and money would be saved.[38]

Fracture treatment was much more advanced in some parts of Europe, Vienna in particular, than in Britain. Johannes Lohmann had a long-standing relation with the Viennese clinic of Dr Boehler, where the first fracture treatment film was made in October 1934.[39] Through Lohmann H.N. Smith therefore arranged for several English surgeons to visit and report their findings. The recovery rate at the clinic was far higher than any that had been achieved in Britain; amounts paid in compensation for permanent disability had been cut by one-third. For certain types of injury the reduction was far greater. A report was sent to the medical authorities, and in 1935 the findings of the BMA enquiry were published. The most important recommendations were that fracture cases should be segregated from the general surgical ward into fracture clinics, that each case should have continuity of treatment, and that one person should be responsible for the patient.

Anticipating the report of the committee which began work in 1933, and perhaps with prior knowledge of its findings, Smith & Nephew made their first medical film in 1934. Called the 'Functional Treatment of Fractures', the film was made under the guidance of Reginald Watson-Jones and Norman

Table 4.3   Potential cost reductions in fracture treatment through clinics and Cellona/Gypsona, 1935

	Traditional treatment	Special clinics and Cellona/Gypsona
Average incapacity period	0.61 yr	0.2 yr
Average yearly wage	£130	£130
Average wages foregone	£79.3	£26
Total number of fractures	200 000	
Total wages foregone	£15m	£5.2m
Total cost reduction	£9.8m	
	(0.37% of national income in 1934)	

Source: calculated from BMA Report on the Treatment of Fractures, 1935.

Roberts, consultants to the Liverpool Royal Infirmary. It was one of the first films made for medical purposes and the techniques demonstrated were the next year endorsed by the BMA report.[40] The film was shown to branches of the British Medical Association throughout the country; as the number of fracture clinics increased so did the demand for Cellona/Gypsona.

Cellona use could only be encouraged with the help of practitioners who early recognized its value. Smith & Nephew attracted some of the most innovative to develop Cellona: Watson-Jones, with whom H.N. played Bridge, K. Hampden Pridie of Bristol Royal Infirmary (responsible for writing the original *Cellona Technique*), W. Sayle-Creer of Salford Royal Infirmary and J.R. Blackburne of Hull Royal Infirmary.[41] A simple estimate of the potential social gains from Cellona and Fracture Clinics is shown in Table 4.3.

CELLONA AND THE TRANSFER OF TECHNOLOGY

As in the case of Elastoplast, Smith & Nephew's manufacture of Cellona/ Gypsona originated with a Lohmann innovation embodied in a licence of 1932. Unlike the case of Elastoplast, Lohmann was not the only contributor. Lohmann AG had invented a solvent-based manufacturing process and commissioned Dr Eichengrun's Cellon-Werke to develop a suitable solvent formula. If relative payments under the licence measure their respective contributions, Johannes Lohmann and Dr Arthur Eichengrun in Berlin were responsible in the ratio 3 to 1 for Cellona.[42] Their relations were turbulent, Eichengrun accusing Lohmann of delaying transmission of Smith & Nephew payments to him, trying, eventually successfully, to reduce Eichengrun's payments, and withholding technical developments in Cellona manufacture from Smith & Nephew, contrary to the terms of the licence. Their dispute was eventually settled in 1938 when Eichengrun conceded that filing a patent for a solvent was a breach of confidence since the underlying invention had been made at Lohmann's.

Transfer of technology was a continuing process and one that was hard to formalize. Very often at the German end it was the result of painstaking systematic trial and error rather than based upon advanced technical knowledge. Transferring the results equally depended on minutiae of production processes which were unsophisticated but which might have taken some considerable time and resources to discover by Smith & Nephew's own efforts. Negotiations for production by Smith & Nephew were well under way by the end of 1931 and concluded in 1932. Licensing and market sharing was a sensible arrangement for products based on new techniques for it avoided duplication of research effort and economized on scarce capital in Germany. (In August 1933 Smith & Nephew granted a loan of about 151 000

RM to Lohmann.[43]) But subsequent difficulties emerged which drew attention to the value of an in-house research department.

The most appropriate processes were likely to differ between countries with the varying availability of chemicals and other raw materials. On the other hand the terms of the licensing agreement (assuming they could be enforced) might constrain the choice of technique. Smith & Nephew originally bought their plaster of Paris from Lohmann's, and paid a royalty of 5 per cent, but since Lohmann's total revenues also depended on total UK sales, he had an incentive to encourage Smith & Nephew to buy cheaper plaster in Britain and so boost sales by reducing prices. Smith & Nephew therefore had to find a suitable domestic plaster, with a greasy feel instead of the usual dry and dusty texture. Achieving the different texture was a matter of coarsely grinding the plaster before burning at about 150°C and then finely grinding it afterwards.

In 1933 Lohmann obtained a new Bindenlack (resin for binding the plaster) from IG Farben, about 25 per cent cheaper than the original and at the time thought superior to Eichengrun's. But Smith & Nephew were obliged by their licence to use adhesive resin from Eichengrun's own company, Cellon-Werke – at any rate in small proportions – in the manufacture of Cellona. Lohmann's plant at Fahr used methyl alcohol advantageously instead of the methylated spirits employed by Smith & Nephew.

Even though ICI had been formed in 1926 from a merger of four established British chemical firms to utilize scale economies, chemicals were often still much cheaper in Germany than in Britain. Methylene chloride, which was needed for the Cellona process, cost 40 per cent less, for instance. This placed a premium on an effective solvent (for the adhesive) recovery plant in Britain. The huge German chemical combine, IG Farben, thought Eichengrun merely mixed methylene chloride with the adhesive to form the paste which Smith & Nephew bought from him.[44]

Five years later Cellabaster was being manufactured at Fahr with both the old Eichengrun process and the new water-based process, which was not altogether satisfactory. Lohmann had found a new binding material but would not tell Smith & Nephew what the formula was. In 1936 Lohmann had applied for a patent on the new process competitive with Cellona in Germany. By contrast with the British process, the shortage of imported raw materials in Germany allowed Lohmann only gauze of poor quality and required them to use a proportion of expensive artificial fibre. Smith & Nephew's May 1938 visit was not welcome, ostensibly because the process was not ready. By then, everybody was expecting the outbreak of war and therefore the ending of information exchange. Smith & Nephew stopped payment of royalties early in 1939.

Fisch were less vulnerable to the cessation of technology transfer, even though they acquired a Cellona licence for France at the same time as Smith

& Nephew were granted their rights. Richard Lohmann, then a young Lohmann AG employee, was assigned to Mulhouse to help René Fisch set up the first plaster of Paris bandage production.[45] But probably because he received less help from Lohmann's, Fisch employed Adrien Notter, a chemical engineer, to work on the process. In 1933 Notter found a new plaster of Paris manufacturing process. After five years, Fisch was able to take out a patent for this 'aqueous' process (by contrast with Eichengrun's 'anhydrous' technique).[46] The French company was therefore already on the way to technological independence by 1939. Even in the British case the transfer of technology was far from complete, and a good deal of local technological ingenuity was evoked. Each of the three companies made plaster of Paris with different machines, with different materials and obtained different quality products.

CONCLUSION

Each of the products that accelerated Smith & Nephew into the big league in the years between the world wars were textile-based, and all except the night clothes, which had begun as an emergency response to collapsing postwar demand, were directed to the health care market (see Figure 4.1). Both the technology base and selling techniques of the company bore the distinctive imprint of H.N. Smith. Early life in Manchester followed by work experience in a draper's made H.N. aware of possibilities in this segment of health care and his contacts allowed him to draw on Lohmann's expertise in this area without committing resources to expensive and risky research programmes. By the late 1930s the difficulties of not operating a company research department were beginning to become apparent.

H.N.'s ebullient and sociable personality was at its most effective in marketing aimed at the medical profession. At the same time his social life enabled him to ascertain what the profession needed and to anticipate findings of its committees.

British companies and individuals are commonly said to have been good at invention but poor at successfully bringing them to the marketplace. The early history of Smith & Nephew is the antithesis of this stereotype. Under H.N. Smith, and subsequently, the company acquired products from Germany that they were to market with great ingenuity and success: Elastoplast in 1929, Cellona/Gypsona, Nivea and finally Lil-lets in 1954. Both H.N. Smith and Ernest Buckley, his long-time protégé, were fluent German speakers with close friends and associates in Germany, from which they, and the company, gained enormously.

Figure 4.1   Smith & Nephew principal products, 1858–1951

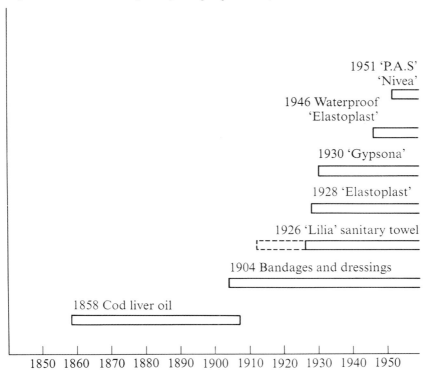

NOTES

1. Communication from Dr Martin Barth, 3 February 1992, recollections of Johannes Lohmann. 'Coming to Fahr [Lohmann's home town] is like coming home', H.N. wrote.
2. Barth to Fryer, citing Lohmann's AI/23, 27. Thereafter Buckley served as Lüscher & Bömper's official accountant from 1905 until 1912 and, in the case of some affiliated businesses, even until 1916. In November 1904, Lüscher & Bömper sold to the Hull firm of Lambert & Lambert surgical dressing manufacturing plant, later shipping cotton wool and other raw materials. H.N. Smith became a director of Lambert & Lambert and the largest shareholder in 1913. *Share Dealing Register – Lambert & Lambert*, Smith & Nephew Archives Hull. The firm was wound up in 1920.
3. 'Meeting HN', *Sanaco News*, I, pt. 1 (1954).
4. G.F. Smith & Son have had long-standing ties with an American producer of high-quality papers, the Strathmore Paper Company or, as it was previously called, the Mittineaque Paper Company. Unfortunately, at the turn of the century the American company only did British business with their established British agents, who would not supply potential competitors. George and Thomas Brooks Smith very much wanted to deal in Mittineaque paper, so much so that when Thomas was on business in America, at the turn of the

century, he decided quite suddenly to call upon the president of the company, Horace A. Moses. He arrived in Mittineaque, Massachusetts, on a Saturday and his return passage was booked for Monday. He decided to call at the Moses' home, being unable to call within proper business hours. When he left, the company of G.F. Smith and Son had become authorized agents of the Mittineaque Paper Company.

The Moses found a crisis on their hands. A special performance of an oratorio had been planned for that evening in the family's local church, but the organist was seriously ill. Fortunately Thomas Brooks Smith, known as just Brooks, was able to play the organ and knew the oratorio in question. After the performance, which incidentally went very well, the Minister reminded the appreciative congregation of 'their debt to this God-sent visitor from another country'. The Moses insisted that Brooks stay with them, arranged for his luggage to be removed from his hotel, and a licence for dealing in the American paper was signed and sealed.

The episode shows the interrelationship between social and business transactions, a facet of life of which H.N. Smith, like Brooks, was to take full advantage. *G F Smith and Sons London Limited*, Commemorative leaflet, Smith & Nephew Archives, Hull.

5. As shown by the acrimonious correspondence between H.N. Smith and B.A. Franklin of Strathmore Paper Co (formerly Mittineaque) Mass., 2 March and 31 March 1916, G.F. Smith & Sons Archives, Hull.

6. The other director was A. Samuel Haller, a Hull ship-owner. The nominal capital registered was £4 000. *Agreement for Sale of Business Dated 25 July 1907* P4 Smith & Nephew Archives, Hull.

7. The first description was by Stanley Duckworth of Colne. The second was by George Whittaker, later Deputy Chairman of Smith & Nephew. See G. Whittaker, *A Handful of Shale*, unpublished ms, S & N, Brierfield, p. 171.

8. George Leavey, then Chairman, in Obituary, *Pharmaceutical Journal*, 17 September 1960, p. 280. His granddaughter Jean visited him when he was 80 while she was studying French literature as an undergraduate. He cross-examined her about her work, which she thought was a long way from any interests of his. Yet a few weeks later she received through the post a package containing a great deal of material useful for her studies. Personal communication from Jean Charlton.

9. *Smith & Nephew Chairman's Annual Report 1949*. Ernest William Buckley was a founding partner of Buckley, Hall, Devin, who became Smith & Nephew's auditors. This firm eventually became Ernst & Young, at the time of writing still Smith & Nephew's auditors. Buckley directed a number of other companies including Eversharp, whose other directors, R.T. Outen and J.W. Hamilton Jones also achieved senior positions in Smith & Nephew.

10. Communication from S.M. O'Neill. H.N.'s brother married six years earlier at a Methodist Chapel.

11. According to Johannes Lohmann's memoirs H.N. learned of a Turkish tender from him. Barth, 3 February 1992.

12. *Time Book: Office Staff 1910–11*, vol. 55, Misc. 6, Smith & Nephew Archives, Hull.

13. Robinson began his career in 1904 with a Manchester firm of printers and boxmakers. Becoming MD of the Manchester subsidiary when it was formed in 1920, he played a leading role in establishing Smith & Nephew's bleachworks in 1937. In 1942 he became a director of Lilia whose affairs he managed for 10 years. He was also instrumental in the takeover of Hindle Warburton after the Second World War.'Sanaco Board Changes' *Smith & Nephew Reporter*, January–February 1961.

14. 'Recollections of S. Daly', *S & N Reporter*, November 1959.

15. *Anglo-French Supplies Minute Book*, Smith & Nephew Archives, Hull.

16. *Sanaco News*, vol. 4 no. 4, Christmas 1956, p. 12.

17. 'SANACO Board Changes', *Smith & Nephew Reporter*, January–February 1961.

18. *S & N Commemorative Brochure for the Visit of Overseas Directors to Brierfield*, 1958. The Smiths of Smith & Forrest seem to have been unrelated to H.N.'s family. The firm began in 1878 as Livesay, Smith & Forrest of Holehouse Mill. The founder, a T. Smith,

had three sons, William, Richard and James, who managed the business in the 1920s. *Times*, 8 February 1919 and 4 August 1928.

19. *Wardle Co Minute book*, Smith & Nephew Archives, Hull
20. Supplement to *Concerning Cotton: A Brief Account of the ACMT Ltd*, Amalgamated Cotton Manufacturers Trust 1920, Smith & Nephew Archives, Brierfield.
21. Dr Martin Barth to Alan Fryer 20 December 1991, citing Lohmann's AI/53,52. AII/101, Forts. 18 July 1925.
22. *A Review of the Merger Between Smith & Nephew (Lilia ltd) Southall & Arthur Berton*, p. 3, May 1961, Smith & Nephew/Southalls Archives, Birmingham.
23. A five-year contract agreed in 1938 fixed the price at 5 1/2 d. per lb. These sheets were cut by guillotine and split into individual towel size on a 'multi-cutter' built in Hull.
24. SANACO Board Meeting, 22 December 1937; *Minutes 1937–1947* pp. 67–8, Smith & Nephew Archives, London.
25. Smith & Nephew Board Minutes, 14 July 1938, p. 94, London.
26. Protected by a German 'Gebrauchsmuster' no.915.938, 4 July 1925. Patent applications were filed in France and Britain 27 May 1926. Barth to Fryer, 20 December 1991, citing Lohmann's AI/68a, AII/139, 151,207.
27. In all Dominions, colonies, protectorates and mandates with the exceptions of Egypt and Palestine.
28. Elastoplast file, Smith & Nephew Archives, Hull.
29. Communication from J.-P. Fisch. Barth to Fryer, citing Lohmann's AI/68a, AII/139, 151, 207.
30. Elasto 7 Agreement of 30 March 1933; Elasto 10 Agreement 30 March 1937. Smith & Nephew Archives, Hull.
31. Transcript of interview with Miss Florence Midforth, 8 May 1990, Smith & Nephew Archives, Hull.
32. Arthur Dickson Wright was a senior consultant surgeon at St Mary's and a member of the Council of the Royal College of Surgeons from 1949–65. Originally he practised general surgery, but branched out into neuro surgery and wrote many papers on the subject. In later years he devoted all his energy to the treatment of cancer. He was a fine after-dinner speaker, and spoke several languages fluently, including Russian. In a television series about 'Great Surgeons', when asked about post-operative mortality, he answered, 'Patients have died under my knife, but not as many as under other surgeons'. He was a consultant to Smith & Nephew from 1928 until his death in 1976. See P.S. Watson, *A Miscellany of Historical Notes Regarding the Development of Some of Our Earlier Products*, 1979, Smith & Nephew Archives, Hull, pp. 4–5.
33. Unna's paste was a well established but inconvenient treatment. Paul Unna (1859–1929) was a well known German dermatologist who had worked with Beiersdorf (whose headquarters are still in Unnastrasse). His casing for the treatment of leg ulcers was made by first spreading on the leg a paste made from zinc oxide, gelatin and glycerine and then covering it with a gauze bandage. The paste had to be softened in a double-pot water boiler before it could be spread. Once cooled it set firm.
34. At the time of writing, Cokkinis was Assistant Director of the Surgical Unit, St Mary's Hospital, London, and Assistant Surgeon at Wembley Hospital.
35. At the meeting of the Medical Society of London where Wright gave his paper, Sir Almroth Wright said he 'considered Mr Dickson Wright's work a great intellectual and humanitarian achievement'. Similarly, Mr Ernest Graham-Little spoke highly of the method in Mr Dickson Wright's hands: 'it had created a revolution in the treatment of this very troublesome condition.'
36. Transcript of interview with Stanley Quantrill 7 August 1990, Smith & Nephew Archives, Hull.
37. *The History and Function of Plaster of Paris in Surgery*, Smith & Nephew 1967, pp. 2–9; Elliott (1964). The chemical formula for gypsum is $CaSO_4.2H_2O$, calcium sulphate dihydrate. Plaster of Paris is $CaSO_4.1/2H_2O$. When water is added to plaster to give a cream, not all the plaster is dissolved at once and a reaction proceeds that deposits interlocking layers of crystals.

38. *British Medical Journal*, Supplement, 16 February 1935.
39. The same year that Dr Schnek from that clinic published his *Die Technik des ungespolsterten Gipsverbandes*, Barth 3 February 1992.
40. Watson, op. cit., note 32, p. 7.
41. Reginald Watson-Jones (1902–72), author of *Fractures and Joint Injuries* (1940), was orthopaedic adviser to the RAF during the Second World War. Seventy-seven per cent of injured aircrew who passed through his hands subsequently resumed full duties. He graduated from Liverpool in 1924. Kenneth Pridie (1906–63) was an innovator who applied engineering and carpentry to orthopaedics.
42. Cellona File, Smith & Nephew Archives, Hull; Barth to Fryer 18 December 1991. Eichengrun made a major contribution to cellulose technology in 1919 (Miall 1931, p. 158) and continued to patent prolificly until after the Second World War.
43. Barth to Fryer, 18 December 1991; Lohmann Documents L1, L2 Smith & Nephew Archives, Hull.
44. *Report of RW Douglas, Chemist*, Cellona File, Smith & Nephew Archives, Hull
45. Barth to Fryer, 18 December 1991.
46. Communication from J.-P. Fisch. French patent no. 842708 applied for 22 February 1938. In 1950 a machine adapted to this process was constructed and installed at Vibraye. The first commercial bandages of this type were Platrix (1952) and Biplatrix (1957).

Plate 1   Thomas James Smith, FGS, MPS, an analytical and pharmaceutical chemist who founded the company in 1856.

Plate 2   Horatio Nelson Smith, who was responsible for developing the surgical dressings side of the business, joined his uncle in 1896.

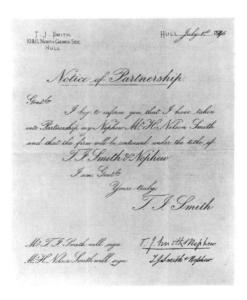

Plate 3   Notice of Partnership between T.J. and H.N. Smith, 1896.

Plate 4   *Whitefriar Gate, Hull where T.J. Smith opened his chemist shop
in 1856.

Plate 5   *North Churchside, Hull. The company moved to larger premises
in 1861.

*Reproduced with permission from Wilberforce House, Hull City
Museums & Art Galleries.

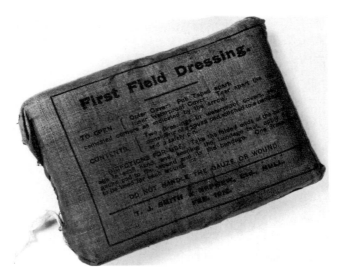

*Plate 6   First World War field dressing. 1914–18, a time of expansion when
staff increased from 50 to over 1 200.*

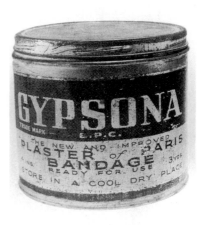

*Plate 7   Elastoplast EAB which revolu-
tionized the treatment of
varicose veins and leg ulcers.*

*Plate 8   Smith & Nephew manufact-
ured the first commercially
produced plaster of Paris
bandage which was later
named Gypsona.*

Plate 9 Sanitary towel manufacturing at Southall Bros & Barclay, 1927.

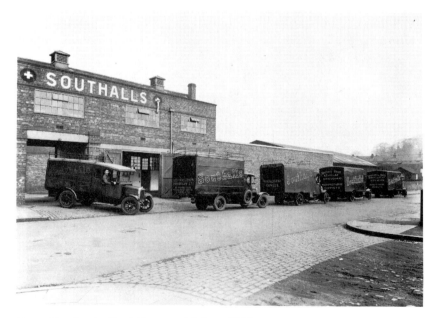

Plate 10 Southalls delivery vehicles, 1927.

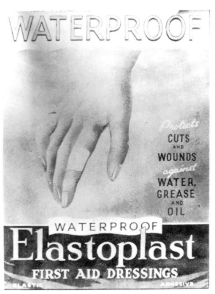

Plate 11   *Waterproof Elastoplast was launched in 1946 and proved an instant success.*

Plate 12   *The purchase of Herts Pharmaceuticals at Welwyn Garden City in 1951 brought laboratories and technical staff to the group and formed the basis of Smith & Nephew Research which was formed the next year.*

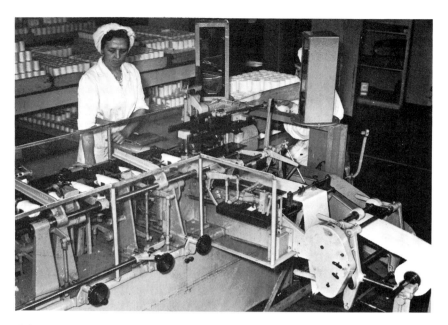

Plate 13 Wrapping Elastoplast bandages, Hull, circa 1950s.

Plate 14 An aerial view of Brierfield Mills, Nelson, Lancashire.

Plate 15   Nivea packaging in Canada in the 1950s.

Plate 16   The factory at Pinetown, Natal in South Africa was opened in 1955.

Plate 17   During the 1960s, Smith & Nephew built a number of factories around the world including the Australian operation in Clayton near Melbourne.

5. Strategy and structure between the world wars

Acquisition of popular brands and imaginative marketing was not the only source of Smith & Nephew's rapid growth between the wars. In some respects in contrast with the older Birmingham company of Southalls they were later to acquire, Smith & Nephew in these years began the transformation from family business to professionally managed multidivisional firm. This organizational step, generally believed more common in the United States at the time than in Britain, allowed H.N.'s company to grow to twice the size of Southalls from a point at the beginning of the century when Smith & Nephew's paid-up capital was little more than one-tenth of 1 per cent of Southalls'. The larger, longer established firm dealt with the organizational issue by retaining a unitary structure and by divestiture of activities in the 1930s, rather than by the establishment of operational divisions.

Both companies retained elements of family management throughout, but Southalls much more so. Smith & Nephew typically imported top managers from companies that they absorbed. By this means a wider range of managerial experience was introduced than was utilized by most British companies, such as Southalls, whose board was typically recruited from those who had spent their entire working lives within the one firm.

ENTREPRENEURSHIP AND THE FAMILY FIRM

A widespead criticism of British entrepreneurship has been that the preferences for leisure of second and third generations lowered business performance. H.N. took his leisure interests seriously but frequently employed them to the benefit of the company. At one time chairman of the Filey Road Tennis Club, Scarborough, home of the North of England Tennis Championships, he did not let negotiations for the Cellona contract interfere with club committee meetings in 1931.[1] His Bridge meetings provided the opportunity to interest Dickson Wright in the potential of Elastoplast in ulcer treatment. His interest in travelling provided him with many sales opportunities. He first crossed the Atlantic in 1906 to Boston. It was probably on this occasion that H.N. travelled all over Canada with a sample case and personal belongings comprising only a toothbrush and one pair of pyjamas. He obtained hospital orders for surgical dressings and on his return bought the cloth to be converted into the necessary bandages and dressings.[2] H.N.'s attachment to table tennis – he was vice-president of the English, and president of the Yorkshire Table Tennis Associations[3] – led him to employ two officials of the Table Tennis Association. Later during the 1930s his travels were not always so helpful to company management. H.N. Smith took '...a keen, but owing to his frequent and long absences, spasmodic interest in many details of company business', the board was told in 1937.[4]

The resemblance to the behaviour of another major entrepreneur of the time, William Morris, Lord Nuffield of the motor industry, is striking (Turner 1973, p. 78). Both did not want to be tied down by their creations but were unwilling to abandon them either. In fact H.N. Smith's flair was in marketing and identifying opportunities. His success owed much to support from his professional advisers and managers, especially Ernest Buckley, whose financial acumen and organizational ability ideally complemented H.N.'s talents, and Fred Medhurst, whose salesmanship was legendary.

Family management played only a small role in Smith & Nephew even before the company went public. Although H.N.'s brother left the paper business at the beginning of the 1920s, H.N. did not employ him. Thomas remained a self-employed tour organizer for trips to the continent.[5] Only H.N.'s son Alister was employed in a senior management position, apart from H.N. himself. Alister became company secretary for a couple of years after holding the post of production manager, but resigned in May 1939. He suffered from a heart complaint and died before H.N.

The contrast with the management of Southalls & Barclay is extreme. Although a public company for much longer than Smith & Nephew, the fecundity and shareholdings of the Southall and Barclay families allowed them to dominate the management of the company throughout this period. When the First World War ended, Sir Thomas Barclay was 79 years old. Since the formation of the public company of Southalls & Barclay 20 years earlier, the board had lost three of its original directors; John Barclay BSc had died in 1903, Alfred Southall retired in the same year and Gilbert Southall retired in 1908. Only four original members remained, Sir Thomas Barclay JP, chairman and managing director, Thomas Barclay junior, Wilfred Southall, secretary, and Alfred William Southall. Thomas Barclay junior became chairman and managing director on the death of his father in 1921 and continued in this office until he died in 1940.[6]

Edward Debell Barclay, third son of Sir Thomas Barclay and half-brother of Thomas Barclay junior, joined the board in 1923. His early experience vividly illustrates the ravages of the First World War on the health and survival prospects of his generation. Graduating from Cambridge, he enlisted and was sent to Mesopotamia. There he caught typhoid and was returned to England. As soon as he recovered, temporary Second Lieutenant Barclay joined the Worcester Regiment on the Western Front in 1917 at the age of 21. After six weeks at the front, he lost a leg in an attack on a machine gun post, for his gallantry in which he was awarded the Military Cross.

Another Barclay, John Innes Monkhouse Barclay, BA (Cantab.), joined the company in 1925. Born in 1904, the only son of Thomas Barclay junior, he was appointed to the board of directors in 1930 and on the death of his father in 1940 succeeded him as chairman and managing director. He started at shop-floor level, later becoming involved in the purchase of raw materials, including raw cotton and wood pulp. During his first 15 years with the company he worked closely with his father in the management and development of factories. Two non-family directors were appointed in 1917. William Ernest Hipkiss became a director and secretary, resigning in 1927. William Ernest Mann, the pharmaceutical chemist who had worked on 'Vitafer' for Sir Thomas, also joined the board in 1917, though he moved to Sangars when they bought the drug business in 1935.

The only other non-family director appointed until the end of the 1930s was, as the local newspapers recognized, unusually photogenic, though her contribution to the company was extremely practical.[7] Florence May Sharpe was made a director of Southall Bros & Barclay in 1924. Mrs Sharpe was a local woman who had joined the company before the outbreak of war, manufacturing surgical dressings. Her industry and drive brought her quickly to supervisory and management levels. Her appointment was unusual but not unique; a female director sat on the Cadbury's board. Since 80 per cent of the workforce was female and the principal products of the company were for women, arguably even in the 1920s a lady director was overdue. Mrs Sharpe started up the works in the morning, and though a director, was expected to continue to do so. That a board member was supposed also to undertake such time-consuming line management tasks goes a long way towards explaining Southalls' relatively slow growth in these years. Problems of long-term strategy and company organization were unlikely to receive the consideration they deserved.

At the end of the interwar years, board appointments at Southalls reflect a professionalization of top management, although all non-financial, non-family appointments still had spent their working lives entirely with the company. In 1938 G.F.M. Lyster, chief accountant for the preceding two years, took up board duties covering investment, accounting and all financial matters, together with the sales policy of the company. Dr Kenneth H. Southall, son of Wilfred F., and great-grandson of William, one of the founders, was appointed to the board in 1941.

Both Arthur Belfield and Samuel S. Smith became board members in 1941. Arthur Belfield entered the company in 1910 at the Lower Priory offices as a boy from school, moving to Saltley after about two years. He developed and managed surgical dressings throughout his career. He represented the company on, and was a leading member in the foundation and running of, the Surgical Dressings Manufacturers' Association which organized the industry for handling 1914–18 war contracts and subsequent war supplies. Samuel S. Smith joined the Saltley works in 1911, becoming works manager in the 1920s. By the 1930s he had assumed special responsibilities in the management and development of the weaving shed, including purchasing of raw materials, packaging and other factory requirements. This entailed forward contracting for supplies of raw cotton, yarns and wood pulp, and weekly attendance at the Liverpool Cotton Exchanges.

The board therefore knew the Southalls' business inside out. Whether they were equally able to identify and manage opportunities for expansion in adjacent fields might be doubted. Of course the goals of a firm owned and managed primarily by a family might differ from those of one administered mainly by professional managers. The first category, in which the objective might be a steady flow of cash for the owners, certainly includes Southalls. Smith & Nephew may fall into the second category, where the goal is more likely to be the long-term growth of company assets.

ORGANIZATIONAL CHANGE IN SMITH & NEPHEW

In step with much bigger businesses in Britain between the world wars, notably ICI, Unilever and Anglo-Persian Oil, Smith & Nephew's management became more professional. Managerial control was extended through a pyramid structure based on semi-autonomous divisions, answerable to a board of directors. Legal changes accompanied this transformation. For the first 50 years of the company's history Smith & Nephew had been a private unlimited concern. In 1907 T.J. Smith & Nephew Limited was registered as a private limited liability company with a nominal capital of £4 000. At the peak of the postwar boom, in April 1920, this capital was increased to £100 000. Smith & Nephew (Manchester) was formed in the same year to manage the company's textile and clothing interests. When the boom burst later on that year, the collapse of demand and overcapitalization caused difficulties for the company that were not surmounted until 1927. Only then did Smith & Nephew resume dividend payments.[8]

The following year, a separate sanitary towel division or company, SASHENA, was established to manage the business of Mclaren & Donaldson and Smith & Nephew's SASHENA assets of eight times the value. Smith & Nephew Associated Companies (SANACO) was launched on the stock market in 1937 with a share capital totalling £0.5m. Of the three 'divisions', T.J.

Smith & Nephew, SASHENA and Smith & Nephew (Manchester), T.J. Smith & Nephew, with the branded lines of Elastoplast and Cellona, judged by profit was the largest and most rapidly growing and the Manchester division the smallest. There were three overseas subsidiaries of T.J. Smith & Nephew in Canada, South Africa (1931), and New York.

Distinguishing whether an organization operated as an unintegrated device for eliminating competition (the accusation frequently made of holding companies), or coordinated corporate functions to bring down costs, the achievement of the multidivisional business can only be discovered from a detailed study of operations. Smith & Nephew's structure in the 1930s almost certainly contributed to rapid growth, in excess of that achieved by Southalls. Separation of a company into quasi-autonomous but integrated product divisions allowed a greater span of control by central management. They could concentrate on strategic functions, especially the introduction and development of new products.[9]

Coordination between companies/divisions was based on the sequence of production in the company that, from 1937 and the acquisition of Oliver Ormrod near Bury in Lancashire, began with textile bleaching. Weaving was still undertaken outside the company. In 1920 Edwin Robinson asked Hindle Warburton in Blackburn to weave gauze and bandage cloths for Smith & Nephew, followed shortly by gauze for SASHENA sanitary towels. Later they also wove leno for Cellona.[10] The purchase control section of T.J. Smith & Nephew at Hull was concerned primarily with gauze, bandage cloth, and cotton wool. Departmental work was so arranged that Smith & Nephew (Manchester) and the cotton carding mill were automatically supplied with information which ensured they regulated production to meet all requirements at the right time. The cotton carding section (Hollinwood) of T.J. Smith & Nephew was controlled by Robinson of Smith & Nephew (Manchester) assisted by the mill manager.[11]

By 1937 the group operated five freehold factories (three in Hull and two in Manchester) and three leasehold plants (one in London and two in Hull).[12] Stocks of materials and finished products accounted for more than the value of the factories or of the plant and machinery. For this reason, when price volatility for raw materials emerged with the Korean War boom, company profits proved vulnerable.

RECESSION AS STIMULUS TO CHANGE

The world depression after 1929 eventually cut demand in all Smith & Nephew markets. In response the company embarked on a drive to improve efficiency and boost sales at the beginning of 1932. Sam Lovatt, the production director, introduced a programme of improved timekeeping, reduction of piece rates, elimination of unnecessary paperwork and better stock control. In selling and purchasing four new policies were introduced: the adoption of standardized order forms (like those of Marks & Spencer and Woolworth's), the proper sequencing of materials orders before production, bargaining for lower suppliers' prices, and offering ideally a 24-hour service, with no order outstanding for more than five days. Branded lines were introduced in 1930. A special section to manage them was created in August 1932 with particular reference to overseas sales. Since advertising, research and sales promotions were previously located outside the branded lines section, their activities were likely to have been hampered. The Branded Lines section in Hull therefore acquired the responsibility for sales promotion from the London-based Research Department. The Research Department, broken up in 1932, was a misnomer, dealing mainly with advertising and relations with medical staff. In addition to the transfer of sales promotion to Branded Lines, out of the department was formed Technical Research, and a 'propaganda department' for general sales and medical relations, that remained in London.

A number of other changes were intended to achieve greater sensitivity to market conditions and a sharper delineation of responsibilities. A margin of gross profit for each product was established, based on turnover predictions, to cover all expenses and a satisfactory return on investment. General Sales were responsible for setting prices that allowed these margins to be earned. New lines were an exception. These prices were to be fixed by the board. Formerly pricing was jointly the task of Lovatt, the purchasing agent and the general sales manager.

The Technical Research Department created at Smith & Nephew in the reorganization of 1932 (shown in Figure 5.1) was not the first technical facility acquired by the company. Noel Akers of Hull, a chemist, was hired in 1913 for a monthly salary of £10 13s. 4d. plus a bonus of £4 6s. 8d. a month.[13] Taking salary as a comparative indication of his scarcity value, chemists were much rarer than clerks, paid between £23 and £65 per annum plus a small bonus. But Lambert & Lambert paid their traveller about the same as the chemist, £3 a week in 1906. Akers 'resigned' in 1921, when the economic downturn brought severe difficulties for the company. The likelihood must be that, cheap as he was, he was regarded as one of the luxuries with which the company could relatively painlessly dispense. By 1932 the loss had been made good and Roderick Douglas was the works chemist in the new Laboratory section of Technical Research. This department, just moved to Hull, was concerned primarily with quality control and sterilization. The development and cost section of Technical Research was concerned with collating data for new lines.

Reforms initiated during the world depression carried Smith & Nephew into a sales boom culminating in the public flotation in 1937, which required

Figure 5.1   Management structure, 1932

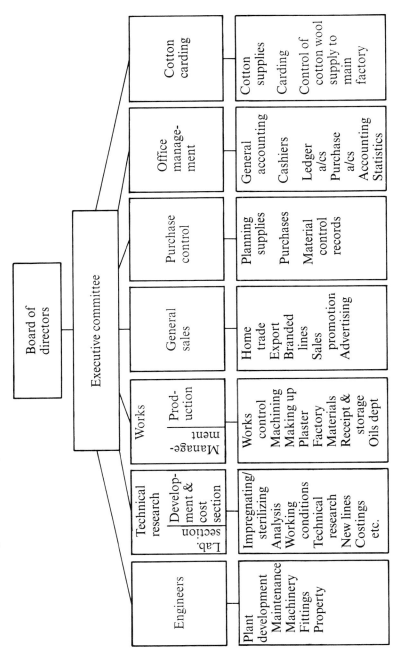

still further organizational changes. Under the constitution established for the public company in 1937, the SANACO board of directors laid down policy while supervision and control of the companies was in the hands of Mr Lovatt as manager of SANACO. The directors of SANACO (especially no doubt H.N. Smith) were enjoined not to interfere. A management committee was established consisting of Sam Lovatt of SANACO, J. McClaren of SASHENA and E. Robinson of Smith & Nephew (Manchester) with Alister Smith as secretary. The importance of these deliberations is underlined by the statement prepared by E.W. Buckley in the minutes. Buckley emphasized the need to build a 'scientific organization' for a public company in which the directors were trustees. Many matters had formerly been referred to Ernest Buckley by the general sales manager of T.J. Smith & Nephew Ltd, by the executive in charge of sales promotion and by directors of subsidiary companies. All such business in future would go through Mr Lovatt. Monthly figures necessary to make management control effective were suggested.[14]

While Smith & Nephew was acquiring companies and new products, Southalls evolved rather differently. The, for them, profitable 1920s culminated in two acquisitions in 1929. Southalls bought outright the Taylor lint property that they had formerly leased and, encouraged by Egyptian government orders in the early 1920s, they opened a factory in Alexandria in 1929, from where the company hoped to expand Middle East sales. The world recession convinced the Southalls board that they could not manage both the textile-related side of their business, surgical dressings and sanitary towels, and pharmaceuticals. In 1935 they sold the chemist and druggist unit to Sangars Ltd, and with it the company's own name so the division could continue to operate under the title of 'Southalls Bros & Barclay (1935) Ltd'. The company thereupon changed its name to 'Southalls (Birmingham) Ltd', operating the 11-acre factory at Saltley and the original Charford Mill at Bromsgrove. Company policy envisaged neither multidivisional organization nor the large research and development expenditures by then essential for pharmaceuticals.

TECHNICAL DEVELOPMENTS AND PLANT EXTENSIONS

Faced with recession, the company focused increasingly on efficient production in the lower technology side of the business. In 1923, 28 years after Robinsons bought their first cellulose-making machine and patent rights from the German paper-maker Jacob Feirabend, Southalls installed a machine to make cellulose wadding from wood pulp.[15] The machine produced a fine tissue sheet with high absorbency and moisture retention, a good substitute for cotton wool. Used in sanitary towels, the cellulose paved the way for the completely soluble article, thus avoiding disposal by incineration. More uses were found for this wadding as production increased. The first machine turned out about 15 tons weekly as compared to 150 tons weekly from four machines in the 1950s.

Special machinery was essential for high-volume surgical dressing and sanitary towel production. In 1920 Smith & Nephew licensed technology from an employee of G. Williams & Co. of London.[16] Machinery was also helpful in selling sanitary towels. By 1928 Smith & Nephew had acquired patent rights in automatic dispensing machines for Lilia products.

Cotton and paper were passed through a sequence of processes demanding considerable supplies of water and power. Cotton was bleached, carded, woven and linted and facilities had to be extended as demand grew. Towards the end of the 1920s there was increasing pressure on the capacity of Southalls' bleachyard, based on the original installation from the turn of the century. If capital expenditure was to be minimized, the problem was to keep the old plant running while designing and building a new bleachyard to cope with increasing demands in the foreseeable future. By 1938 the new bleachyard, completely designed by the company's staff, was in production. From a flow line production of six kiers (boilers), each with a capacity of 2 tons, over 80 tons of bleached cotton could be delivered weekly in the carding machines to meet the demands of the factories for cotton fleece used in the manufacture of dressings and sanitary towels. The plant also provided increased facilities for bleaching surgical bandage cloth and gauzes, towel coverings and loops. The downside of this low-cost ingenuity was the decade that passed before it was operational.

Bleaching required large quantities of water. After the First World War, Birmingham's water supplies were expected to be restricted and boreholes were therefore sunk on the factory site. By 1950 four boreholes between 800 and 1 000 feet deep were able to supply the factory's bleaching needs with a pumping capacity of 20 million gallons a year. Power for 150 years had been generated by the mill wheel driven by the pool water. The wheel finally ceased operating when electricity was brought to Bromsgrove in 1923.

Southalls weaving plant increased from 50 looms in 1906 to 1 000 looms making various surgical gauzes and bandage cloths early in 1940, in addition to tubular gauzes and knitted tubing for sanitary towels. Paradoxically this capacity expansion came when Lancashire, the traditional nineteenth century weaving centre, was in decline. Clearly there was by now a premium on integrated production which could only be managed by large firms.

RETAILING ORGANIZATION AND SALES

The world depression concentrated Smith & Nephew's corporate mind on retailing, on national advertising, and in particular on the benefits of direct marketing to retail chemists. The largest chain of retail chemists was Boots. Begun in 1877 by Jesse Boot of Nottingham, the son of an agricultural labourer, Boots, then under American ownership, operated 900 retail establishments by 1930. Jesse's son John proudly opened the thousandth shop in 1933, the year control was won back (Miall 1931, pp. 146–7; Chapman 1974, p. 193). There were 16 000 chemists in the country and the average takings on plasters, like Smith & Nephew's Elastoplast, of an individual chemist was 15s. a week. These figures implied an annual aggregate sales value of £624 000, of which the manufacturers could expect £340 000.

Most major manufacturers of nationally advertised lines employed between 15 and 20 representatives calling on retail chemists and soliciting business either directly or by encouraging ordering through wholesalers. In nearly every instance the chemist preferred to place orders with the wholesaler that he used regularly. Evidence from manufacturers employing their own reps to visit chemists showed that 75 per cent of sales went through a wholesaler. Chemists handled thousands of lines and were strongly averse to opening new accounts. They could also generally get better service from a wholesaler unless the manufacturers kept large stocks throughout the country and had an extensive transport section. In any case, over 1 000 chemists were prohibited from making direct purchases because they were tied to a wholesaler. Smith & Nephew policy was that if a chemist of good financial standing wanted to place a direct order then he was to be allowed to do so, but he would not benefit from any price advantage.

When a manufacturing company employed its own reps and undertook national advertising, wholesalers were willing to accept a decrease in their percentage, to between 10 per cent and 12.5 per cent. In Smith & Nephew's case this represented a saving of 7.5 per cent which could be redirected towards the costs of advertisements and the enlarged sales force. The wholesaler's selling was done for him and he would benefit from increased turnover, but he still had to bear the risk of the account, to give service and to grant credit (notoriously long in the chemists' sundries trade). Where national advertising and direct selling were not adopted, in such lines as Elastoplast and Gypsona bandages, the wholesaler would still receive 20 per cent of the profit on sales.

Seventy per cent of Smith & Nephew's trade in general dressings took place through wholesalers and their goodwill was very important. With direct selling, wholesalers would have to accept a cut in their percentage profit from 20 per cent to 12.5 per cent but would benefit from increased turnover. Retail traders knew Smith & Nephew's name, for the firm had been a well respected supplier of dressings for several decades, as well as the manufacturer of several highly regarded specialities and of the recently introduced Elastoplast. The company had established relations with 1 500 chemists by the beginning of January 1933, though orders went through wholesalers. Nearly every chemist approached had been willing to give a prominent position in his shop to Smith & Nephew's showcards.

The dressings side of operations provided the greater proportion of Smith & Nephew turnover in 1932, but was not really profitable. The Branded Lines section had to earn the profits, through increases in sales, as was the pattern in other manufacturing businesses. Even though only in operation for a short time to encourage sales abroad, the Branded Lines section was already showing returns. Despite falling sales in Montreal and Johannesburg, Lilia earnings overseas were 50 per cent higher in 1932 than they had been the previous year.

NEW PRODUCTS

With Elastoplast and Gypsona, Smith & Nephew had acquired very successful brands, but the company continued attempts to add new products to its portfolio. Experiments in Germany and Austria with radium bandages in the 1930s suggested that they gave relief from rheumatic and other pains. Smith & Nephew therefore considered marketing a radium-impregnated version of Elastoplast. The news in 1933 that the British Medical Association was likely to recommend a ban on all substances using radium put this project to rest.[17] The ever intellectually fertile Lohmann originated Viscopaste, a bandage that contained Unna paste, a treatment for leg ulcers (Chapter 4, note 33) which required heating before use. No patents were involved and Smith & Nephew gained without payment the know-how for marketing in Britain and the Commonwealth in the early 1930s.[18]

The US by 1937 was becoming a source of medical innovation for Smith & Nephew. Castex, a cotton gauze bandage soaked in a resin/acetone mixture, individually sealed in tins with special opening devices, was imported from the Tower Company, Chicago. Gloves had to be worn during application of Castex and a hair drier employed to evaporate the solvent. The cast was light, very strong and water-resistant. Sales remained small, however, until the outbreak of war cut off imports.[19]

Two new product lines were considered in 1938, a benzedrine inhaler for colds and catarrh, and Lemoquin, a mixture of lemon and quinine for colds. The board did not approve the second product because of their previous decision not to adopt internal remedies for the time being (presumably on the grounds of greater patient risk and therefore company liability). For the same reason they also vetoed Quinimaxa, another quinine-based product. Betacol, the benzedrine inhaler, was dropped in 1940 with the board expressing their disappointment at the way the product had been handled from the beginning.[20] In short, there was an element of luck in the acquisition of new brands: of a number tried, only a few paid off, but, with lifetimes of more than half a century, those that did, sold spectacularly well. They provided the financial base for further market experiments.

RELATIONS WITH COMPETITORS

New products were the ultimate competitive weapon but there were others such as advertising and pricing. The legal and economic environment of the years between the world wars did not favour price competition and there were some forms of competition that were wholly unacceptable to the industry. Cuxson Gerard & Co. complained to Smith & Nephew's SASHENA division in 1929:

> We have been informed that your lady representative in the Manchester district is decrying our products and is even going so far as to show a specimen, and characterising it as very inferior.
> We feel sure that you are unaware of this procedure and that it is entirely without your knowledge and approval.

SASHENA's managing director John McLaren replied diplomatically:

> ... we have now obtained the results of the enquiry held amongst our Manchester representatives. One of these admits that she encouraged comparison of quality between your Cotton Wool towels and our own. She categorically denies that she in any way decried your goods.
> Should any one of our representatives in any excess of zeal ever have done this, we feel sure that the seriousness of the views we put forward at the enquiry will prevent their ever doing it again.[21]

As this correspondence suggests, cooperation came relatively easy to the industry. One of the largest, if not the largest, enterprise in their sector during the early 1920s, Southalls played a leading role in industry organizations. Thomas Barclay junior headed negotiations with the Ministry from 1919 over surplus surgical textile disposal. In recognition of this service he was appointed the first president of the Surgical Dressing Manufacturers' Association in 1928.

The shares of each manufacturer in the total bought back from the Disposal and Liquidation Commission give some idea of their relative sizes.[22] Gross sales in 1923 were:

Southall Bros & Barclay	£137,722
T.J. Smith & Nephew	£96,985
Robinsons of Chesterfield	£97,034
Vernon & Co.	£96,632
Benjamin Lees & Co., Oldham	£40,337[23]

A positive side of this comfortable relationship between the companies was that during wartime, they readily cooperated in overcoming materials shortages. Cuxson Gerrard were prompt in helping Smith & Nephew out by supplying first aid cabinets and providing Tannic jelly for a delayed Russian Red Cross order of 1942. Equally quickly Cuxson Gerrard offered information and practical assistance in testing for the sterility of dressings for government contracts during 1944.[24]

Trade associations for information and state control, totalling about 500 in 1919, had grown up throughout the economy during the First World War. The case of Sorrel v Smith in 1925 set the tone for their operation: restrictive practices were legal if they were intended to forward the trade and no wrong was committed. No wider public interest was acknowledged. But industry organizations such as the Surgical Dressings Manufacturers' Association (SDMA) and the Plaster Makers' Conference which aimed to control prices were always liable to be undermined by the withdrawal of members who could no longer afford to hold up prices or who judged it more profitable not to do so. Southalls withdrew from the SDMA price arrangement in 1937.[25] They were not subject to the rough treatment of the Americans Johnson & Johnson. Johnson & Johnson's resignation from the Plaster Makers' Conference and their price cuts at the beginning of 1939 led to Conference reprisals. The Association policy became one of attacking Johnson & Johnson's soap cylinder patent by infringement.

EMPLOYEE RELATIONS

Competitive success required harmonious industrial relations as both Southalls and Smith & Nephew readily acknowledged. At the 1924 annual company meeting Southalls' managing director remarked: 'We remain on friendly terms with our workpeople whose spontaneous help has done so much to bring about the good result'.[26]

This recognition of the employee contribution to the high dividends – effectively 15 per cent – that Southalls & Barclay achieved through the 1920s, was clearly more than merely conventional. The company aimed to encourage and reward loyalty. Thomas Barclay junior and Mrs Sharpe presided at the company dance for employees to celebrate the opening of the

New Works in 1926, and in 1927 a recreation hall for employees next to Charford Mill was investigated. Wages for at least some employees were high. The 'tacklers' in Southalls' Preparations Department in 1921 earned a standing wage of £4 18s. a week, almost a professional income by the standards of the time.[27]

Southall & Barclay established a pension fund in 1927. This arrangement was pioneering because it was open to both staff and hourly-paid employees, men and women, with benefits on the same basis for all. The fund was also unusual in that instead of being administered through an insurance company, as were many at the time, it made and managed its own investments.

In Hull the port location allowed the National Union of Dock Labour to negotiate, generally amicably, on behalf of the Smith & Nephew workforce.[28] Smith & Nephew introduced staff shares in 1920 but financial difficulties prevented any payouts until 1927. H.N.'s interest in sport was reflected in the introduction of annual company games. It is indicative of the better health and fitness of higher paid salaried workers that at the Hull company second annual games in 1936 the office staff beat the other section teams in all contests except the tug of war.[29]

CONCLUSION

By the outbreak of the Second World War, Smith & Nephew was considerably larger than Southalls, measured by capitalization. Southalls' authorized share capital in 1935 was £286 000 while Smith & Nephew's in 1937 was £500 000.[30] These relative sizes the two companies were to maintain until the 1958 merger. They show the effects over a generation of a high growth rate sustained by a multidivisional organization, new products and strong marketing, by contrast with a policy of a unitary production-oriented organization. Because of H.N.'s acquisition policy, outside management was brought into Smith & Nephew (McLaren and Lambert), unlike Southalls, and a series of internal management reports addressed company organization and strategy. Though still a comparatively small company, Smith & Nephew embraced the types of organizational changes that the very largest market leaders were adopting.

In their impacts on the two firms, the two recessions of 1920–22 and 1929–32 differed markedly. The first downturn hit the expansionist Smith & Nephew hard. However it proved a catalyst for the creation of a professional management organization that carried the company through the second depression and into a phase of rapid expansion. The more sedate Southalls weathered the first recession well but, failing to adopt organizational reform, was obliged to reduce their range of activities during the 1930s.

NOTES

1. H.N. Smith to E.W. Buckley, 29 December 1931, *Cellona File* Smith & Nephew Archives, Hull.
2. 'Our Companies Overseas: No 2 Canada', *Sanaco News*, 1958.
3. *Daily Express*, 20 July 1936.
4. Memo by E. Buckley, 3 March 1937, *Sanaco Board Minutes*, 1937–47, p. 24, S & N/L.
5. Transcript of interview with S. Quantrill, 8 July 1991, S & N/H.
6. T.B. Powell and J.N. Hillman, '*The History of Southalls (Birmingham) Ltd 1820–1957*' unpublished ms, n.d., Smith & Nephew/Southalls Archives.
7. *Birmingham Gazette*, 8 March 1924; *Southall Bros & Barclays Directors Minute Book 1898–1926* 20 December 1923 p. 232, S & N/S.
8. *Minute Book*, 1 July 1927, p. 132 Smith & Nephew, Hull.
9. Although the group looked like a holding company, coordination between companies made each operate more like a division within a multidivisional enterprise (M. form). From the perspective of British industrial history this observation suggests that castigations of British industrial organization between the wars as lagging American practice may be misplaced in some instances (Chandler 1990).
10. Smith & Nephew Commemorative Brochure for the Visit of Overseas Directors to Brierfield 1958, Smith & Nephew/Briefield Archives.
11. *S & N Plan of Organisation*, 25 October 1932, Hull, p. 4.
12. 'S&N Offer For Sale', *Morning Post* 23 February 1937.
13. E10 Agreement, 22 October 1913 S & N/H. By way of comparison, the huge Bleachers' Association decided to equip a chemical laboratory only in 1906 (Jeremy 1993).
14. *SANACO Board Meeting Minutes, 1937–47*, 3 March 1937, p. 23, S & N/L.
15. See Porteous (1965), p. 165; Powell and Hillman op. cit., note 6.
16. Correspondence with G. Leavey 1920, ST 3, S & N/H.
17. J. Cochrane, *Report on EMSA Radium Bandages*, 1933, Smith & Nephew Archives, Hull.
18. P.S. Watson, *A Miscellany of Historical Notes regarding the Development of Some of Our Earlier Products*, 1979, pp. 13–14.
19. Ibid., p. 8.
20. *SANACO Board Minutes*, 13 May 1938, pp. 88–9; 14 July 1938, p. 107, 13 February 1940, p. 174, S & N/L.
21. J. McLaren to Cuxson Gerrard & Co., Oldbury 16 August 1929, Smith & Nephew Archives, Hull.
22. Disposal and Liquidation Commission to T Barclay, 2 October 1923, Smith & Nephew/ Southalls Archives.
23. Robinsons, who had traditionally supplied Smith & Nephew for a number of purposes, were larger than these figures suggest. In 1927 they employed 2 400 people in five Chesterfield factories. *Manchester Guardian Commercial Supplement*, 24 March 1927.
24. P. Clifton to A.D. Gerrard, 17 June 1942, Cuxson Gerrard to F. Medhurst, 16 June 1944, Smith & Nephew Archives, Hull.
25. *SANACO Board Meetings Minutes*, 1937–47, p. 36, 112, S & N/L.
26. *Times* 20 March 1924, Southalls & Barclay Company Meeting.
27. *Cotton Factory Times*, 19 August 1921.
28. *T.J. Smith & Nephew Minute Book of Directors Meetings from 9 April 1920–16 July 1920*, pp. 7–8, S & N/H.
29. *Hull Daily Mail*, 27 July 1936.
30. For comparison, another Hull company, Reckitt & Colman, achieved an estimated market value of capital of £33.6m in 1930, becoming the eleventh largest UK manufacturer.

6. The health care environment since 1940

A new, more affluent, era was ushered in by the 1940s. The depressed 1930s and then the war had encouraged smaller and deferred families. With the return of peace and full employment in 1945, a baby boom compensated for the backlog of births. But this upsurge of fertility proved only temporary in the West and slowing population growth soon began to raise the proportion of older people, with different and greater health care needs; treatments for cardio-vascular diseases, rheumatics, Alzheimer's disease and cancer. Obvious man-made health problems, road accidents and tobacco smoking, assumed a new significance. During the 1980s the destruction of the body's immune system by AIDS presented a new range of social and medical research challenges.

Pharmaceutical and medical device innovation accelerated, but maintaining the impetus required greater investment in research and development and longer gestation periods, in part because of tighter regulation. Products became more directed at particular problems, more effective and more expensive. TB and polio were virtually eliminated from the West.[1] All Western health services were expected to cover the entire population, with the consequence that in all advanced countries governments were obliged to concern themselves with the cost and effectiveness of health insurance and medical treatment.

Scientific advance made possible entirely new, more effective and usually more expensive treatments. Successful innovation involved various forms of interaction between medical practitioners, academics and business. Innovators were not necessarily good developers and failure to be an innovative firm did not preclude success in a second wave. From a position of net imports before the First World War, and primarily since 1945, British pharmaceuticals and medical devices companies have exploited these relationships rather successfully to establish theirs as one of Britain's most internationally competitive industries.

In poorer countries higher living standards and Western medical technology radically cut death rates, causing a postwar population explosion of dimensions never experienced in Europe. Their populations were dominated by the young and they generally lacked the income to pay for all the sophisti-

92

cated health treatments of the West, as well as the organization to absorb them.

HEALTH AND POPULATION TRENDS

Changing health needs were responses to previous medical successes, to rising living standards, to demographic change and to the transformation of the social and biological environment. But the 'clinical iceberg of sickness', identified in the Peckham experiment (Chapter 3), persisted (Last 1963). Medical advances enhanced the ability to treat this vast number of cases in which treatment was not sought, as well as those in which it was. Deaths from TB in England and Wales which fell by about one-third between 1930 and 1940, dropped by one-half in the decade which saw the introduction of streptomycin/PAS/isoniazid and by almost three-quarters during the 1950s when these treatments became widespread. Deaths from pneumonia and influenza showed a similar but less obvious trend following the discovery of sulphonamides, penicillin and other antibiotics. The effects of rising standards of hygiene and living were likely to be running into diminishing returns, so the increase in the rate of decline of deaths from 30 to 55 per cent between the 1930s and the 1940s was especially striking, and almost certainly attributable to the new drugs (Reekie 1975, pp. 11–12). The Office of Health Economics extrapolated death rates for 1–14-year-olds from the 1901–35 trend to 1968 and predicted 1 207 per million compared with an actual rate of 496. Over half of the implied improvement was attributable to the near eradication of deaths from five diseases: pneumonia, tuberculosis, diphtheria, measles and whooping cough, responsible for 1 570 deaths per million children a year in 1931–35. By 1968 the rate had been reduced to 51, of which 46 were due to pneumonia.

Hospital beds occupied due to mental illness fell from 151 000 in-patients in 1956 to 103 600 in 1971. Tranquillizers from 1952, and antidepressants from 1960, brought about a large share of this reduction, which continued partly as a result of changes in treatment policy. Between 1978 and 1988 bed–days due to mental illness fell at an annual average rate of 3.2 per cent, for reasons about which some now express reservations; 'care in the community' brings its own distinctive problems.

Disease risks facing infants and children declined markedly in Britain and the US between 1935 and 1954 as new immunizations and chemotherapies protected them from, or curtailed the course of, common diseases. Both the risks of dying and of falling sick decreased. This was not true of the US 15–24 and 25–34 age groups, where sickness risk rose among the new survivors, who would not have been around to fall sick without the revolution of 1935–

54 (Riley 1989, Chap. 8). War and road accidents killed a smaller proportion of victims but left a higher number of injured and debilitated who would be more liable to fall ill.

Cigarette smoking, widespread since the 1920s, took its toll. Realization that the 15-fold increase in lung cancer between 1922 and 1947 in England and Wales was due to tobacco smoking came only at the beginning of the 1950s. By 1947, tobacco consumption had doubled from an average of two pounds per person a year in 1901. Yet the *British Medical Journal* felt justified in giving smoking a clean bill of health in 1947 (Bartrip 1990, p. 307). Clear American research evidence was published in 1950 in the *Journal of the American Medical Association* and in Britain by Doll and Bradford Hill in the *British Medical Journal* (30 September, pp. 739–48).

The contribution of the motor vehicle to road accident injuries was rather more obvious. As the most motorized country in the world, the United States led the way. Already in 1929 motor accidents were the tenth most important cause of death there. For 15 developing countries in 1972 road accidents accounted for 17 per cent of deaths, a proportion exceeded only by mortality from enteritis. Medical science was increasingly effective in saving lives of the rising numbers of those injured. Speed limit, seat belt and drink and driving legislation reduced injuries. Compulsory seat belt laws markedly lowered the number of fracture cases dealt with in British hospitals (Foreman-Peck 1987).

US death rates during the 1960s increased for the age groups 15–24 and 25–34; homicide, suicide and motor accidents appear to play a role. During the 1970s death rates resumed their decline helped by lifestyle changes and earlier diagnosis. The reduction in US heart disease deaths in the 1980s was clearly due to changes in behaviour, including diet and exercise. Since 1945 in the West the opportunity to overeat was no longer confined to a minority. Weight standards based on insurance mortality statistics suggest that in England and Wales middle-aged men in the 1980s were on average 20lbs overweight and Americans were even heavier. Men more than 25 per cent above the average for their age and height had a death rate twice as high as those within 5 per cent. The difference was particularly due to ischaemic heart disease, diabetes, cerebrovascular disease, chronic nephritis and accidents. Fraudulent adulteration of food was no longer common but chemical preservatives, pesticides in the food chain and mercury contaminated water absorbed into fishes, may all adversely affect health (McKeown 1988, Chap. 9).

Investigation of the sickness and mortality records of London Transport bus drivers and conductors in 1953 demonstrated the importance to health of physical exercise. The study revealed an inverse relationship between physical activity and coronary artery disease, with drivers suffering a higher incidence than conductors; their disease appeared at an earlier age and was more frequently fatal. Similar results were obtained for government clerks and postmen. Physical inactivity also raised blood pressure and insulin activity. Differential alcohol consumption undoubtedly explains the ten times higher cirrhosis of the liver death rate in France than in Britain.

In international comparisons of death rates, Germany scored badly especially on maternal but also on infant and perinatal mortality until the end of the 1970s. Sweden and the Netherlands achieved relatively low rates for most of the period. (Some differences between countries in causes of death may stem from differential rates of misdiagnosis, however.) How much this type of mortality data depended on income distribution is shown by wealthy Kuwait, with almost three times the infant mortality of the UK or Germany in the early 1980s. Poor Ethiopia, where Smith & Nephew failed to establish a profitable pharmaceutical subsidiary in the 1960s, suffered 12 times Britain or Germany's infant mortality at the beginning of the 1980s.

The number of persons in the UK aged 65 and over increased by 4 per cent between 1982/3 and 1987/8, but those of 75 and older rose by 12.6 per cent (Social Services Committee 1989). By the end of the century nearly 14 per cent of the US population will be over 65 and in the year 2010 47 per cent of the elderly population will be 75 years or older. The primary diagnoses of these age groups admitted to hospital were most commonly circulatory diseases, then digestive and respiratory diseases, followed by cancer and hip fractures.[2] People who were 65 or older (of whom there were 32 million in the US) entered hospital three times as often as other age groups and stayed more than 50 per cent longer. The elderly accounted for 34.5 per cent of all US hospital admissions in 1990. By the mid-1990s they were responsible for more than half of hospital in-patient days. They absorbed 38 per cent of all health care expenditure although they accounted for only 13 per cent of the US population.

Some health problems were a by-product of treatment, such as hospital cross-infection or even bed sores. Improved health care, raising the life expectancy of paraplegic patients and of the population in general, increased the number of patients at risk of developing bed sores.[3] In the UK 30 000 hospital patients suffered from pressure sores at the beginning of the 1980s. In Denmark, Sweden and Scotland, between 3 and 9 per cent of hospital in-patients developed them. In 1973 it was estimated that the prevention and treatment of pressure sores in the UK cost the NHS £60m. The cost of preventing and treating the condition worldwide in the early 1980s was likely to have been in excess of £2 000m (Smith & Nephew n.d.). Adequate nursing could largely eliminate bed sores but that is increasingly costly. It can also lead to a rise in back problems among nurses, often of relatively slight build, required to shift heavy patients. Sophisticated beds that move the patients' pressure points automatically can substitute for nurses but are expensive at present.

The most extraordinary change in the bacteriological environment after 1940 was the spread of AIDS in the 1980s. Some 20 to 50 000 people were thought to be infected with the AIDS virus in England and Wales by the end of 1987. In 1988 a 40 per cent annual growth in the full-blown AIDS population of England and Wales to the end of 1992 was predicted.[4] New infections have little influence upon prevalence of AIDS over a five-year span because of the long incubation period. The Cox report assumed low survival times after diagnosis of full-blown AIDS – only 18 per cent surviving for more than two years. Wellcome's drug Retrovir radically extends this life so that 50 per cent of newly diagnosed patients could expect to survive for at least two years. The AIDS population is therefore larger than the Cox prediction. In the US the virus was much more widespread than in Europe and the incidence of AIDS is much higher. Within Europe, France, Germany and Italy have higher numbers of AIDS patients than the UK, both absolutely and relatively, and the total number of AIDS cases in continental Europe increased much faster than in the UK (Kleinwort Benson 1988).

HEALTH CARE EXPENDITURE

An ageing population with more demands on the service meant that only maintaining, rather than increasing, health care output was hardly an option. Moreover medical advances allowed new forms of treatment that were more expensive (Culyer *et al.* 1990). Health care spending as a proportion of GNP therefore rose quite strongly in richer countries (Table 6.1). As a labour-intensive service with little increase in labour productivity this trend is almost inevitable, even without the pressures already identified. The proportion of UK regional hospital board expenditure accounted for by salaries and wages rose from 58.8 per cent in 1954/5 to 68.9 per cent in 1973/4. Even holding health care output constant, the need to match wages and salaries in the rest of the economy, where productivity was increasing, pushed up real costs every year.

The British proportion of health care spending to GNP was among the lowest in the group of richer countries by the mid-1950s and it failed to increase in line with the others. Perhaps a more efficient British organization gave better control of costs. Alternatively restricted spending reflected low wages of health service personnel, or because of an inadequate supply of health services. Proportions do not indicate absolute amounts of service; the high-income US not only spent a higher proportion than most other countries but a far greater total. On the other hand since American wages were higher, the services that expenditure bought were not proportionately greater. Increases in the share of national income spent on health cannot all be accounted for by

Table 6.1   Health care spending as % of GNP, 1950–90

	1950	1960	1970	1980	1990
UK	3.9	3.8	4.3	5.6	6.1
Australia[a]	–	5.0	5.5	7.5	7.5
Canada	4.0	5.6	7.1	7.1[c]	9.0
France	3.4	4.7	6.4	8.4[e]	8.9[f]
Germany (West)	–	–	6.4	9.2[d]	8.1
Italy	–	–	6.1[b]	6.4[c]	7.7
Netherlands	–	4.5	6.3	8.2[c]	8.0
Sweden	3.4	4.7	7.4	9.8[c]	8.7
Switzerland	–	–	–	6.9[c]	7.4
USA	4.5	5.3	7.6	9.5	12.4

Notes:
[a]   Fiscal years to 30 June
[b]   1971
[c]   1977
[d]   1978
[e]   1979
[f]   Germany

Source: Maxwell (1981); 'International Health Comparisons', Public Money March 1984; OECD (1990).

rising income, population trends and technical developments. Changes in organization played a part in the 1960s, especially in the US with the introduction of the federal health insurance programmes Medicare and Medicaid.

The extraordinary chemotherapeutic revolution since the end of the 1930s has encouraged the identification of health care with pharmaceuticals, but when expenditure is analysed by components that is seen to be drastically wrong; in the UK and the US pharmaceuticals have accounted for only about one-tenth of health care costs. Hotel costs of hospitals, staff costs, and elective surgery all push up expenses beyond the budgets allocated by insurance schemes. Cost-saving policies cut hospital stays from 9-day averages in the mid-1970s to 5.5 days at the end of the 1980s. Improvements in cataract operations allow patients to be in and out the same day. Cartilage operations are down to 48-hour stays. Over the decade 1978–88 UK in-patient cases treated rose at an average of 2.3 per cent, the average length of stay fell 3.1 per cent, and day case admissions rose at 6.5 per cent (Social Services Committee 1989, Annex B).

Another strategy for cost containment is the introduction of more cost-effective treatments and devices that substitute for more expensive health resources. Smith & Nephew's Allevyn, like other new dressings, are cost-effective though more expensive than the treatments they replace (see Chapter 4 for earlier comparable products).[5] Dressings that speed recovery allow a greater patient throughput for a given number of hospital beds. They may also economize on scarce time of skilled nursing staff by allowing application by less highly trained personnel. A general trend is for products to become more specific, in the case of dressings, by targeting particular wounds. Even so NHS spending increased in real terms between 1986 and 1989 at over 4 per cent per annum to reach a total for 1989–90 of over £14bn.

High-price new medicines continued either to replace old products or to create entirely new markets. With an annual real growth of 10 per cent in this market, pressures to constrain costs became worldwide towards the end of the 1980s. Most European countries legislated to restrict cost rises, and even in the US, largely a free market, price controls on intraocular lenses were introduced in 1990.

HEALTH SERVICE ORGANIZATION

Among the national health services that undertook most health expenditure and attempted to satisfy health care needs, there were marked institutional differences. Some were financed out of central taxation, others by contributions of insured persons and/or by earmarked taxes. Some health organizations allowed medical practitioners to charge a fee per service; others paid them directly. All faced the problem of matching rising aspirations against a limited budget. For organizational reasons they did not all respond in the same way, as the following comparisons of four health services shows.

British national health service reorganization after the Second World War was obliged to address the institutional legacy of 'an early start', as was industrial policy. Small units exercising their independence failed to use existing resources efficiently (or so it was claimed) and provided inadequate coverage for all groups and locations in the country. The interwar attempt to integrate private, voluntary and local authority provision without sacrificing independence or committing large sums of public money was widely perceived as inadequate, against the background of what war conditions had demonstrated could be achieved by a concerted national effort.

Under the legislation of 1946, from 1948 not only the worker but the whole family could attend the doctor and dentist free at the point of service. Compulsory national insurance payments contributed, but nowhere near covered the costs of the service, which was supported by general taxation. Rationing was still by queueing, often for arbitrary lengths of time, depending on the region in which the client was situated (Cartwright 1977, Chap. 10).

Preventative medicine was not integrated with curative, and social medicine remained a local authority concern. The hospitals were nationalized but family doctors preferred to continue to work from their surgeries. Despite the less than total integration of the 1946 Act, the reforms concentrated demand and so encouraged domestic health care business, as the French director of May & Baker predicted by analogy with the French reforms. The NHS drug bill rose from £6.8m in 1947 to £55.6m in 1955–56 and the enlarged demand drew in multinational pharmaceutical subsidiaries, especially from the US.

Within the three branches of the post-1948 NHS, hospital and specialist services accounted for by far the greatest proportion of expenditure. It also rose from 55.7 per cent in 1951 to 67 per cent in 1974.[6] Reorganization in 1974 introduced a single administrative structure in England and Wales encompassing hospital, GP and most of the community health services formerly provided by the local authority. The idea was to improve coordination within the health service and enhance responsiveness to local needs. Efficient management required 'facing up to the traditional authoritarianism of the medical profession, which ... so frequently in the past flouted the advice of central circulars' (Culyer 1976, p. 136), an objective attempted by the reforms proposed in 1989. These placed primary and secondary care under control of regional health authorities (Social Services Committee 1989). Whereas secondary care was already subject to cash limits, for the first time some cash limits were imposed on primary care. To create an internal market, improve competition and drive economic change, the old NHS service role was divided so that the purchaser of goods and services was no longer the provider of those same services. To ensure that resources flowed to where there was greatest need, the regional, district and Family Health Service Administration budgets were based on their respective resident populations. Fixed budgets exerted downward pressure on prices, particularly on prescribing costs.

Germany initiated and persisted with the principle of social insurance which prevailed in Britain between the world wars. Social insurance provided free medical and dental care and cost-sharing arrangements existed for prescription drugs, dentures and suchlike. The system was regulated by government but carried out principally by a large number of sickness funds. These funds operated as autonomous bodies but were required to report to the provincial governments which supervised their financial stability. The main source of finance was a payroll tax and employee contributions. The government made direct payments to hospitals, some of which were publicly owned, some private and some charitable. Doctors were paid on a fee per item of service basis by the funds. Deficits in funds and hospitals were recurring problems. Average length of patient stays were longer in German than in British hospitals in 1971, consistent with the daily charge and hospital income maximization. Higher German hospital admissions, because of few out-patient facilities, were in turn attributable to fee per item payment which encouraged local physician specialization. The German drug bill was very high, at around 28 per cent of total health expenditure, compared with the UK's average of about 10 per cent. The British government were more successful in holding down drug prices. At the end of the 1980s Germany changed the reimbursement system for drugs to bring down the National Health Insurance fund's bill by DM12.4bn by 1992.

Canada's health system was primarily financed by the government and physicians were paid on a fee per service basis. Doctors could bill patients for a portion of the fee. Health care was less comprehensive than in Germany or Britain. Billable services were encouraged and physicians were not controlled centrally so they could and did increase patient demand for health care. Federal–provincial cost sharing was a further incentive to spending. Hence the rapid increase in Canadian health care. Canadian doctors were given an incentive to place patients in hospital whether or not it was essential (Andreopoulos 1975, p. 3). Costs therefore escalated at 12–16 per cent per annum in the early 1970s, a rate estimated to raise health expenditure to equal the entire Canadian GNP by the year 2000.

US Medicare and Medicaid programmes began in 1966. Medicaid was originally intended to cover the costs of health care for the medically 'needy'. The federal share of costs ranged from 83 per cent in the lowest-income states to 50 per cent in the highest-income states. Eligibility based on income encouraged uniform benefits. Medicaid covered hospital care and physician services. Expenditure, rising at 25 per cent per annum, was $2.5m in 1967 and $9bn in 1973. Governments were obliged to restrict benefits as spending rose beyond budget limits. Medicare provided uniform benefits to all elderly people covered by the social security programme for hospital insurance. Supplementary medical insurance also covered physicians' services. The programme was extended to include those with chronic kidney disease and some disabled persons under 65 (Davis 1975). Only 10 per cent of US hospital expenses were paid directly by the patient in the early 1970s but in 1973 42 per cent of physicians' bills were paid directly. Prescription drugs were paid almost totally directly. Eighty per cent of the population under 65 had some form of private medical insurance for hospital care and almost as many were covered for physicians' services in hospital and surgical clinics. Medicaid reached large numbers of the poor and increased the frequency with which the lowest-income group consulted a physician. On the other hand 40 per cent of all black people under 65 and 75 per cent of poor children had no hospital insurance cover.

The operations of US health maintenance organizations (HMOs) extended during the 1990s. Companies placed contracts with these organizations which managed the health payments of participating individuals. Companies facing heavier bills pressurized the HMOs to cut costs. The HMOs in turn negotiated with doctors, hospitals and pharmaceutical companies. Imposition of diagnosis-related groupings (DRGs) on the health care system indirectly reacted on prices. Insurance companies did not raise cost allowances within DRGs in line with costs. Hospitals put pressure on manufacturers and used cheaper medication. In July 1988 the government saddled itself with a new expensive welfare programme providing finance for the reimbursement of drug costs under the Medicaid system for people not previously eligible. Unfortunately there were insufficient funds to meet this commitment. Moreover, the prospect that all Americans would be covered by health insurance seemed distant in 1994.

HEALTH CARE BUSINESS

Duncan Reekie's time series of pharmaceutical patents registered (Figure 6.1) in London succinctly illustrates the acceleration of pharmaceutical industry activity in Britain from 1945 to 1966, that underlay some of the increasing effectiveness, and expense, of medical treatment. Glaxo isolated Vitamin B12, the vitamin which countered pernicious anaemia in the liver, in 1947. Glaxo's first major in-house commercial pharmaceutical product, griseofulvin, originated in a research programme of 1952. It was developed first as an agricultural product, but later proved to be a systemic fungistatic for human and veterinary applications and was launched in Britain in 1959 (Davenport-Hines and Slinn 1992, Chap. 9). Although ICI only formed their pharmaceutical division as an independent entity in 1957, during the war the company had successfully developed antimalarial drugs. ICI conducted research into griseofulvin before Glaxo but abandoned commercial investigation on the grounds that the antibiotic appeared too expensive. Much later ICI researchers under James Black discovered beta-blockers for control of high blood pressure, and launched them in 1964. Black subsequently joined Wellcome. A generation earlier, Wellcome discovered polymyxin, the second antibiotic to originate from the UK. 'Actifed', the antihistamine and nasal decongestant, also emerged from work at Wellcome in the late 1940s. By 1980 the group research budget was around £80m (Burroughs Wellcome 1980). Boots' research team began working on rheumatism in 1952/3 and after 17 years developed 'Brufen', a treatment for rheumatoid arthritis and osteoarthritis which sold well in many parts of the world. Despite a lack of success in the early 1950s with amino acids and antitubercular drugs, Beecham launched the first semi-synthetic penicillin in 1959, boosting pharmaceutical sales from £2.8m in 1960/1 to £44.2m in 1969/70.[7]

As this selection of innovations suggests, by the early 1960s the British pharmaceutical industry was large and important.[8] The total value of produc-

Figure 6.1   *Chemico-pharmaceutical patents in five-year periods and total*
           annual patent sealings, 1910–66

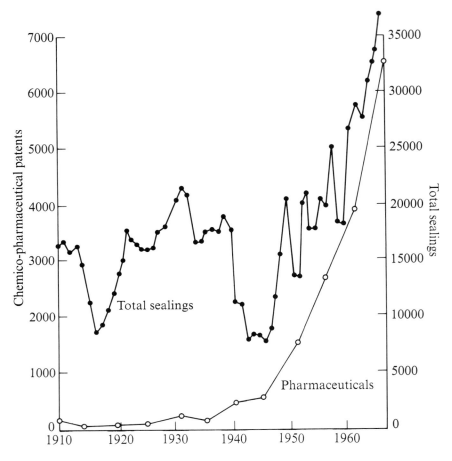

Source: Reekie (1973), p. 249.

tion had risen to £218m in 1961 from about £30m in 1948 (Association of
British Chemical Manufacturers 1949). Of the 1961 figure, 34 per cent (£74m)
was sold to the NHS, 22 per cent (£48.8m) represented export sales and the
remaining 44 per cent (£95.2m) was accounted for by over-the-counter sales
in pharmacies, veterinary products and so on. The industry as a whole employed 66 000 workers in production and 4 000 in research (of whom 2 600
were graduates). Total research expenditure had risen from only £2.8m in
1953 to £9m in 1961; the corresponding 1961 figure in the US was £80m.

How much £1m of research bought differed markedly between countries. A research worker in a British department was estimated to cost one-quarter of an American worker in the 1960s and there was little evidence to suggest their productivity was lower (Cooper 1966, pp. 168, 181).

Twenty out of the 50 leading pharmaceutical firms in the UK were subsidiaries of American, French or Swiss firms. The fruits of research undertaken by the parent companies in the home country were naturally passed on to the subsidiaries without contributing to research expenditure in the UK. An estimated figure of world-wide research expenditure in 1962 was £150m – US £100m, UK £10m, and 'others' £40m. Others included Switzerland, with an estimated research outlay of £15m, whose pharmaceutical industry supplied the British market of the early 1960s with the best selling Librium and Valium.[9]

Allen & Hanbury's respiratory research project began in 1963 giving rise to their well-known Ventolin, for the relief of asthma, in 1966 and later Becotide, a treatment. The American company Smith Kline & French marketed Tagamet in 1976, transforming the treatment of peptic ulcers by reducing the need for surgery. By 1981 in Tagamet they had a best-seller, grossing $620m in that year. Glaxo's Zantac, a more selective treatment launched the same year, surpassed Tagamet to become at the time of writing an all-time pharmaceutical best-seller (Tweedale 1990, pp. 217–25; Chapman 1974, p. 201). By the 1980s it was clear that a less half-hearted commitment to pharmaceuticals would have stood ICI in good stead. In 1982 pharmaceuticals accounted for 6.2 per cent of group sales but 28.5 per cent of trading profits (Pettigrew 1985, p. 77). By the time Zeneca was formed as an independent pharmaceutical company from ICI's assets in 1993, half of ICI's stock market value was accounted for by pharmaceuticals.

The British pharmaceutical industry in the 1980s was the third largest medicine exporter, with output up by 40 per cent over the decade. Britain held the third largest share of world market economy exports in medical and pharmaceutical products (SITC 541) with 12.61 per cent in 1988, compared with the US's 14.66 per cent and West Germany's 17.47 per cent. After 1970 Britain slightly closed on the two leaders over a period when the British share of world trade in manufactures had fallen; the medical and pharmaceutical proportions then were UK 12.48 per cent, West Germany 18.27 per cent and US 15.71 per cent.[10]

Less glamorous but no less essential health care products experienced considerable progress as well. At the beginning of the period surgical gloves at Perry's Ohio plant took about eight hours to make. Rubber arrived from plantations in bales of thin sheets of pure gum that were then dissolved in a tank with naptha. Forty to 60 glove forms were mounted on a tray lowered into the tank by an operator who would turn a crank to control the movement of the mounted glove forms. They were dipped in rubber seven times before the desired thickness was obtained. The gloves were individually beaded and hand-stamped with the correct size. Next the gloves were cured with sulphur and heat, hand-stripped by a worker, then paired by another worker before packaging. Output and employment were inevitably low under these conditions.[11]

Perry introduced the world's first pre-packaged disposable surgical glove in October 1958. Productive efficiency and capacity grew rapidly so that more than 50 000 pairs of gloves a day could be made in 1960. Acquisition by United Industrial allowed Perry to double capacity again: in 1963 Perry supplied about 40 per cent of the US market for surgical gloves. Pre-sterilized surgical gloves joined Perry's product line in 1965, using Perry's own ethylene oxide gas sterilizer, the world's largest. A new state of the art microbiological testing laboratory checked for sterility.

Disposable non-sterile latex examination gloves in 1970 replaced plastic. AHP-Europa in Brussels from 1971 supplied the European conversion from disposables that was just beginning, lagging the US market. The British Standards' Institute approved Perry gloves for use in British hospitals, a distinction no other foreign producer had achieved. Perry was also the only medical glove manufacturer to conform with FDA guidelines for 'good manufacturing practice'.[12] Efficient manufacturing techniques meant that when the AIDS scare boosted the demand for examination gloves, they could be supplied relatively cheaply. The other side of the coin was that as the product became standardized, it could be manufactured in low-wage locations more competitively, although problems over quality could surface. Only by moving up market, by innovating, by raising quality, or by differentiating the product to meet more closely the needs of various market segments could high-wage plants remain competitive.

PRODUCT INNOVATION AND DEVELOPMENT

Medical innovation since 1940 has been so voluminous and complex that here we only discuss four major advances that originated in Britain: penicillin, wet-wound healing, intraocular lenses and replacement hips. Innovations typically require utilization of advances in other fields, which themselves often need a large market and strong demand. Inner ear hearing devices connecting to nerve endings can now restore hearing to those who have lost it, thanks to microelectronic circuitry. Laser technology is employed to take out the natural lens in lens replacement operations. Materials developments in glue, plastic and metals were essential for artificial hips. X ray irradiation produced high-yielding mutant strains of penicillin from a mould growing on a cantaloup melon in the fruit market in Peoria, Illinois.

Penicillin

In an industry transformed by scientific and medical advances, the antibiotic penicillin was one of the principal innovations of the chemotherapeutic revolution. Howard Florey and Ernst Chain at Oxford proved penicillin was an effective treatment for lethal doses of streptococci and staphylococci.[13] Florey and Chain's research was largely financed by the US Rockefeller Foundation, although the UK Medical Research Council earlier provided a smaller grant. Burroughs Wellcome declined to help production of penicillin in 1940 because their resources were stretched preparing blood plasma and supplying vaccines. They felt penicillin would not be of great significance for the war effort. Before leaving for the US carrying his mould culture, with expenses paid by the Rockefeller Foundation, in 1941 Florey approached ICI and Boots but also to no avail. The Medical Research Council secretary advised him to proceed with the visit since no British manufacturer was in a position to help (Sneader 1985, pp. 306–7).

Patenting was not then regarded as ethically appropriate for medical products and in any case at that stage of development of penicillin it was unlikely to have provided much commercial protection. British manufacturers later were obliged to pay the US royalties on penicillin made in the UK, but payments were for new development undertaken in the US (Macfarlane 1979, p. 369). Chain blamed Florey for not patenting penicillin because he felt that he was thereby deprived of the funds necessary for further work. He left Oxford in 1948 to direct chemical microbiological research at the Institute of Health at Rome. The penicillin episode did change official British attitudes. The National Research Development Corporation was set up and promptly patented cephalosporin which generated some offsetting royalties.

During Florey's US visit, Merck agreed to proceed with penicillin production at once and to exchange information with interested parties. Later other US companies formed consortia. At Peoria, Illinois intensive efforts were being made to find a strain of penicillin mould that would grow in deep tanks and deliver a higher yield. This was achieved in the second half of 1943. The US government spent almost $3m subsidizing penicillin research, sold its penicillin plants after the war to private manufacturers at half the cost and allowed accelerated depreciation on private construction. The upshot was a mushrooming of drug research. Nineteen US companies produced penicillin in 1944 (Temin 1980, p. 66). Japhcott of Glaxo bought the rights from the US for the deep fermentation process in 1945.

With Waksman's 1943 isolation of streptomycin by screening soil samples, the method was widely adopted in the US and Parke Davis came up with chloramphenicol, the first broad spectrum antibiotic, in 1947. Several companies were reluctant to commit themselves to this fermentation process because they expected it quickly to be made obsolete by a synthetic method. They turned out to be wrong. Merck, which made the largest commitment to penicillin synthesis, lost out to fermentation rivals. By 1945 the structure of penicillin was determined but with the ending of the war the collaborative programme between Merck and Oxford was wound up and all laboratories working on the synthesis programme abandoned it.

By late 1942 the British Ministry of Supply established a penicillin chemical committee to coordinate manufacture in much the same way as in the United States. Boots, Burroughs Wellcome, Glaxo, ICI, Kemball Bishop and May & Baker eventually produced penicillin by the surface culture method. The Ministry of Supply refused Chain, or Allen & Hanbury, the resources to manufacture by the deep fermentation process which was to dominate production. But because of their interest in Yeast, Distillers (DCL), who lacked a research team or even a pharmacologist, were appointed in 1994 to build a penicillin plant using the deep culture method at Speke at the Ministry's expense. Glaxo also established an antibiotic factory at Barnards Castle, Co. Durham in 1944 and another in Ulverston two years later.

One Merck scientist, John Sheehan, pursued the synthesis of penicillin at MIT, supported by Bristol Laboratories, New York and achieved his goal in 1957. His method would have been difficult to scale up for commercial application but that was unnecessary for, at about the same time, a new Beecham research team advised by Chain produced a more successful synthetic penicillin. Chain in Rome had been persuaded to become a consultant to Beecham in 1955, in which role he encouraged their move into antibiotics (Lazell 1975, pp. 138, 141). Beecham isolated the basic core penicillin in 1957 and in 1959 marketed their semi-synthetic penicillin Broxil. As Chain predicted, there were 200 new penicillins by 1959.

Beecham invested heavily in penicillin plant, much more heavily than they had originally planned. Research was supported by revenue from Lucozade. Sheehan and Beecham became locked in a dispute over patent rights to the synthetic penicillins for many years. In 1979 the US Board of Patent Interferences ruled in Sheehan's favour. Beecham's late partnership with Chain showed how a lead in commercial production of penicillin could be recovered a decade later when a manufacturer was prepared to make the financial commitment and enlist the right advice. Recovery was supported by the 1944 British Finance Act, which revolutionized the treatment of research expenditure, thenceforth an expense for tax purposes.

Moist-Wound Healing

Unlike the case of penicillin, the innovatory lead in moist-wound healing products was never lost from Britain, although it quickly came to be shared.

The discoverer of the principle, George D. Winter (1927–81), initially qualified in zoology, and was awarded a PhD in Physiology ('Wound Healing in the Domestic Pig') at the London Medical School. There he detailed the anatomy of healing cutaneous wounds, laying the foundations for current ideas about wound healing. He then joined Professor John Scales at the National Orthopaedic Hospital at Stanmore. Winter played a major role in the development of bio-engineering in the UK but was especially interested in wound dressing and orthopaedic implants. In 1962 and 1963 he published the two papers on moist-wound healing rates in *Nature* which stimulated interest in this area at Smith & Nephew. The significance of moist-wound theory is that in many circumstances wounds heal considerably faster if they are allowed to remain moist, as long as they are also free from bacterial infection. The body's normal reaction to tissue damage is to release a fluid, 'inflammatory exudate'. This fluid actively promotes healing. Dressings, such as Opsite (Chapter 9), that maintain a bath of exudate around the wound, are therefore more efficient.

Smith & Nephew did not collaborate continuously with Winter but later they did use their relationship with Dr Winter on other topics.[14] Winter's resources enabled Smith & Nephew to study the phenomenon of ossification of implanted polyHEMA sponge (published in *Nature* in 1969), and to carry out systemic toxicity studies on the burns cream Flamazine (silver sulphadiazine) developed in the early 1970s. Shortly afterwards, Winter left Stanmore to join a pharmaceutical company in the US.[15]

Intraocular Lenses

The three most important advances made in ophthalmic surgery during the past century have been the intraocular lens (IOL), the operating microscope, and microsurgical techniques including sophisticated cataract extraction procedures. The last two innovations were the cumulative result of many researchers but IOLs were mainly pioneered by Dr Harold Ridley, who introduced implantation in Britain in 1949.[16] Worldwide 12–15 million people are blind from cataracts, a problem that will become more severe as population growth deceleration raises the mean age of the world's population. A pharmacological preventative treatment still seems to be many years away. Surgical treatment and, increasingly IOL implantation therefore remain the only viable alternatives.

Ridley felt compelled to develop his artificial lens when a medical student, observing a cataract operation, remarked to Ridley that it was a pity the cataract could not be replaced with a clear lens. Ridley was aware that both glass and acrylic appeared to be inert within body tissues. During the Second World War, aeroplane cockpit and gun-turret canopies were made from an acrylic plastic, perspex. When a canopy was shattered by gunfire, fragments of perspex sometimes entered the eyes of aircrew. After examining several of these airmen,

Ridley concluded that unless a sharp edge of plastic material rested in contact with a sensitive mobile portion of the eye, the tissue reaction was insignificant. Ridley's protoype IOL was therefore made from ICI's Perspex CQ (Clinical Quality) by Rayner of London. J. Pike of Rayner provided important technical assistance in the production of this lens design by calculating the dimensions of early lens prototypes. Ridley performed the first IOL operation on a 45-year-old woman at St Thomas's Hospital in London on 29 November 1949 in an operating suite that had changed little since it was photographed in 1904. After the implant had remained in place for 17 months, Ridley lectured on the procedure in July 1951. Most early implantation work was also carried out in Britain and in continental Europe. Not until 1952 were IOL operations performed in the US, using Ridley lenses. Ridley's work was met with great professional hostility in Britain and the US, which limited research advances. Ridley himself was ostracized from mainstream ophthalmic surgery for a while. Only in 1986 was he elected a Fellow of the Royal Society.

Much of the original work, both theoretical and applied, throughout the history of IOLs has been carried out by ophthalmologists in private practice and by individuals in private industry. Often these lens designers later became associated with large corporations having ample research and development facilities. Posterior chamber lenses, following a long period out of favour after the Ridley lens was discontinued, were reintroduced in the mid-1970s and early 1980s. Thereafter they became the dominant type.

With notable exceptions, in the US the new procedure first gained popularity in the Sun Belt, the South-West and South. The high population of elderly retired people in these areas and the relatively conservative stance of many physicians in other regions seem to be responsible. Estimated IOL implants totalled 70 300 in the US in 1977–78, rising rapidly to 1 million in 1985–86. The lead in production clearly passed to US companies by the 1980s despite the British origin of the innovation. When Smith & Nephew chose to move into this field they bought an American company, Ioptex.

Total Hip Replacement

John Charnley, the total hip replacement innovator, and Charles F. Thackray Ltd of Leeds enjoyed a more successful business relationship than Ridley and Rayner, but at similar times. Neither pair managed to make a major impact on the American market although their innovations did. Charnley was a pupil of Platt, one of the remarkable group of orthopaedics specialists traceable to the Liverpool school, whose direct lineage reaches back to 'bone-setters' of the eighteenth century. In 1950 his *The Closed Treatment of Common Fractures* was published. Charnley's great contribution was his total replacement of the hip joint: the excision of the diseased joint surface and the interposition of synthetic materials. He was certainly not the first to undertake the operation successfully. G.K. McKee in Norwich produced an all-metal prototype replacement joint in 1940 and published his results in 1951, while Robert and Jean Judit used a perspex femoral head in a Paris operation of 1946. But Charnley's approach was eventually adopted worldwide (Le Vay 1990, pp. 598–602).

Charnley's seminal paper appeared in 1961: 'Arthroplasty of the Hip – a New Operation'. Charnley was deeply interested in engineering problems but his manufacturing connections were largely a matter of luck. Bone cement played a key role in the Charnley system. This originated with D.C. Smith, a chemist working at the Turner Dental Hospital in Manchester in 1956 or 1957. A decade later Charnley was emphatic that the Americans still were unfamiliar with the necessary cement.[17] Charnley was in luck when he operated on F. Hawtin, who turned out to be a director of the Dental Manufacturing Co. In his gratitude to Charnley, Hawtin offered the services of the company to make the cement even if Hawtin had to pay for it himself, because production was uneconomic. For manufacture of the implants themselves, Charnley was directed to Thackray by the instrument curator of the Manchester Royal Infirmary.[18]

Thackray's craftsman Arthur Hallam worked closely with Charnley on the implants. Thackray took over manufacture of the high molecular weight polyethylene acetabular sockets from Charnley in 1963. They paid £1 into his Wrightington Hospital research fund for every prosthesis sold. In 1968 a socket was sold for £3 and a femoral prosthesis for £12. In return Thackray received sole manufacturing rights, while Wrightington maintained quality control. A larger-headed model, the Charnley–Muller, proved more popular in the US but Charnley was not keen to introduce it. Thackray experienced problems achieving the volume of output required and so called in Leeds Polytechnic Industrial Liaison Unit for advice. The resulting works organization report led to a reorganization and the hiring of senior production personnel. Thackray were making 9–10 000 hip prostheses a year. Charnley in 1970 advised an output of 100 000 to avoid falling behind the competition but no Thackray response survives.

Charnley's stainless steel models did not sell in the US where chrome-cobalt was preferred. But when Thackray did make a special steel version, that did not sell either. In the earlier stages of the technique, to ensure quality control, Charnley insisted surgeons might only buy the prosthesis after initiation at Wrightington. By the early 1970s the technique was sufficiently established for this requirement to be abandoned.

Seventy per cent of hip replacements in the US during the 1980s were of the type innovated by Charnley, cemented metal on plastic, but probably only 2–3 per cent *were* Charnley's. In the rest of the world the proportion was about 20 per cent and in the UK about 50 per cent. In 1983 there were about 78 000 US hip implants and 57 000 knees. By 1988 these numbers had increased respectively to 129 000 and 105 000. The trend growth was expected to continue at about 5 per cent, twice the rate of population increase, reflecting the ageing population and the greater need for implants among older people (Shearson Lehman Brothers 1991). In 1990 Thackray, with revenues of over $30m, was acquired by De Puy, an American subsidiary of the private German firm of Boehringer Mannheim. As with intraocular lenses, by the 1980s the lead had passed from the innovator to US companies, one of which, Richards, was bought by Smith & Nephew in 1986.

REGULATION

Whether or not medical products perform as expected can be a matter of life or death. Inevitable failures and errors of judgement led to the creation of state-managed rules for establishing and supervising the safety of new drugs. The UK at first relied on voluntary regulation, which we have seen deterred Smith & Nephew from introducing radium bandages in the 1930s (Chapter 5). During the 1960s the voluntary Committee on Safety of Drugs exercised supervision until replaced in 1970 by the Committee on Safety of Medicines under the 1968 Medicines Act (Davies 1967, Chap. 4). Compulsory licences for drugs were introduced in September 1971.

Additional US legislation was precipitated earlier by a quicker reaction to the thalidomide tragedy. The 1962 US Drug Amendments Act made the FDA an active participant in the approval process: drugs now had to be effective. This however did not address the problem posed by thalidomide . Safety was not equivalent to effectiveness; innocuous drugs could be ineffective. Thalidomide was an effective tranquilizer but it was not safe. The makers of thalidomide had been requesting US approval from 1960 but each time the application was turned down on the grounds that insufficient information was supplied.

More liberal approval procedures in Europe allowed the drug into use earlier. Distillers, still without a pharmacologist, were persuaded in 1957 to buy the rights to thalidomide from Chemie Grunenthal. By late 1961 thalidomide had been identified as the source of an outbreak of phocomelia in Germany, Britain and elsewhere. Parents of 62 deformed children took action against Distillers for negligence. By 1969 all but two had been settled by compromise, the parents being advised that their claims were unlikely to succeed. However some 266 fresh actions were begun in 1968 by parents dissatisfied by the compromise. After a campaign by the *Sunday Times*, city institutions, Ralph Nader and others, these were finally settled in 1971 when DCL set up a charitable trust for the children.[19]

Was stricter regulation, which led to fewer new drugs and delayed the introduction of those that were eventually approved, desirable? Greater safety had to be traded off against fewer effective treatments, an issue highlighted by Drazine in Chapter 9. Stricter regulation included longer and more numerous clinical trials. The disincentives of tighter regulation were a continuing complaint of pharmaceutical firms who pointed to the launching of twice the number of new drugs in the lightly regulated UK compared with the more tightly controlled US between 1962 and 1971, despite the UK being a market six times smaller. A major drug took perhaps seven to eight years from screening to launch. By 1976 only one US firm was in the top five companies launching new products in 1976. Lengthier validation procedures also discouraged development of products with only minority uses (Grabowski 1976).

The European Community's regulatory regime is administered by the Commission's Committee on Proprietary Medical Products, charged with control over the granting, suspension and withdrawal of registration. Not only new products but retrospective launches are monitored. This last provision implies that fewer resources will be spent on new products and more on improving existing ones (Reekie and Weber 1979, pp. 56–7). Under EC legislation the producer is liable even for those defects that could not have been foreseen in the light of the scientific and technical developments at the time the product was launched. The prescriber of a generic was no longer liable for adverse consequences, perhaps encouraging generic use in preference to more expensive brand names.

By the 1970s pharmaceutical regulations were fairly consistent among the Western advanced economies but controls over increasingly complex medical devices were minimal. Once again the US was in the forefront of the introduction of legislation, with the 1976 Medical Device Amendments to the Federal Food and Drug and Cosmetic Act. The FDA thereby gained greater authority to ensure the safety and effectiveness of devices intended for human use. As with pharmaceuticals, the UK evolved voluntary controls and other countries adapted existing medicines legislation. Electrical safety standards were developed to regulate powered medical devices. But even in the mid- to late 1980s some advanced European countries, such as Denmark, lacked any formal medical device legislation. The introduction of the European single market in 1992 required the harmonization of the various national positions to permit free trade in health care products.

The length of time that approvals take from submission of required documentation depends on the complexity of the device and the urgency of its need as well as on the idiosyncrasies of national legislation. In the UK even medicated dressings now are classified as pharmaceuticals and therefore are subject to those approval procedures. A simple dressing might be held up for perhaps 18 months in the approval process. Tongue-depressors, as medical devices of the simplest kind, might clear the FDA in six months. Devices the failure of which has serious or life-threatening consequences, such as heart pacemakers, officially take 18 months to clear the FDA but three years would be a more accurate assessment. Part of the approvals delay is incurred before submission, in complying with the extremely detailed specific information requirements of the approval process, where for example intraocular lenses are concerned. For a comparison with pharmaceuticals, drugs which are merely variations on existing products might hope to get approval in two years, whereas the thirty-third different beta-blocker might take 12. A treatment for AIDS would be rushed through extremely quickly.

More stringent legislation in the US was passed with the Safe Medical Devices Act of 1990 and other large markets, such as Japan, South Africa, Australia and, as discussed above, the EEC, acted similarly.[20] Greater complexity of medical devices contributed to the evolution of this legislation. A design fault in a heart valve causing a breakdown is a frequently cited reason for the tighter legislation. Some half of all device recalls have been attributed to design defects.

At the same time, a greater emphasis was placed on the FDA drug approval process as a result of the generic drugs scandal. The large sums of money at stake over their decisions puts substantial pressure on the FDA. The generic drugs business in the US depends in part for its profitability on getting approval for a generic drug immediately the patent expires on the product the generic is imitating. Approval is much simpler for a generic product, for applicants are only obliged to demonstrate equivalence with the innovative drug that has already been approved. Without incurring the costs of research and development or the lengthy approval procedure, the generic manufacturer can sell at a much lower price than the innovating firm, but profits also depend on getting to the market before other generic suppliers.

Approval requires the submission to the FDA of a dossier containing technical data on the drug. Towards the end of the 1980s some FDA officials were found guilty of taking bribes to review certain dossiers before those of other companies. The result of the 'generic drugs scandal' was that the FDA was subject to detailed scrutiny by Congress and understandably became reluctant to approve applications. Smith & Nephew at the time was awaiting permission to manufacture and market a number of products at the new Solopak Elk Grove (Chicago) facility. Delays in approval procedures resulted in Solopak recording substantial losses in 1990.

There is no doubt that the passing of the Safe Medical Devices Act of 1990 and closer scrutiny of drug applications has made the US the most demanding of nations as far as regulation and enforcement are concerned. Such rigour is however unlikely to deter producers of medical devices or pharmaceuticals from locating in the US because of the pull of the enormous US market and because exporters to that market are also subject to FDA approval and inspection. Fisons' shares plummeted when the FDA took an adverse view of their UK manufacturing facilities. In any case the 1990s are seeing convergence in regulation and reporting among trading blocks. The US Medical Devices Reporting Regulation requires the reporting of 'events in use' of appliances wherever they happen to have been sold and the EC is moving towards a similar system. When in place the new European regulatory system will be much more stringent and resemble that of the FDA (which is itself tightening up).

Regulation in the form of standard-setting can function as a competitive, or an anticompetitive, weapon. In Europe the new EC Medical Devices Directives, to be implemented in the mid-1990s, must somehow integrate the different regulatory approaches of member countries. The specification and interpretation of the new requirements and regulations to ensure fair and consistent application will pose new challenges for both industry and regulators. If barriers to trade in medical devices are to be eliminated, national reimbursement schemes in particular will require special attention.

CONCLUSION

Measured by improved life expectancy, the years since the end of the Second World War have seen remarkable improvements in health. In what proportions these changes should be attributed to rising living standards, to better health service organization and to more effective medical technology remains controversial. But there is no doubt that the capacity of the medical profession to save and maintain the quality of life has been greatly enhanced. Close relations between practitioners, researchers and medical business have been essential to the development of new medical products, and to national competitive advantage in this field; Chain and Beecham, Ridley and Rayner, Charnley and Thackray, Winter and Smith & Nephew have all been instances of this constructive interchange that has converted ideas, experimental evidence and prototypes into practical benefits to mankind. In the interests of safety, state supervision of new products has become more detailed, with inevitable consequences for final costs and for the probability of a beneficial drug or device being blocked. More expensive medical technology and increased demand, partly from an ageing population, impose an increasing burden upon national health organizations, which are forced to find new methods of serving patients at lower unit cost. Since manpower is such a large and rising proportion of health care costs, any products that reduce this component are particularly welcome.

NOTES

1. Although TB appears to be returning at the time of writing.
2. 'Hospitalization of the Elderly', *MedPRO Month*, Vol. 1, July/August 1991, p. 106.
3. All living cells require an adequate supply of nutrients and oxygen to survive. Deprived of these essentials, cells differ in the length of time they can survive. Pressure on the skin can distort blood vessels sufficiently to interrupt blood supply which can lead to cellular death and the start of a pressure sore.
4. In the report of the Working Group on the prevalence of AIDS in Britain, chaired by Sir David Cox.
5. Bactigras, a medicated antibacterial dressing launched in the later 1970s, falls in this category.
6. *Compendium of Health Statistics*, 2nd ed. 1977, Table 1.3.
7. T.A.B. Corley, 'The Beecham Group in the World's Pharmaceutical Industry 1914–1970', University of Reading, unpublished.
8. Smith & Nephew's share in the market was extremely small. Sales were only 0.3 per cent of the total while the corresponding share in total research expenditure was 0.8 per cent.
9. A.E. Smith, *Pharmaceuticals*, Smith & Nephew Archives, London, 1963.
10. The position had changed even more radically since 1958 when US exports were more than double British, but West German exports, not fully recovered from the war and its aftermath, were less. See United Nations *Yearbook of International Trade Statistics* (New York) various eds. Trade shares are only a partial measure of competitiveness in an industry where foreign investment is so important.
11. The company president, John D. Ferrero, would often arrive at the factory to work the midnight shift. As owner of the Venice Spaghetti House in Massillon, he also provided a place where Perry employees could guarantee their pay cheques would be cashed.
12. R.A. Camp, *The History of Smith & Nephew Perry*, 1990, ms.
13. Staphylococcus is a type of rounded bacteria which grows in clusters when cultured; streptococcus grows in chains.
14. Although from time to time contacts with academics were valuable for Smith & Nephew, since 1958 most progress was made 'in-house', and there was no continuous active research collaboration. Occasional contact could and did open up new areas to Smith & Nephew's benefit, such as Haemocol.
15. J. Howes, *Research at Smith & Nephew*, ms 1991; J.C. Lawrence (1984).
16. The following paragraphs are based on Apple *et al.* (1989).
17. Waugh (1990), pp. 139–40,145. This account differs from Le Vay's where it is asserted the cement had been used in dentistry in the US from the 1930s and that Charnley identified it on a visit to California.
18. Like Smith & Nephew and Southalls, Thackray began life as retail pharmacists, but in 1862 in Leeds. Again like Southalls and Smith & Nephew but later, Thackray diversified into manufacturing and wholesaling, with the purchase of a sterilizer for dressings in 1905. From 1918 paths diverged as Thackray focused on surgical equipment, and on orthopaedics from 1947.
19. Temin (1980); communication from Dr R.B. Weir.
20. B. James 'Medical Devices Regulation', unpublished 1991. The 1990 Act included the option of suing individuals in companies for up to $1m by civil petition.

7. Health care and cosmetics

When Smith & Nephew bought the rights to Cellona/Gypsona and Elasto-plast they could hardly have hoped that the brands would have been so successful for so long. Yet after the Second World War they repeated the achievement of the interwar period with the acquisition of Nivea in 1951. These brands were necessary conditions for rapid and profitable growth but not sufficient. New but related product lines were developed continuously and production processes were improved. Growth was maintained by acquisitions in other health care areas, such as hypodermic syringes and needles. Close attention to the medical services allowed as quick a reaction to the 1958 report on hospital cross-infection as to the 1935 BMA report on fractures. Nivea was a natural spring-board for diversifying into the fashion cosmetics market. That goal was attained when Gala was bought between 1970 and 1973.

WAR

Health care firms inevitably faced increased demand for at least some of their services during wartime. Like the rest of society, they also suffered great disruptions. For Smith & Nephew, the Second World War was marked by difficulties in getting raw materials, the bombing of factories and offices and the call-up of a substantial proportion of male employees. An office building in Lancashire was hit in 1940. The same year the main works at the Hull site established duplicate plants at Lomeshaye Mill (bought from Nelson Corporation) to ensure continuation of production if the Hull site was bombed. Out of a total of 92 600 houses in Hull, 82 378 were damaged in 82 air raids and 1 148 people killed. Yet suprisingly Smith & Nephew's Hull facilities were relatively unscathed. In 1941 one factory was hit but the dislocation was not serious. About 40 per cent of prewar male employees were by then in the armed forces.[1]

SASHENA Ltd changed its name to Lilia Ltd in 1942. Sales to the women's services and the general public boomed. Labour had become an acute problem, with less than half the prewar employees left. Married women and part-timers partly compensated for the lack of skilled labour. Smith & Nephew

(Manchester) began making utility garments in 1943. Labour and materials were scarcer still, but a government scheme to ensure material supplies, reflecting the importance to the war effort of all the company's products, provided sufficient quotas to maintain essential output.

As in earlier conflicts, medical professionals and the health care industry rose to the new demands made upon them. One case among many illustrates their achievement. A man was injured on 18 July 1941 when his ship was bombed and machine-gunned. He suffered a divided lower lip and a loss of soft tissue of the chin and of the mandible from the right molar region to left incisor. Over two years he was rebuilt with great ingenuity and patience according to the following timetable:

29 August 1941	Two tube pedicles were raised on the neck, and lengthened four weeks later.
22 October	Scars were excised from the face and the two pedicles attached.
11 November	The pedicles were divided.
24 February 1942	A bone graft was inserted.
26 June	An acromio thoracic tube pedicle was raised.
22 July	The pedicle was lengthened.
31 July	The pedicle was attached one end.
24 September	The pedicle was attached the other end.
2 February 1943	A further bone graft was inserted with Gypsona plaster of Paris headcap and plaster between each pair of pins.
20 October 1943	A chin dimple was made.

The Canadian subsidiary did not let this reconstruction go unrecognized. The above case history, with illustrations, appeared as an advertisement for Gypsona in the *Canadian Hospital*.

After the war the company shifted towards export markets as required by government policy. Fuel shortages hampered production in 1947 and inadequate supplies of labour in Lancashire textile factories were a problem for the whole industry. Almost all Smith & Nephew's profits came from Elastoplast and Gypsona in these years; other lines at best broke even.[2]

THE DRIVE FOR EFFICIENT PRODUCTION

Peace did not bring an end to privation, for the British economy was in dire straits. Britain's overseas assets, that cushioned the balance of payments in earlier years, had been sold to pay for the war and in their place were debts. Only a massive increase in exports would allow the country to maintain even wartime living standards, now American aid had ceased. As well as rationing raw materials to favour activities that would benefit exports, the government hoped to achieve the same end by raising productivity levels closer to those achieved by the Americans. A study published in 1948 showed that American manufacturing industry on average produced twice as much per worker as the British industry (Rostas 1948). Productivity circles were formed and American methods were studied with a view to improving British practice.[3]

Karl Dolezalek, a German engineer friend of Ernest Buckley, had persuaded H.N. and Leavey before the war to build at considerable expense a colossal plant at Hull for Elastoplast manufacture. Hostilities required the plans to be shelved, but the construction of the half-million square foot Neptune Street factory began at last in 1949. Dolezalek also worked with Hull's chief design engineer, Jack Page, to apply biscuit manufacturing technology to making Elastoplast. Page visited the German Bahlsen biscuit company to study their ovens so that the drying process could be applied to Elastoplast.[4] Teething troubles with the Elastoplast line required assistance from the research and development staff at the Hunsdon site of the newly acquired Herts Pharmaceuticals. Continuing problems eventually prompted Hull to establish a technical department.

Before the move to the new factory, conveyor filling raised Elastoplast output but the savings were rather less than hoped. In 1948 Elastoplast tins were filled by each operative having a supply of different dressing sizes, paper liners and outers spread on the bench, and being paid individual piece rates. This process was one of the first where Smith & Nephew's development/motion study section of the engineering division systematically introduced new machinery and work practices. The belt was handed over to Smith & Nephew on 29 August 1949 with details of suitable speed and arrangement.[5] Anticipating further improvements, the development engineer did not want to set piece rates at the time. But the production department, noting that operator effort was slackening off in August 1949 as the novelty of the belt evaporated, felt works management should take over and give the incentive of piece rates. As soon as the cruciform liners for the tins were available, works management therefore set a piece rate on the basis of an earlier memorandum and without the engineer's consent. Subsequently, the engineer rearranged the feeding of 2" × 3" dressings to the conveyor. Had the rate been properly set *after* these modifications, savings would have been about £1 100 more annually, based on operators' earnings 40 per cent above the basic rate, with the output actually achieved.[6]

Previously the joint industrial committee, the company and the union had agreed that rates were to be fixed so as to give from one-quarter to one-third above the time rate. Smith & Nephew agreed with the union that they would measure actual earnings in each department for three months and adjust rates

Table 7.1 *Savings from new machines and methods, 1949–51*

	Year installed	Gross saving p.a. (£)	Capital cost (£)	Annual cost (£)	Nett saving p.a. (£)	Savings in direct labour or materials?
Elastoplast tin-filling conveyor	1949	830	283	28	802	D.L.
1-yard Elastoplast drsg strips	1949	1 138	100	10	1 128	D.L.
Elastoplast cloth – four slitting machines	1949 (2) 1950 (1) 1951 (1)	2 980	430	43	2 937	D.L.
American bandage rolling and cutting machine (modifications)	1949	390	NIL	NIL	390	D.L.
37" plaster	1949	6 090	571	57	6 033	D.L. & M.
Dematol lint haspel	1950	207	94	9	198	D.L.
Crinoline on Elastoplast bandages	1951	350	NIL	NIL	350	M.
Single-wrap W.O.W. bandages	1951	350	253	25	325	D.L.
Guillotine (Jelonet cloth)	1951	110	55	5	105	D.L.
Waterproof plaster laying-up and cutting – 2½" × 1" and 1½" × 1" (four machines)	1950 (2) 1951 (2)	6 150	1 080	270	5 880	D. & M.
Plastic cross cores (Gypsona)	1951	12 000	4 470	447	11 553	M.

where the existing figures were insufficient to allow the average worker to earn 25 per cent more than the new basic time rate.[7] There was of course a strong incentive to go slow while production was being measured for rate-setting purposes. If workers could afford to forego income for the three months, they could more than recoup their losses by working normally once rates were set. An 'ideal' system of setting rates would have avoided this particular difficulty but would have been less acceptable to the union. The upshot could be that workers managed to capture a substantial proportion of the gains from introducing new machinery and organization and so reduce the incentive for management to implement these changes. That affected long-term competitiveness.

Smith & Nephew were unable to reach an adequate agreement until the 1970s, in a modest way. The development section suffered the consequences of this confusion over piece rates. Their work was liable to be undervalued because the gains to the company were not so apparent. Table 7.1 shows the

Figure 7.1a   Learning curves on the Elastoplast line, 1949–53

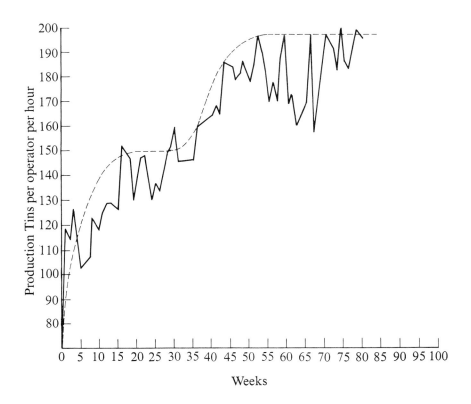

Figure 7.1b   Learning curves on the Elastoplast line, 1949–53

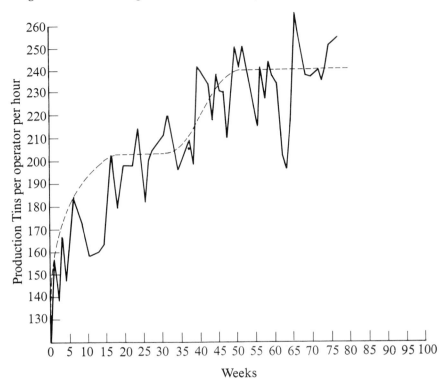

calculated financial gains between 1949 and 1953 on the assumption that annual machine costs were 10 per cent of the purchase price. There can be no doubt that the costs of the section were more than covered since savings were made in perpetuity whereas the section could be shifted on to another process once the new methods had been introduced.

Learning effects of flow-line production were quite dramatic, as Figure 7.1 shows. Learning curves, the rise in labour productivity as experience is gained, had been noted with the volume production of aircraft and ships during the war. The Elastoplast curves show a rise of two-thirds from the end of the first week through to the end of the first year of conveyor belt operation. Renardson in 1955 clearly felt development work was not appreciated despite such evidence.[8] Whatever the truth of Renardson's complaints, there is no doubt that by then Elastoplast production was on a sound and profitable basis, helped by continuing automation, as the next section shows. Engineering staff began modernizing the Lancashire weaving mills at the same time.

Recognition of their continuing and increasing usefulness in the group led to the transformation of the engineering division into Smith & Nephew Engineering Ltd.

ELASTOPLAST MANUFACTURE IN THE 1950s

Perhaps the most important stage in the manufacture of Elastoplast was the work done in the cloth processing department at Hull. There the initial stages of washing, shrinking and dyeing the cloth in preparation for the finished Elastoplast and Elastocrepe products took place. After drying the cloth was ironed by large steam-heated machines known as calenders. At this point a meter checked the length of the cloth and confirmed that adequate shrinkage had taken place; much of the elastic quality of the cloth depended on correct shrinkage. Although the initial treatment of all the cloth was broadly the same, there were a few variations. Some of the cloth was dyed and in this instance the temperature during the washing process, in which the dye was added, had to be considerably higher.[9]

The cloth was passed on to the spreading department in 250-yard rolls. By a continuous process it was passed through a machine which not only spread adhesive evenly but also blew air through the cloth so that the adhesive was made porous and was dried at the same time. In the subsequent slitting and making-up processes, a slitting machine processed the large rolls of cloth into $1^1/_2$-inch, $2^1/_2$-inch and 3-inch widths.

Three main types of Elastoplast first aid dressing were manufactured at Hull in the mid-1950s. At first the making-up of the first aid dressings, including the application of medicated gauze pads and the protective covering (the only component of the dressings not made within the group) had been manual. By the 1950s the job was entirely carried out by automatic machinery which not only performed the above tasks but also cut the dressings to their appropriate lengths. There were 14 machines, each one modified for the size to be produced.

The dressings were passed by the conveyor belt to a team of 34 female operatives who packed them into tins. The bright red Elastoplast tins arrived at the factory with their lids on so the first job in the packing process was to remove them. Each operative used only one hand to remove each lid so that she could work with both hands at the same time in order to double the throughput. Printed liners were put into tins and then the assorted sizes of dressings were packed, nine in the medium tin and 14 in the large tin. Between 50 and 60 000 tins left the packing belt each day.

Plastic film for the manufacture of waterproof Elastoplast and Airstrip was made at Hull. The processes of manufacture were exactly the same as for original Elastoplast with the exception that in the case of Airstrip the adhesive was applied in a lattice-like pattern which left the dressing half unspread. This was essential since Airstrip's most important function was to allow the wound it covered to breathe (see below). The dressing therefore needed to be air-permeable.

In the first stage of production, various chemical powders and colouring pigment were mixed together to form a pink 'dough'. This dough was kept hot and eventually fed into a machine where it was rolled into a thin film. While still hot, the film was rolled inside damp strips of cretonne so that it took on the embossed pattern of the cloth. The film was then ready for the spreading operation. Initially a tie-coat was applied so that the adhesive would hold better to the base film. When this had been dried in an oven, the plastic film was coated with adhesive and wound on to large 60-yard haspels, where it was left for two hours to air-dry. Making-up took the same form as that of original Elastoplast.

NEW DRESSINGS

Waterproof Elastoplast was introduced in 1946. An instant success, shortages of materials held back production. Trials that led to 'Airstrip' Elastoplast were reported shortly afterwards. The aim was to supply a dressing that would, like tropical clothing, be impervious to liquid water (and so keep off tropical rain) yet be pervious to water vapour, and so allow perspiration to evaporate. Uncoated cellophane and nylon derivatives were pervious to water vapour, while PVC and polythene were very resistant to water in liquid and vapour forms. Nylon-derivative films were chosen for the experimental occlusive dressing because they were also barriers against micro-organisms. Such dressings were particularly valuable in industrial environments where waterproof dressings were required by statute but adversely affected wound healing because the skin became sodden. Mean healing times in clinical trials of nylon dressings improved on those of waterproof dressings by one-quarter (Bull *et al.* 1948; Schilling *et al.* 1950). Ultraplast joined Smith & Nephew's range of dressings in 1958 with the acquisition of the Scottish company Wallace Cameron.

A decade later, the quality of the products was recognized by the award to Smith & Nephew of a Royal Warrant as suppliers of Ultraplast First Aid Dressings to HM the Queen. Roughly 75 per cent of all adhesive bandages sold in Great Britain by 1961 carried the Elastoplast mark, but this position could only be maintained with constant vigilance (Carr, Sons & Co. 1962, p. 5). Through a visit to the US in the 1950s Smith & Nephew learned of the apparent success of a new type of dressing named Telfa, marketed by Bauer

& Black. Although Telfa was covered by several UK patents, it was not sold in Britain. Smith & Nephew therefore tried to make a product that avoided these patents. Bauer & Black used their own Webril as a superb absorbent backing material. Smith & Nephew had to fall back on Absorbent Lint BPC. ICI supplied a suitable grade of Melinex film but making holes in the film was problematic because the only apparent suitable method was again patented by Bauer & Black. Smith & Nephew's alternative hot-needle process caused small flaps to be punched out which gave a rough surface to the film. Finally, patents prevented heat-bonding the film to the absorbent pad and a water-based adhesive was employed instead.[10]

The dressing that emerged was far from perfect but it was marketed in 1959 at a low price. The trade name Melolin was selected, derived from 'Melinex on Lint'. Some sales were achieved and a number of hospitals reordered. The only way open to Smith & Nephew to improve the product was to buy a licence from Bauer & Black, which they did. Machines were designed in Hull to use the two basic patents, the perforation of the Melinex film and the heat-bonding of the film to the absorbent backing. When a better backing, Lantor, was found, a completely new dressing was marketed in 1964 under the name Melolin XA. How successful this version was may be judged by the 1979 sales of £640 000.

One of the more quickly designed dressings, which also illustrates interaction between practitioners and business, was Airstrip Theatre and Ward Dressing in 1963. A consultant had visited the research company and was being entertained to dinner at a night club and restaurant in Piccadilly, London. He enquired whether the company had thought of making a large adhesive dressing. There and then, with Smith & Nephew personnel, a design was decided upon.

GYPSONA AND SPLINTING DEVELOPMENTS

The second of Smith & Nephew's two most profitable products lost the German original name in 1946 when Cellona became Gypsona.[11] The same year Smith & Nephew learned that the Tower Company had developed and marketed a new bandage made from yarn constructed from fibreglass and rayon acetate and woven in the form of stockinette. The bandage, Aire-lite, was activated by dipping in acetone.[12] Tower had not patented the product in the UK or in a number of other countries, leaving the field open for Smith & Nephew to manufacture Glassona in 1950. The advantages of Glassona were lightness, porosity and resistance to water but it was slower to set than Gypsona. Gypsona therefore continued to dominate casting. About one third of Gypsona production was exported in the mid-1950s. Sixty-five operatives worked 8³/₄ hours a day for five days a week. They mixed, cut, machined, wrapped, packed and crated. All processes were coordinated to ensure a continuous and even flow through the entire department. Eight men worked through the night mixing, spreading and slitting so that the girls on the day shift were not held up.[13]

Lohmann introduced a melamine formaldehyde reinforced plaster of Paris bandage named Cellamin, which Smith & Nephew followed with their own version, Gypsona Extra, in 1956. Initially a very satisfactory product, serious sensitivity problems emerged six months after first marketing the product. Some patients were affected but plaster technicians were the principal victims. Consequently Gypsona Extra was withdrawn in 1957. However the Canadian subsidiary continued to market Extra that they made themselves. Either Canadians have tougher skins or the use of gloves in Canada prevented the occurrence of the British problems.

The work on Gypsona Extra was not wasted for it led to the discovery of a means of increasing strength by using improved adhesives. This meant that more plaster was retained in the cloth after soaking and the amount of waste plaster in the bucket, on the floor and on the hands was reduced. Low Plaster Loss Gypsona (LPL) was introduced in February 1958, just in time to counteract the entry by Johnson & Johnson into the market with their Velroc. Quality problems struck LPL Gypsona, giving rise to a large number of complaints. Johnson & Johnson therefore quickly captured more than 20 per cent of the market. Then Johnson & Johnson also ran into quality difficulties and their share fell to 15 per cent. Failing to achieve the decisive victory they had expected, after three years they retreated from the field.

Close company relations with customers were helpful in new splinting product development, as the following three examples show. Arnold Lucas (director of the medical division) was on very good terms with the director of the Army Medical Services in the late 1950s, Lieutenant-General Sir Alexander Drummond. Drummond decided he must develop a system of splinting fractures for the treatment of mass casualties following a nuclear attack. Influenced by Lucas, he asked Smith & Nephew to propose how Gypsona might be used. At the Research & Development division, Smith & Nephew invented a technique of using gutter-type splints for all the common types of fracture. The resulting 'mass production' splinting was adopted by the Royal Army Medical Corps and became part of the training of all orderlies. With the help of the RAMC, Smith & Nephew devised the Gypsona Emergency Pack in 1960.

A slab dispenser for Gypsona was introduced in the same year. Smith & Nephew were given the idea by a young house surgeon at a Lancashire hospital. For his efforts the company paid him £25, with which he appeared well satisfied.

The Canadian subsidiary brought out San-Splint in 1967. Smith & Nephew UK discussed the product with W.H. Tuck, manager of the workshops at the Royal National Orthopaedic Hospital, Stanmore, that year. Tuck told the company he was experimenting with a much more interesting product of far greater potential, Plastazote. Smith & Nephew immediately contacted the manufacturers, Expanded Rubber & Plastics Ltd (part of the Bakelite-Xylonite group) and eventually signed an exclusive marketing agreement for the sale of Plastozote for medical purposes throughout the world.

IMPROVEMENTS AND RATIONALIZATION OF MEDICAL SUPPLIES

The problem of hospital cross-infection, highlighted in 1958 by the Nuffield Provincial Hospitals Trust Report, encouraged Smith & Nephew to introduce a whole range of disposables: face masks, sterilizing boxes and the like. Washable cotton cellular blankets were also provided to replace the rarely washed woollen covers that offered a safe haven for germs. In keeping with the tradition established in the mid-1930s, the company made a film 'Hospital cross-infection; Ward dressing Techniques 1960' to protect patients by encouraging changes in dressing techniques. Unlike merely promotional films, this depicted articles manufactured by competitor companies as well as by Smith & Nephew. The value of the film was recognized by a bronze medal from the British Medical Association, by an American hospital award and by the Italian hospital authorities. Ten years after the première, the film was still employed on the Hospital Nurse Training Curriculum.[14]

Standardization of nurses' dresses in 1960 with Trimsona was a Smith & Nephew innovation calculated to reduce hospital operating costs. The variation between hospitals in style and materials was tremendous, with consequent delays while manufacturers produced bespoke garments, and with idle stock as hospitals were left with clothing unsuited to the dimensions of new staff. Teaching hospitals had each evolved distinctive clothing styles which were jealously guarded. Trimsona was intended to be a dress that would fit 85 per cent of nurses. The Trimsona despatch service of 14 days particularly impressed hospital supplies officers. By contrast, when the Ministry of Health in 1968 suggested a 'national' dress for nurses and set up a working party which recommended such a dress, the proposal was not well received.

Smith & Nephew composite pre-packed surgical dressings helped combat cross-infection from 1959/60. Pre-packed dressings in 'soft pack' form for hospital supply were pioneered in a joint project with the South Eastern Region Hospital Board in Scotland and Johnson & Johnson. Service plus the packing of dressings under aseptically clean conditions were the selling points. The hospital board saved £0.25m capital costs on the central sterile supply department (CSSD) that they did not have to build, and the annual cost of £200 000 for the 15 standardized packs, agreed by the project committees, was much less than needed to *run* hospital CSSDs. From 1 October 1969 the two companies supplied the 93 hospitals, clinics and nursing homes in the region under a three-year contract.[15]

COMPETITION

Parenthetically the contract points out the paradoxical relationship between the large health care companies. In general they competed vigorously when they thought it profitable to do so, as the Johnson & Johnson entry to plaster of Paris bandages in 1958 showed. But that did not preclude selected cooperative projects when they were more in the public interest than competition. Patenting, as we have seen, was and is a vital competitive weapon. Although in the case of Melolin, Smith & Nephew were unable to invent round the key patents, competitors found substitute technology for air-permeable dressings. Smith & Nephew innovated porous first aid dressing but then other firms, by mechanical innovation, introduced perforated dressings and thus maintained their position.[16]

Branding was a competitive weapon that Smith & Nephew came to late in surgical dressing. While Johnson & Johnson, Vernon & Co., Robinson & Sons, A. Carus & Sons Ltd all competed with brand names (mainly for swabs) in 1970, Smith & Nephew had not branded any of their surgical dressings with the exception of 'Crinx', conforming bandage. Other competitors were Newsome & Co., Barton & Co. and Bailey & Co. It is impossible not to notice how long-established some of these names were and how different were their sizes relative to Smith & Nephew a century earlier.

A key to Smith & Nephew's growth continued to be the sales force. Originally called 'ethical representatives', Smith & Nephew employees from the beginning visited hospitals, factory first aid centres, varicose and fracture clinics to give demonstrations and advice on techniques and on proper use of the company's products. They were not salesmen in the sense that they did not take orders; they were more like teachers. Later they were renamed technical representatives, but their job was the same. Their expertise made them especially welcome when a clinic was faced with a particularly difficult fracture to cast. They kept in close touch with medical developments which they were able to relay back to research, so as to generate new products. During the 1950s there were ten medical representatives but they were reinforced from a total of ten in 1961 to 18 by 1970. By comparison, Everetts' (see below) sales force had consisted of one representative and one export sales manager, who was out of the country much of the time. Their policy, unlike Smith & Nephew's, had been to employ wholesalers. They therefore lost opportunities to obtain information from users about product performance and potential new product areas. The close contacts with the Royal National Orthopaedic Hospital, Lancashire house surgeons and with the RAMC, already referred to, demonstrate the importance of such interchanges. To facilitate this process, in late 1966 the representatives were divided into those selling textile products and those specializing in surgical equipment.

HYPODERMIC SYRINGES AND NEEDLES

At first a successful acquisition in the core health care market established Smith & Nephew in the supply of hypodermic needles and syringes. As technology and medical demands changed, the company failed to cope with foreign competition and eventually withdrew after two decades. In 1954 Smith & Nephew bought S. & R.J. Everett & Co., an old established and well-known company manufacturing hypodermic syringes and needles. They held the greater part of the home market and a considerable share of overseas markets as well. Smith & Nephew–Southalls were given responsibility for marketing and selling Everett products both in home and export markets four years later.

A hypodermic needle had four main features: the bevel of the point, the gauge or diameter of the cannula, the length of the cannula and the fitting of the hub or mount. Whether or not the injection of the patient was painful was determined by the sharpness of the point. The medical profession had asked for so many varieties of needles since the First World War that by the 1950s 1 800 types were produced, which militated against long production runs. Disposable needles in five standard gauges and lengths began to sell from 1959 and over ten years superseded traditional needles for general ward work in hospitals and for local authorities. American companies Gillette, Becton, Dickinson and Argyll entered the market and production methods were transformed, not very successfully in Everetts' case.

Hypodermic syringes were made at the S. & R.J. Everett & Co Ltd factory at Camberley in the 1950s and 1960s; they were essentially machine-made rather than hand-produced.[17] An S. & R.J. Everett & Co. Ltd factory at Lewes was originally opened during the Second World War as a shadow factory to the main unit at Thornton Heath. Between the end of the war and 1950 production ceased at Lewes, but thereafter, due to high demand, a factory on a different site was reopened. By the late 1950s the factory employed 190 workers and produced many thousands of needles a day.

Manufacture at Lewes was confined to the production of two types of needles: the ordinary surgical type for the medical profession and needles for dentists. The factory was supplied with 15-inch pieces of metal tube already prepared for manufacture into needles from Thornton Heath. Once the needles had been made they were returned to the main factory for final packing.

A Smith & Nephew sterile syringe service centre was set up in the aftermath of the report of the Nuffield Hospital Trusts team. The team was formed to investigate the sterilization of needles and syringes in hospitals, by means of boiling in water for five minutes. Boiling had been severely criticized because it does not kill all germs, particularly those varieties collectively called bacterial spores. The investigators supported the criticisms and stressed the need for organized syringe sterilization services to hospitals throughout the country. In December 1958 the new subsidiary company of Smith & Nephew pioneered the first commercial sterile syringe and needle service to hospitals in Birmingham and London – Hospital Instruments Ltd of 149 Alderson Road, Birmingham. Commercial operation of the scheme at this time was a considerable achievement, for the plant at Birmingham had been created only a few months earlier, purely as an experiment.

Constructional, administrative, technical and production problems were rapidly solved in order to turn 'experiment' into a functioning service. The service ensured that hospitals received only chemically clean, mechanically sound and truly sterile syringes with sharp needles attached, ready for instant use. Disposables rendered the service obsolete. Disposable syringes arrived at the same time as needles. Smith & Nephew's original product was 'Aseptor'. Made from polypropylene in the first instance and sterilized by Gamma irradiation, these were initially a success. Unfortunately the effects of irradiation on polypropylene were not then fully understood and after a few months the syringes were showing signs of discolouring and brittleness. They were withdrawn and replaced by polystyrene syringes, the molecular structures of which were unaffected by irradiation. Over the decade of the 1960s the price of a 2ml. disposable syringe fell from 6d. to 2d. because of economies of scale, learning and competition.[18]

The small Grahams Medical Products, well known for their disposable syringes, was bought in 1967 to increase capacity and mechanization. Smith & Nephew's brand name Aseptor was dropped in favour of Grahams, and production concentrated at Grahams' Berkshire plant. Everetts was rationalized by closing Lewes and Camberley and expanding operations at Mitcham. This strategy turned out to create very substantial training problems because the local labour forces did not want to move and the Mitcham labour supply had markedly changed in character since the plant was first established. Difficulties with the installation of new machinery at the same time as American competition was intensifying lost the company export market share from 1968, because of quality problems and supply shortages. The expiry of

Grahams' site lease in 1970 gave rise to further supply problems while production was transferred, as did teething troubles of the new unit.

Despite production handicaps new products were introduced. The success of the Viggo intravenous needle persuaded the organization to market a quality intravenous cannula under the name Venflon. Hospitals acknowledged the unique advantages of this 'long-stay' needle which could be inserted while the patient was still anaesthetized in theatre. In 1969 a new system of distribution of syringes, needles, swabs and intravenous needles was evolved under the title of Unit Pack Distributors. A selected list of wholesalers undertook to service hospital contracts negotiated by Smith & Nephew. The scheme permitted an average 48-hour delivery service to hospitals and was an unqualified success.

NIVEA CREME AND HERTS PHARMACEUTICALS

Nivea Creme came into Smith & Nephew earlier than hypodermics, with the purchase of Herts Pharmaceuticals in 1951. It proved an astonishingly popular product and encouraged Smith & Nephew to diversify into cosmetics. Smith & Nephew entered the toiletries market in 1948, with a facial cleansing pad called 'Flicks',[19] but within a year this product was withdrawn. The Nivea range in 1951 was much wider, consisting of Nivea Creme, soap, skin oil, hair oil (for men), shaving cream and sunning preparations. By 1955 Nivea was contributing almost half as much to home market sales of public products as Elastoplast and derivatives (Table 7.2). Moreover the contribution in overseas markets was equally healthy. Canadian sales of Nivea were almost double Canadian public sales of Elastoplast dressings.[20]

Table 7.2   Sales of T.J. Smith & Nephew in the UK, 1955 (£m)

Public products	
Elastoplast dressings, plaster, Airstrip etc.	0.96
Nivea products	0.44
Blue Velvet	0.04
Technical tapes	0.29
Medical products	
Elastoplast bandages, Jellonet, Gypsona	1.01
Surgical dressings	0.46
TB drugs and Dilatal	0.27

Nivea was invented as a simple soap at the turn of the century by Herr Doktor Beiersdorf, who marketed the famous Creme in 1912 (Krikler 1991, p. 17). Beiersdorf subsidiaries operated in every European country by the 1930s and ensured their Nivea Creme sold well and widely. Almost every German household owned a tin of Nivea. The British subsidiary in Welwyn Garden City undertook production but all research and technological support was at Beiersdorf headquarters in Hamburg. When war broke out in 1939 the British staff had to improvise for themselves the facilities that had been available in Hamburg.[21] They needed to find out exactly what made Nivea unique. The key was lanolin, a fat obtained from washing lambs' wool; the drains of Bradford were often blocked with it. Lanolin is easily absorbed by the skin and possesses some antiseptic properties. Cholesterol (which Don Seymour showed could be used for making Vitamin D3, see Chapter 8) and stearols are the principal components of lanolin. These stearols treated with wool alcohol made Eucerite. Since all the materials for Nivea were originally imported from Germany and were no longer available, understanding the constituents of Nivea was a vital first step towards finding replacement materials. Other ingredients were paraffin wax, oil, earth wax, 70 per cent was water and the perfume contained 26 ingredients such as lavender oil, orange oil, bergamot oil, synthetic amber and lilac 24. Nivea Creme is a water in oil emulsion, a mixture of oil and water that needs something to stop it falling apart. The British analysts were obliged to identify those ingredients from the many small quantities of apparently arbitrary substances, like magnesium sulphate, that were added in manufacture.

Frank Moore, trained as a pharmacist, assumed management of the subsidiary for which he had worked since 1932. Formally the German company was under American control, the shares being held by Duke Laboratories of Connecticut. Beiersdorf UK (changing its name to Herts Pharmaceuticals) not only manufactured Nivea but also a heart preparation made from digitalis lanata, Tricoplast and Hansaplast wound dressing. In pursuit of technical information about dressings, at the beginning of the 1940s, Moore visited the Manchester dermatologist P.B. Mumford. Mumford pointed out that Moore's company could not hope to operate without a chemist and directed Moore to the Manchester University department where Alexander Todd (a Chemistry Nobel Prize winner in 1957) was then professor and F.S. Spring was reader. Spring recommended to Moore a graduate student, D.E. Seymour, who was to be a powerful influence on Smith & Nephew's development. During the war Herts engaged in R & D for their full range of products, not just pharmaceuticals: Nivea, plasters and tapes for Ministry of Supply aircraft production. The chief pharmacist at Southend Hospital, Adamson, drew Moore's attention to the need for May & Baker's sulpha drugs, for drugs for diarrhoea and bowel infections and for Acumerol (for heart failure). Herts then made all these and sold them to the Ministry of Health. After the war Herts bought Hunsdon, formerly one of the largest night fighter command stations in the Home Counties, for the manufacture of PAS (Chapter 9).

The acquisition of Herts by Smith & Nephew allowed a much better use of space at the new Hull factory. Herts' fine chemical plant was transferred to Hull where production of Therapas, Nupasal and Propyl Salicylamide was undertaken. Nivea production followed soon after. Labour difficulties at the Welwyn factory accelerated the move of the industrial tape section in 1956.[22] Smith & Nephew Engineering made major contributions to improvement in manufacturing processes. One instance was their production of an industrial tape tunnel drier capable of making 50 000 running yards a week, by comparison with the pre-existing double shift capacity of 16 000 yards.

NIVEA MANUFACTURE

The first stage in Nivea production is the separate preparation of the water and oil bases. In the 1950s Eucerite, the refined form of lanolin unique to Nivea products, was blended with other ingredients in a hollow-sided vessel called a 'kettle' and steam-heated to the required temperature. The resulting liquid looked like clear golden honey. In the 'mixing vessel' the water base of the creme was similarly blended and heated. When both preparations had reached the correct temperature the oily base was pumped through overhead pipes into the mixing vessel, where giant paddles stirred the mixture into a creme. The process took about four hours and during the last hour the Nivea perfume was slowly added, drop by drop. As the creme was stirred and cooled it gradually turned from a yellowish colour to pure white. Finally the creme was milled – it was pumped through overhead pipes to special apparatus that ground the mixture down to superfine quality. The Nivea was then pumped into bins and fed into tins by a filling machine which was operated by a foot pedal and adjusted to deliver enough creme to fill one tin. The filled tins slid down a ramp on to a conveyor belt and as they moved along a row of female operatives in white caps and overalls levelled off the top of the creme, put on the disks of protective silver paper, fitted the lid and gave the tin a final polish.[23]

Nivea Creme soap manufacture began in large soap-boiling pans, 13 feet in depth and 12 feet square, of about 40 tons capacity. High-quality oils and fats were boiled together with other ingredients until a neutral soap was formed. The soap was then left to settle for two or three days, after which time the skin of 'neat' soap was skimmed off and stored in tanks for the next process. From the tanks it was pumped to a spray-drying plant where it was passed through hot air to drive off moisture, until the end product became a powder. The powdered soap was fed into a mixer where Nivea perfume and Eucerite were added. It was fed through two triple-roll mills which compressed the soap into a more solid form. The soap emerged as a continuous solid block which was automatically cut into tablets while still warm and pliable. The tablets passed into the stamping machine which impressed the 'Nivea' name on both sides of the tablet at the rate of 100 per minute. Finally an automatic machine wrapped an inner waxed wrapper, a cardboard stiffener and a printed outer wrapper round the completed tablet of soap.

Blue Velvet Hand lotion was made very much like Nivea Creme, but it was blue and much more liquid. When the mixing of the lotion was completed it was filtered to ensure purity and then transferred in large stainless steel containers to bottle-filling machines. Although worked by hand, the filling machines were semi-automatic; as soon as the bottles were taken away the supply of lotion was shut off. Caps were put on manually and then tightened by machine.

By the early 1960s little had been achieved in extending the Nivea product range because of very high promotional costs and risks. Smith & Nephew held a strong position in one cosmetic market segment and felt little need to break into others. Roughly 40 per cent of all general-purpose skin cream sold in the British market during 1961 originated from Smith & Nephew (Carr Sons & Co. 1962, p. 5).

THE TOILETRIES AND COSMETICS MARKET IN THE UK

The whole British cosmetics market of 1963 was worth about £50m in retail selling prices and growing at a rate of between 12 per cent and 15 per cent per annum (see Table 7.3). Manufacturers' selling prices were approximately half retail prices, yielding a market value of £25m. (Total consumers' expenditure was about £20 000m in 1963.)

The market was split into three price categories. The medium- to high-bracket products were sold through department stores, while 70 per cent of the lower two categories was sold through retail chemists. The remainder was distributed through Woolworth's and other such stores. Some products, like shampoos, where the customer needed no advice, were, in addition, sold through supermarkets and grocers. Distribution depended on type of outlet; high-price products were distributed selectively, with representatives visiting stores, while traditional universal distribution characterized low-priced items.

Although forms of cosmetics and toiletries had been popular for centuries, from the late 1950s a substantial commercial market was established and increased dramatically. The cosmetics and toiletries market was and continues to be vastly changeable because of fashion. Shampoos, eye cosmetics,

Table 7.3   UK cosmetics/toiletries market in 1963 (at retail selling prices)

Product group	Market value, £m.
Hair products	17
Creams and lotions	10
Lipstick	8
Powder (all types)	5
Eye make-up	3
Deodorants/anti-perspirants	3
Perfumes/toilet waters	18
Depilatories	0.5

Note: Deodorants, depilatories, mens' toiletries and sunning preparations are not true cosmetics but are included in the table. Hence the difference in the table total and the earlier
figure.

foundation creams, face powders, lipsticks, deodorants and men's cosmetics
give an idea of the range of the market in the early 1960s.

Sales of shampoos were increasing, especially the medicated sector of the
market, and 40 per cent of women used some type of shampoo at least once a
week. Inversely related to shampoo sales were those of home perms – the
percentage of women using this product fell from 29 per cent in 1959 to 17
per cent in 1962. Postwar highly structured coiffures were giving way to the
more 'natural' look. Hair sprays were relatively new but expansion was
rapid; 20 per cent of women used spray as a method of 'hair-fixing'.

Growing use of eye cosmetics – eye shadow, eye liner, mascara and eye-
brow pencils – was the biggest single change in the cosmetics market between 1957 and 1963. These products were mainly bought by the 16–18 age
group and so continued growth was virtually assured. Although the largest
growth area, the market for eye cosmetics was still relatively small in 1963,
having an estimated value of £3m at retail selling prices (Table 7.3).

Fifty-six per cent of all women used some type of foundation/vanishing/
cold cream. All-purpose creams were most popular, the product leader being
Nivea, followed by Ponds, Astral and then Yardley. Perhaps the most widely
bought product for the skin, though, was powder. Eighty-three per cent of all
women used one or other form of face powder, but cream powder clearly
dominated the market. Another very commonly used product type was lipstick. Eighty-five per cent of all women put on lipstick at one time or another;
79 per cent used it regularly. Sales were estimated at £8m per annum at retail
selling prices, but the market was relatively static. Max Factor and Yardley
held 40 per cent of this market between them.

Deodorants and antiperspirants were relatively new products, and in the early 1960s the toiletries industry expected their popularity would increase considerably. The market was dominated by four products: Body Mist, Mum, Odo-ro-no and Arrid, with a host of minor brands in competition. Forty-eight per cent of women had used one of these products at some time, while an equal percentage had never used one. The Lilia-White organization of Smith & Nephew was actively considering entering this market in 1963.

The men's toiletries market had always been seasonal, with women buying products for men at Christmas. In 1963, seasonality was decreasing but the market as a whole continued to be a major disappointment for manufacturers. In the mid-1950s the market was forecast to be worth £10m per annum at retail selling prices by 1960. Instead, by 1963, sales were nearing the £6m mark, of which 50 per cent was accounted for by hair dressings. The resulting £3m was divided between approximately 60 brands; Unilever's and Beecham's disastrous experiences trying to develop sales in this market persuaded them to withdraw from the field completely. A market investigation by Smith & Nephew reported:

> Women, with the hope of making their menfolk as fragrant as themselves, appear to have been more enchanted by these preparations than men and still two-thirds of all male toiletries are bought by women. After-shave lotions have made some impact but pre-shave lotions, cologne, body rubs, talc and deodorants are still too much for the average British male. Undoubtedly the market will progress and perhaps really 'arrive' one day; the time to enter the market does not seem to be now. ...

Smith & Nephew supplied preparations for the face, hands and hair – the last through shampoo only and the first two mostly because Nivea was an all-purpose cream. Atrixo, as a hand care preparation, was already reasonably accepted and by the end of 1963 this product was expected to equal or exceed sales of the brand leader, Nulon.

Organic Development

If acquisition proved impossible, the plan in the early 1960s was to increase Smith & Nephew's share in the cosmetics market by development of its own products. However, in the initial stages, expansion into rapidly growing sectors of the market (hair and eye make-up) was avoided. The group tested the water in the facial cream sector where it was already familiar with manufacture and marketing.

In the cosmetics market it was, and still is, vital to publicize the brand name. Once a name is established other products, and even products for other cosmetic purposes, can be added to the range comparatively inexpensively.

The Nivea name was well known and associated with quality. With its direct association with skin care, there was an undoubted advantage in new products being thought of as a 'Nivea product'. Although association with Nivea would have benefits, the company did not want the name used for branding cosmetics: 'the Nivea name has little of the mystique and glamour of the recognised cosmetics companies'.

Instead the name 'Serene' was registered to cover groups of cosmetics before the recommendations were put before the board in readiness for quick action. Initially, the marketing angle was to be 'Serene by Nivea', imparting a feeling of quality and know-how in skin care. The 'by Nivea' was to be dropped once the range was established. A cream powder had been developed, and was the first product of the potential range. It was envisaged that cold/vanishing cream, foundation cream, cleansing cream and eventually lipstick would follow. If they were successful, expansion into products for the hair and eyes, and for dipilatories was foreseen. Advertising expenditure of not less than £100 000 was essential, and turnover was estimated at between £500 000 and £750 000 at the end of five years. Net profit was estimated to be in the region of between 25 per cent and 30 per cent. New products were in the medium price range and were introduced through test marketing. Test marketing permitted detection of any imperfections in the product, or unsuspected consumer resistance, and also considerably limited the initial financial risk.

With hindsight, Smith & Nephew were quite correct that this was a dynamic market. Spending on toiletries and cosmetics in 1972 rose by 19 per cent. By then the cosmetics market was worth £260m, and toilet requisites £130m, an increase in nominal terms of six times since 1963.[24] But as television came to dominate cosmetics, advertising fixed costs were boosted and a viable company needed to capture a larger share of the market than before. Safety and efficacy now required more pre-launch investment. More pre-launch testing inevitably braked fashion changes, both for reasons of expense and because of the delay and uncertainty of testing. Long experience in Britain gained under the poisons legislation effectively applied negative listings to exclude undesirable substances from cosmetics. For this reason toxic constituents, such as belladonna and arsenic, were no longer included in cosmetics (van Abbe 1974). Fantasy advertising became less acceptable to consumer lobbies and under the Trade Descriptions Act. But a real consumer demand for positive efficacy would manifest itself in a demand for more therapeutic rather than decorative cosmetics, and that has never been very apparent.

Growth by Acquisition

Smith & Nephew decided that, in view of the growth potential of the toiletries and cosmetics market in the early 1960s, they should take the considerable financial risk of developing wider interests in the field. Ideally they would acquire a company that would give the group immediate access to all sections of the market. Management expertise in the field was of prime importance and the type of thinking, the ability to sense and quickly provide a new fashion, and flair for design and presentation, were all so vital that success was unlikely to be achieved without a company background in cosmetics.

The ideal company, Gala, was acquired in 1971. Gala originated in 1846 when an American music hall owner, Henry Clay Milner, began to manufacture his own make-up. Myram Picker, a qualified pharmacist, founded the Crystal Chemical Company in New York and bought Miner's business in 1928. Visiting England on holiday, Myram, with his daughter Rhoda, launched the Outdoor Girl range of cosmetics. Bulk manufacture began in 1934.

During the war the British government forced the amalgamation of factories. Outdoor Girl, Miner's and Gala of London joined forces first with Brylcreem and then with Max Factor. At the end of hostilities Myram's son Stanley set up a factory on the Kingston by-pass. Mary Quant cosmetics were launched in 1966 and a second factory was opened the following year. The Queen's Award for exports was won in 1968.

Among others, Roland Smith, professor of marketing at University of Manchester Institute of Technology, extolled the virtues of applying Smith & Nephew's rigorous cost controls to Gala (Gala were certainly desperately short of cash at the time) and enabling Gala to use Smith & Nephew's international distribution network. At first, when Smith & Nephew owned only 57 per cent of Gala, all went well. Gala increased turnover by 19 per cent in 1973 and profit by 16 per cent, despite shortages of packaging and raw materials during the second half of the year, when the first world oil crisis struck. In 1974, as the world economy turned down, Smith & Nephew acquired all of Gala. Profits were disappointing, at less than half those of the previous year. But worse was to come. The following year Smith & Nephew's chairman reported '…that a fundamental error relating to 1974 came to light during the year in our Cosmetic Division which has necessitated a material correction of the 1974 figures. As a result, a £3.3 million write-off net after tax relief has been made…'.

Unenforceable sales agreements were incorrectly accounted for as sales, and as a consequence an unduly favourable assessment was made of the saleability of similar goods included in the inventories held at the end of 1974: 'The heavy loss has been a traumatic experience for us all and we must accept our share of the responsibility and blame for having allowed this to occur'.

Nivea Creme, Atrixo Handcream and other toiletries products sales were buoyant during 1975 in the UK, and in overseas units. But the American cosmetic business continued to be a problem and a loss of £1.2m was written off in the 1976 trading figures.

> In cosmetics where there was a decline in UK consumption particularly in the first half of the year, profits improved again in 1977 helped by exports, rationalisation and improved efficiency. We were able to hold our UK market share in Mary Quant, Miners and Outdoor Girl. Whilst not achieving the targets required, cosmetics are now showing a reasonable return on the capital employed. The situation in our US cosmetics company, where there was a loss of £0.5 million continues to be very unsatisfactory.

There was, the company believed, considerable scope for further development in toiletries, particularly if they used more effectively the group's medical technological resources. Therefore a new toiletries division was formed and closely linked to the group's R & D activities, as well as to the pharma-med division. Manufacturing practices needed for toiletries were becoming increasingly similar to those required for ethical pharmaceutical products and called for similar standards and disciplines.

Cosmetics in the UK sold exceptionally well in home and export markets during 1978. Even the American company showed improvement. Unfortunately the broader political and economic environment ensured that the turnaround was short-lived. Profit declined in 1979 as the world slipped into the recession triggered by the second oil crisis and tight monetary policy in the US (as well as in UK). Cosmetics operations in the UK were very disappointing and hardly profitable. Much ground was lost at the beginning of the year because deliveries to customers were disrupted by the national distribution strike and adverse weather conditions. This was followed by a shortage of components and lack of production. The cosmetics operation in the US had been reduced substantially in previous years and moderate write-offs were absorbed in 1979.

Early in 1980, in view of the extreme pressure on both the profit margins and the volume of activity, the board decided to discontinue the clothing and cosmetics businesses. Accordingly by the end of 1980, Smith & Nephew abandoned all major involvement in the making up of clothing or the cosmetics trade. The company continued to operate successfully in the toiletries sector with the established brand names of Nivea and Atrixo. Enforced redundancies involving some 1 900 people were unavoidable. These closure costs (less tax relief where appropriate) represented a large part of the £3.9m written off in 1980.

CONCLUSION

As Smith & Nephew acknowledged when they bought Gala, they lacked the experience or perhaps the corporate culture to operate in fashion markets, even though their existing product range was in some respects close to those markets. Had they restricted themselves to an acquisition purely for the UK then, as the results indicate, the move might have been successful. As it was, the attempt to break into the US, which had always until then defied them, and into new products markets as well, was too much to handle. Thereafter Smith & Nephew chose successful geographical expansion within the more tightly circumscribed health care product ranges.

NOTES

1. *Smith & Nephew Annual Report*, 1941
2. G. Whittaker, *A Handful of Shale*, p. 188 unpublished ms.
3. The Anglo-American Council on Productivity issued a stream of well publicized reports on various industries. (Crafts 1991 p. 279.)
4. Seymour interview. P. Watson communication, 4 February 1992. Page had joined Smith & Nephew from Meihle Press, a US printing press manufacturer. Dolezalek gained his early experience in the aircraft industry. (Dr Martin Barth communication, 3 February 1992.) Although the introduction of moving production lines is generally associated with Henry Ford and the motor car, in fact British biscuit factories were using conveyor belts more than half a century earlier.
5. 10 feet per minute with a production of 34/35 000 large or 48/50 000 small tins per day with 30 operators.
6. That presupposes the production department resolved its other problem of raising the input rate as faster throughput caused stocks to dwindle.
7. E. Robinson to E. Coulson, 7 April 1949; *Report of a Meeting between the Development Engineers and the Production Department of T.J. Smith & Nephew Ltd 25 August 1949*, Smith & Nephew Archives, Hull.
8. H. Renardson to M. Webster, September 1955, Smith & Nephew Archives, Hull.
9. 'The Beginnings of Elastoplast', *Sanaco News*, Autumn 1958, pp. 4–6.
10. P.S. Watson, *A Miscellany of Historical Notes Regarding the Development of Some of Our Earlier Products*, 1979, Smith & Nephew Archives, Hull.
11. Ibid., p. 8. For this section generally see Smith & Nephew (1967), pp. 33–7.
12. The name was subsequently changed to Airecast.
13. 'Making Gypsona', *Sanaco News*, Spring 1955.
14. *Smith & Nephew-Southalls Limited 1958–1970*, p. 6
15. 'A New Form of Partnership', *British Hospital Journal and Social Service Review*, 19 September 1969, pp. 1734 and p. 1759.
16. *Research Report*, 1964, p. 3, *Smith & Nephew Archives*, London.
17. 'Spotlight on Camberley', *Sanaco News*, Autumn 1957, pp. 24–6; 'A visit to Lewes', *Sanaco News*, Summer 1958, pp. 24–5, 'A Service for Hospitals', *Sanaco News*, Spring 1959, pp. 33–5.
18. *Smith & Nephew – Southalls Limited 1958–1970*, pp. 23–8.
19. *Toiletries and Cosmetics Report*, September 1963, Smith & Nephew Archives, London.
20. *Advertising Proposals 1956*, Smith & Nephew Archives, London.
21. Frank Moore interview, 1991.
22. *Managing Director's Report*, August 1956, Smith & Nephew Archives, London.

23. 'A Recipe for Christmas', *Sanaco News*, Christmas 1958, pp. 18–21.
24. *Chemist and Druggist*, 8 December 1973, p. 792.

8. Textile developments

The Smith & Nephew organization underwent three important changes during the 15 boom years after the war ended: acquisition of textile plants (vertical backward integration), merger with competitors Southalls and Arthur Berton (horizontal integration), and diversification into pharmaceuticals with the purchase of Herts. Each move created new and different opportunities for expansion.

Having spent his early years in Lancashire, H.N. Smith always favoured textiles. During the First World War he had owned an integrated textile and medical dressing company that he sold in 1920. His interest initiated the purchase of Glen Mills by Smith & Nephew in 1953, thereby bringing into the group a management team that was to influence strongly the development of Smith & Nephew over the next three decades. By dint of very considerable investment and management effort, Smith & Nephew built up during the 1950s the most efficient integrated textile business in the country, and more important, one that was internationally competitive. The logic of this strategy was that as a large textile user, primarily in feminine hygiene but also in surgical dressings and clothing, the company would benefit from high-quality, low-price, guaranteed supply. Complementary was the integration of the three companies' feminine hygiene production and marketing operations. Together with reduced material prices from the textile plants, the reorganization cut costs markedly and ensured a very substantial source of profits for further expansion.

THE LEGACY OF THE INTERWAR YEARS

Although Smith & Nephew processed substantial quantities of textiles, for most of the interwar years the company was content to buy entirely from other firms, rather than manufacture in-house (Chapter 5). In 1920 Edwin Robinson, a close associate of H.N. Smith, first contacted the firm of Hindle Warburton in Blackburn, an old-established weaving business, to supply Smith & Nephew. By 1932 Hindle Warburton was manufacturing Elastoplast cloth. Many of the cloths required by Smith & Nephew needed bleaching, and therefore Oliver Ormrod of Bury, Lancs was acquired in 1937. Smith & Nephew could now buy cloth in the grey state and bleach it to the company's own requirements. Because of the severe restrictions imposed on the industry during the Second World War, in 1940 Smith & Nephew decided to secure supplies of textiles by purchasing 51 per cent of the shares in Hindle Warburton.[1]

The years between the world wars were ones of humiliation, decline and industrial conflict for Lancashire's cotton industry. By contrast with the US and Japan, productivity stagnated, world markets were lost and union restrictive practices ensured that new investment would not be profitable. Between 1913 and 1937, production of cotton cloth fell from 8 000 million to 3 320 million linear yards. Although synthetic fibres had been introduced by 1937 production amounted to only 482 million linear yards – representing only approximately 10 per cent of the decline in cotton cloth production.

The textile industry in Britain had been based on a 'horizontal system', with separate spinning, doubling, weaving and finishing plants. The new industries growing up all over the world were organized vertically. Verticalization and the ability to adopt modern machinery from the start gave 'new' textile industries a great advantage over the traditional Lancashire operations.[2] The textile industry in Britain, so well established and traditional, was slow to react to changes in technology and in the world economy.

During the 1950s and later Smith & Nephew invested enormous effort in overcoming this legacy. In doing so the company was greatly influenced by George Whittaker. In turn he was reacting to the experience of the years between the world wars and was determined to do what he could to restore Lancashire's and Britain's textile fortunes. His career between the wars therefore ultimately bore upon Smith & Nephew closely. George Whittaker left Mill Hill School in 1921 and went to work in the mill his father managed for David Whitehead & Sons (DWS), while he decided on his career:

> At first I hated the mill and was much nauseated by the smell of dirt grease and dust. The noise was deafening, the danger from unguarded machinery with their forest of belts and overhead shafting was frightening. The stinking toilets, the almost complete lack of washing and eating facilities was repulsive. The people were almost foreigners to me, so little could I understand of what they said with their broad Lancashire accent. ... I had to eat with the workers at the machines, play cricket or football with them on the tip during meal breaks and in every way to identify myself with them. ...[3]

In his economics evening class, then necessary for his professional qualification, he learned of the growth of textile industries in the US and the East, in particular Japan, and noted the Japanese buying up closed mills at scrap value for shipment back. At the Bank of England's initiative the Lancashire Cotton Corporation was formed and by 1930 had bought 96 firms and 9.3 million spindles, almost one fifth of the Lancashire total. By 1939 it had scrapped 4.5 million spindles. The Spindles Board set up by the 1936 Spindles Act scrapped another 6.2 million.

The Second World War allowed the conservative or perhaps stubborn attitude of British textile manufacturers to survive longer. During the war textile production had top priority. With peace the industry also experienced a highly profitable era, but by 1951 the honeymoon was over. The industry had been given the opportunity to reorganize, to take on a vertical character in order to face competition in the future, but little had been done. Perhaps the most pertinent reason was lack of managerial experience. Generally managements had not been trained in the various sections of the industry, and as a result were not capable of verticalizing the particular businesses with which they were connected. By 1962/63 the industry had begun to realize the necessity of creating vertical operations; excuses of flexibility, unsuitability and size of markets were constantly put forward to defend the horizontal system but they gradually lost credibility. Tangible ways of connecting dispersed textile operations were sought; in particular emphasis was placed on the need to integrate manufacture with distributing concerns. However a large percentage of the British industry remained wedded to the old organization. Five of the largest Lancashire operations controlled effectively less than 10 per cent of the looms and about the same percentage of the fabric trade; in the US the percentage controlled by the five largest firms was far greater at 25 per cent.

Most of the problems originated from the textile trade itself, but some criticism may be aimed at the government. Government 'assistance' through legislation such as the 1948 Cotton Spinning Industry (Re-equipment Subsidy) Act and the 1959 Cotton Industry Act, supported and even encouraged the horizontal system, effectively reducing capacity and discouraging any constructive moves towards verticalization. In 1961 only 40 per cent of looms were operated by combined manufacturers – firms owning looms coupled with either spinning or merchanting. All American textile concerns were combined operations. When examples of full verticalization are sought for the same date, probably only 5 per cent of the UK industry could be included in this category. Simply owning facilities in all sectors of the trade did not constitute verticalization; the sections needed to be integrated commercially, administratively and technologically.

ORIGINS OF SMITH & NEPHEW TEXTILE DIVISION

Smith & Nephew continued to acquire textile mills after the war in order to guarantee security of supply. Primrose Mill, Darwen, then owned by the Beecham Group for canning and lard refining, was bought in 1948, completely modernized and equipped with the latest automatic looms and ancillary machinery. Textile policy and prices were dictated by the Hull factory, who always paid excessively low prices. There was no standardization of mill output and innumerable small orders.[4]

As yet Smith & Nephew did not spin any of its own yarn. Very large quantities were being purchased for the company, frequently at prices considerably higher than could be borne in more difficult periods of trading. Glen Mills at Colne and Rawtenstall possessed a modern spinning plant operating a three-shift system and therefore was purchased in 1953. At the same time Hindle Warburton, which had also been severely hit financially by the cotton price collapse, was bought entirely.

Glen Mills was acquired by Smith & Nephew through the personal intervention of H.N. Smith, now in his energetic 70s. The managing director of Glen Mills, George Whittaker, together with a management team including his nephew, Kenneth Bradshaw, as spinning manager, and Gren Hazlitt had transferred from David Whitehead's (now part of Lonrho). They had started the business with some subscribed share capital from outside directors and some of their own. Having just joined the Methodist church at Colne, Whittaker was introduced to H.N. at a social event in 1948, to discover that H.N. was passionately interested in Whittaker's newly ordered (and unpaid for) tennis court. This social contact bore fruit when Whittaker's board of directors decided to dismiss him for visiting Canada and taking orders there. H.N. provided the capital for Whittaker to buy out the directors, advised by Smith & Nephew Chairman G.E. Leavey.

George Leavey was most impressed by the success of Glen Mills in avoiding the losses that Smith & Nephew (and Southalls) suffered when cotton prices collapsed at the beginning of the 1950s.[5] A spectacular rise in American and Egyptian cotton prices pushed up costs in 1948. In 1950 Smith & Nephew used its cash resources to build up raw material stocks, especially cotton and rubber. Prices began falling from the end of 1951, slashing the value of the company's stocks, and imposing substantial losses.[6] Glen Mills had matched the maturity dates of contracts to sell finished products at given prices with those for delivery of raw materials, so avoiding these losses. When Leavey put the Smith & Nephew offer to Glen Mills, Whittaker persuaded his doubtful colleagues to accept the offer by announcing: 'If we can run this successfully, we can run Smith & Nephew successfully', a judgement which with hindsight seems prescient.[7]

H.N.'s indirect influence on Smith & Nephew policy continued by placing Whittaker's daughter as an au pair with the owner of the highly productive Joanna Cotton Mill in South Carolina. Whittaker received an invitation to visit the South Carolina mill because his daughter had proved so valuable and saw how best practice productivity was achieved. During that visit to the US he also saw for the first time denim jeans worn as casual dress.

Coral Mill, Newhey and later Dale Mill, Rochdale, were acquired, making available to Smith & Nephew a total spinning capacity of approximately 170 000lbs of yarn weekly, with an annual turnover of cloth of just over £3.5m. Thus the company owned an organization in 1955 covering every stage of textile production, but in 21 locations.

The choice facing the company was whether to sell or close the textile business and buy from the Far East, or to try to halt the apparently inexorable decline in British textile competitiveness. A study showed that production could be competitive with the Far East if three-shift working was introduced, traditional work loads were abandoned and £0.5m was invested. All 15 unions agreed to the proposals, contrary to expectations, but they required an official application from the textile employers' association to conform with their collective agreement. The employers were convinced that modernization would not pay. Only by enlisting the support of the national press over three months were they persuaded to cooperate.[8] All mills were joined together as one company, Smith & Nephew Textiles, in January 1956.

PRODUCTIVITY GAINS FROM INVESTMENT

Research into American methods where productivity per machine was three times the Lancashire average helped in the planning of this programme. It meant a reduction of just over one-half of the textile production labour force. Three-shift working was introduced in consultation with the unions, as was redundancy. For more than a generation the group's production had been unhampered by labour disputes. Between 1959 and 1961 labour productivity doubled.[9] The story is a remarkable contrast to conventional accounts of Lancastrian inertia and decline in the face of foreign textile competition in these years and one that reflects creditably on the textile division, managed by Kenneth Bradshaw between 1958 and 1971 (Singleton 1986; Lazonick 1986).

Smith & Nephew realized the need for vertical integration well before others in the industry and between 1951 and 1958 the group's textile activities were increased dramatically so as to become completely independent of outside suppliers. By industry standards Smith & Nephew's operation was reasonably efficient but the production units remained scattered. The purchase of Brierfield Mills, at low cost, enabled the company to concentrate its textile efforts and operate at optimal efficiency. In the early 1960s, the number of production units was reduced from 12 to three.

The verticalization achieved by Smith & Nephew, unparalleled in British industry, allowed the company in the early 1960s to take maximum advantage of full automation. An independent survey of 52 Lancashire spinning mills found Smith & Nephew's Brierfield Mills among the most efficient.[10] Total spindle hours expected to produce the actual Brierfield output on the basis of German data was divided by the actual spindle hours used at Brierfield. The resulting index of machine productivity of 1.147 showed that the German standard required 14.7 per cent more spindle hours than did Brierfield to produce Brierfield's yarn output. Briefield's machine productivity was considerably higher than the standard. A similar calculation underlay Brierfield's index of labour productivity of 1.137, with much the same conclusion. The two partial productivity indices were combined in a total productivity, or whole mill, index for Brierfield of 1.143.

Similar indices calculated for other Lancashire mills showed that Brierfield was some 10 per cent more productive than the best. Compared with some of the worst it was more than twice as productive. In a world context, the most efficient firm known to the world's leading textile consultants attained a whole mill (total productivity) index of 1.3 (more efficient than Brierfield). An American mill was known to have an index of 1.0. The index is not necessarily an indication of the relative costs of operation, for wage rates and overhead costs may have varied from mill to mill.

Projections showed that when Smith & Nephew's plan of development was complete in 1964, the whole mill index would increase to 1.284, the world best practice level. Introduction of new automated machinery was expected to raise the index of labour productivity considerably. The projected indices were:

> Index of machine productivity = 1.205
> Index of labour productivity   = 1.414
> Index of operatives employed   = 1.173
> Index of whole mill   = 1.284

Unfortunately there was no similar scheme to measure efficiency in weaving, a far more complex process, and there were no comparative figures for the UK. Originally hand-fed looms required the weaver to 'kiss the shuttle' when the threads broke, as they often did, especially with poorer-quality yarn; the loom was stopped and the shuttle was rethreaded manually. (American) Northrop automatic looms introduced in the 1930s dropped a pin whenever threads broke, stopping the loom and feeding the shuttle automatically. Later the German and Swiss Sultzer looms superseded Northrop. Smith & Nephew operated more Northrop automatic looms per weaver than anyone in the UK. How many looms a single weaver could manage depended on the probability of a thread breaking. That in turn was determined not only by yarn quality but also by the type of cloth and warp thread. Cloth with 100 ends (or warp yarns) across a loom had 100 chances of breaking and cloth with more ends had correspondingly more chances. Light gauze cloth could be woven with over 90 looms per weaver, because of the relatively low chances of thread breakage, but no other UK mill wove gauze cloth. Elastoplast cloth required fewer than 20 looms per weaver. Nonetheless, that leading textile machinery manufacturers considered Brierfield Mill 'the show-piece of Lancashire' was proved by the ever-increasing number of overseas visitors sent by the machine-makers to view the plant. The textile division noted:

> Our reputation over the last ten years has increased out of all recognition, and has spread to many parts of the world, ... this publicity will intensify with the starting up of the prototype plant we are now installing, in conjunction with T.M.N. (Research) Ltd. (Stone Platt Group)... This opinion is also held by the Cotton Board and many other organisations in the textile industry.[11]

SEQUENTIAL TEXTILE PROCESSES AT THE END OF THE 1950s

By the end of the 1950s the vertically organized Smith & Nephew textile division bought raw material in the form of raw cotton, transforming it all the way up to fashion clothes, as well as supplying the cloth for the quantitatively more important surgical dressings and feminine hygiene products in other divisions. In addition denim production was sold to other companies.

Spinning

Egyptian, South and North American and South African raw cotton was spun into yarn at a large number of mills owned by the company in the mid-1950s. Raw cotton was carded, opened out so that the fibres were practically separated and lay parallel to each other (a process in ancient times performed with a thistle or a teasel on sheep's wool). The rope of cotton fibre was attenuated and twisted on roving frames so that the cotton could be wound on to a bobbin without stretching, and wound off by its own strength. The resulting yarn or thread was wound on to small spindles if it was weft, or on to beams, giant cotton reels, if it was warp. The final process was sizing, giving the thread a protective covering. The small Dale Mill, built in 1905 near Rochdale, was the eleventh mill bought by Smith & Nephew. Coral Mill at Newhaye in Lancashire, originally a woollen mill, was converted to cotton spinning in 1908 and bought by Smith & Nephew Textiles in 1953.[12] During the 1950s the mill underwent a gradual modernization in which old and new machinery worked in unison. The increased efficiency of the modern machinery installed was spectacular, as the beaming department showed. A new automatic beaming machine could wind yarn on to beams at a maximum speed of 900 yards a minute, twice as fast as the traditional machinery. The labour force of the mill was predominantly female: compared with 50 men there were 250 women employees, for whom there was a 'housewife shift' between 6pm and 10pm. Radical even by today's standards was the provision of a nursery at the mill, albeit run by the cleaners, which on average served 20 children's needs. Neva Mill, acquired with Arthur Berton (see below), was bigger than either Coral or Dale. Ultimately all spinning was concentrated at Brierfield or Rawtenstall, although Coral was kept on for plastics production.

Weaving

Smith & Nephew saved a great deal of money when they bought the 386 000 sq. ft mill at Brierfield near Burnley in 1957, for they did not have to build a new mill for their integrated operations. Even so, the expense of the investment caused the board some anxiety.[13] New spinning machines were installed allowing one operator to look after 3 000 spindles, about three times the Lancashire average. Automatic looms were introduced that needed only one weaver for between 72 and 100 looms, by contrast with the traditional mill employing one weaver to 10 looms. Brierfield supplied all the group textile requirements from 1961 with the help of two other mills as compared with 10 mills in 1958. Brierfield wove the group's cloth, spun the weft and all the yarn required for sanitary towel covers, and produced cotton wool and surgical dressings.[14] Nearby, Rawtenstall spun the warp yarn, doubled the Elastoplast yarn and prepared the combed yarn for many cloths required by the group. Glen Mills became the bleach works and raised, finished, sanforized and yarn-dyed the print clothing cloths.[15] Rationalization of textile plant was aided by state funds for the cotton industry. Old mills were compensated for scrapping old plant. The sums were placed in reserve, more than offsetting the levy which the government planned to raise from the industry over the next decade.[16]

Automatic looms attained increasing heights of sophistication. In the 1960s came automatic cone-winding, intermediate spinning and weaving. The big development was in spinning where the need for six machines was reduced to two. For weavers paid by the measured length, automatic remedying of breakages was a matter of great importance. Manual rethreading was more work yet reduced payment.

Most of Smith & Nephew's long established mills maintained a family tradition of employment among their workers, spanning half a century or more. But during the later 1950s and 1960s labour shortages emerged in the reorganized textile division, increasingly filled by Asian immigrants. A total of 2 600 people worked in the textile division in 1958, operating 2 600 looms and 150 000 spindles. More than 600 square miles or 40 000 acres, were required to grow the division's annual total cotton consumption.

When the 'jeans' fashion spread from America, Smith & Nephew textiles were well placed to meet the new demand for cloth, because of the wartime experience of its management. Denim was first produced in Nimes, France, as 'Serge de Nîmes'. Woven from a blue warp and undyed weft, denim became the universal dress of French peasants at work. Subsequently both the German and British armies adopted the material and in the 1950s workers' overalls were made from denim. Then jeans became all the rage. From the 1960s the Victoria and North Valley Mills supplied the Blue Bell Corporation of New York with denim for its European jeans business. Under an agreement in 1971, Blue Bell guaranteed to take a minimum of 3 million linear yards a year of indigo-dyed blue denim for two years in the first instance.

Bleaching

By 1958 the Birtle Bleach Works were processing 80 per cent of the grey coarse cloth woven in Smith & Nephew Mills into a fine, smooth and spotlessly white product.[17] The Works were supplied with the large volume of water needed for their operation from three reservoirs which in total held 20 million gallons of water, a sufficient supply for ten weeks. Three distinct bleaching processes were carried out at Birtle, all with the same action but with methods varied according to the material to be bleached – cotton wool, gauze or heavy cloths (lint, heavy bandage cloth). Each type of material was loaded into kiers with chemicals and detergents and boiled for an average of 12 hours; it was then washed, bleached, washed again and dried. Differences in the process of bleaching occurred because of the ways in which the materials were handled during and in between each stage, which in turn depended on the relative strength of each cloth type.

Besides bleaching, two other processes, both medicating treatments, were carried out at Birtle. The cloth for the familiar yellow gauze and lint absorbent pads of Elastoplast dressings were medicated there and then transported to Hull for application. Similarly, raised lint was treated with a solution of boracic acid and dye which medicated the cloth and gave it the pink coloration by which boric lint was known.[18]

Clothes

Smith & Nephew's relatively small Manchester division during the 1950s manufactured nightwear and many other types of women's and children's wear, under the trade names of 'Land o' Nod' and 'Trimsona'.[19] It employed 600 workers who were based in four different factories in the Manchester area. In the late 1950s a new factory was built on Baxter Street, Hollinwood (within a few hundred yards of the original and century-old Park Mill) to house nearly 200 sewing machines and over 200 skilled employees. Music played morning and afternoon in the new factory and, during the lunch break, the young operatives brought in their own records to play.

The company designed a wide range of clothing – pyjamas, nightdresses, beach suits, dressing gowns, petticoats, jeans, shorts and blouses. Not only day clothes were influenced by fashion; nightwear was becoming increasingly fashion-conscious too, and designs changed season by season. Materials were of tremendous importance; the popularity of certain colours and textures came and went. Detailed knowledge of the machines used for manufacturing the garments and methods of production was necessary for the design. Styles had to be shaped to the limits of the machines used for manufacture. Designs and samples of material from inside the group and from external sources were sifted, sorted and discussed until the right design for the right fabric and the most attractive colour combination had been selected.

Once the initial ideas for style and type of cloth had been decided, designs were transferred from the drawing board to the fabrics and made-up samples. It was of course necessary to see if the machines were able to make the garments – a curve may have been too steep or a seam too intricate, in which case the design was modified to conform to the machines. When ready for production the design was transferred to fabric by a perforated paper pattern, through which chalk was rubbed on to the cloth. The material was cut with an electrically operated knife which sliced through 12 dozen layers of material at a time.

Smith & Nephew (Manchester) Ltd now operated five factories, each of which was responsible for a certain type of garment. Once orders had arrived each unit was responsible for complete production, from cutting out to packing and dispatch. When the range for the coming season had been decided, photographs were taken and sent to the company's sales representatives and wholesalers who eventually sold the garments to retail outlets. Professional models and some of the factory girls featured in the publicity material. At the end of the 1950s the company held their first fashion parade, with two factory girls and one professional model.

FEMININE HYGIENE

Apart from clothes and medical products, another use to which Smith & Nephew's textile production was put was feminine hygiene products. But other materials were required as well, the most important of which was cellulose wadding.

Cellulose Wadding

Cellulose is the chief component of plant cell walls. Cotton wool is almost the pure form. As well as being used in the fibrous state as cotton, cellulose is also accessible in wood pulp. Between 60 and 70 per cent of all paper in the 1950s was made from wood pulp, instead of the rags used a century earlier. Wood pulp is simply timber that has been broken down by mechanical or chemical action to individual fibres, that are then mixed with water. The best source timbers for pulp were coniferous softwoods, spruce, fir and pine; some hardwoods such as birch, beech and aspin were also used. Not surprisingly then the principal sources of wood pulp were the Scandinavian countries, Western Canada and the US.

Machines producing 700 feet of paper a minute were worked on a three-shift system at Lomeshaye Mill, the Nelson factory of Southalls, which had the capacity to store 550 tons of wood pulp in 1959. Under the supervision of Mr A.E. Lucas (Smith & Nephew adviser on paper and cellulose wadding) the mill processed imported wood pulp into handkerchief tissue, hand towels and perhaps most importantly, cellulose wadding, a vital constituent of sanitary towels and surgical dressings.

On arrival at the mill wood pulp was quality-tested and then remixed with water to return it to the original 'porridge' consistency. The basic principle was that wood fibres were first separated and suspended in water and then knitted together to form a continuous sheet. If approved, the pulp was transferred to another machine where it was further beaten and more water added before being pumped into a regulator which controlled the consistency of the pulp. At the end of the initial stage of mixing and liquifying, the pulp was 99.75 per cent water.

This very liquid pulp was passed on to a rapidly moving, continuous wire-mesh belt. There the wood fibres spread evenly and became interlocked, as water was drained off by suction boxes and rollers. From the wire-mesh belt the 'paper' was passed on to a drying cylinder to reduce the water content further by steam-heating. The next stage of the process was to pass the paper through 'the crepe doctor' which then gave it the appearance of crepe paper. The final process in the manufacture of wadding entailed feeding single sheets of cellulose paper on to large rotating drums, the number of layers depending on the ply of the wadding; 25-ply wadding required 25 windings of the drum. Then the wadding was slit into narrower strips ready for manufacture.

By the summer of 1959 the Group operated seven cellulose wadding machines, two at Lomeshaye Mill and five at Charford Mills. The bulk of the wadding produced was used within the group in the manufacture of sanitary towels in the three Southalls' factories in Birmingham, Nelson and London (this last was closed down soon afterwards). An alternative use, similar to sanitary towel manufacture, was in the production of nappies. Smith & Nephew manufactured its own brand, 'Golden Babe'. Perhaps the most 'everyday' form of cellulose wadding was in packaging and disposable table accessories. Embossed wadding was used as 'fancy pads' in presentation packs of soaps and chocolates, inside jewellery boxes and in gift-packing generally. High absorbency by the many layers of fine soft tissue made cellulose wadding suitable material for beer and table mats. Other uses of the wadding included the protection of aluminium and metallic foils during transportation, the upholstering of furniture, the lining of television sets and loudspeakers to absorb sound, the packing of bananas for their voyage from the West Indies, to both protect the fruit and aid in its ripening, and last but not least, wadding-lined coffins.[20]

Increasing demand for disposables, be they nappies or surgeons' caps, encouraged Smith & Nephew in 1962 to reach a 50–50 agreement with Wiggins Teape to rationalize their paper products into Associated Tissues. £1.25m of investment was allocated for this project in 1963, which also gave Smith & Nephew access to Wiggins' £60m government-assisted pulp mill at Fort William, enhancing competitiveness relative to the Scandinavians.[21]

THE SOUTHALLS, ARTHUR BERTON AND SMITH & NEPHEW MERGER

After the reorganization of textile production, the next target was the principal textile use, sanitary towel manufacture. These products, produced mainly by the three companies Smith & Nephew, Arthur Berton and Southalls, benefited from very strong brand loyalty and so price competition was ineffective. Rather than finding other methods of competing, merger was a cheaper and quicker way of reducing industry costs and prices, given Smith & Nephew's financial and managerial advantages. But a number of distinct steps were necessary to achieve that end.

Southalls' business performance in the 1950s was clearly weak.[22] A loss was recorded in 1952 for similar reasons that Smith & Nephew experienced a fall in profits: stock losses and reductions of stocks by distributors. Profits then improved until 1954, when plans for expansion of production were implemented. Thereafter profits fell; in 1956 the first of the two cellulose machines was approximately eight months behind schedule with consequent depressing effects on profitability.[23] In 1957 when Berton earned 36.7 per cent return on net assets, and Smith & Nephew 21.2 per cent, Southalls achieved a mere 4.1 per cent. On the other hand Southalls' dowry included £2m cash.[24] Smith & Nephew sales and profits were much more buoyant despite Ministry of Health imposition of maximum rate of profit on the group's sales to the Health Service.[25]

A major new product had been introduced just before the merger. Despite some cultural and medical resistance, the use of tampons, in home-made form, was accelerated by wartime shortages of sanitary towels.[26] In 1954 Smith & Nephew's 'search for the perfect tampon' culminated in a board room experiment. The six elderly male directors were each issued with a beaker of water and three different tampons.[27] They then proceeded to dip each one into the beakers of water after examining them. As a consequence of these deliberations or experiments, an agreement was reached with the German company Dr Carl Hahn AG (subsequently acquired by Johnson & Johnson) under which Smith & Nephew produced Lil-lets on German-made machines. By October 1956 Smith & Nephew were selling 3 000 dozen packets per week and the board noted they were one of the most encouraging aspects of Lilia production.[28]

Competition from Arthur Berton was heavy and prompted the centralization of towel production in Nelson at Lomeshaye Mill at the end of 1955. During the annual general meeting of 1956 George Leavey announced that the group had entered into an arrangement with 'our friends Arthur Berton & Co, under which we had formed a joint Marketing Organisation of their main products and those of ... Lilia ltd'. The organization was intended to lower costs and improve distribution. In nine months the arrangement exceeded expectations and the companies agreed early in 1957 also to merge their manufacturing facilities in a new business, Lilia-White Associated Companies.

The truly dynamic member of the troika was Arthur Berton and the drive behind them was S.N. Steen. Mr Steen, a barrister, joined Arthur Berton in 1943 and began transforming the company from a comparatively small manufacturing unit producing a large number of lines into a volume producer of a limited range of products. In expanding sales, the female sales force he built up was especially effective.[29] The Dr White's sanitary towel he developed became the best selling combined towel on the market. Competitiveness was enhanced by the knitted cover for Dr White's towels being made from rejected rayon supplied by Courtaulds. Because of Steen's good relations with C.F. Kearton of Courtaulds, the rayon was very cheap.[30]

New plant was established at New River Mill and Old Street London. Just as Lilia Ltd, having almost completed their centralization programme, were about to introduce their new combined towel, intended as a serious competitor to Dr White's, Arthur Berton were exploring the possibility of manufacturing a soluble towel to compete with Lilia.[31] On 21 December 1957 Smith & Nephew announced that they had reached agreement with Southalls on the terms for a merging of interests. On 15 January 1958 the world was told that the merger was to be enlarged to include Berton. Smith & Nephew acquired the whole of the existing capital of the other two companies, including the very substantial holdings of the Southall and Barclay families. The merger was justified by the substantial economies in marketing, production, distribution and administration.

After the merger the principal activity of Smith & Nephew was still the supply of surgical dressings, Gypsona, Elastoplast and other health care products to the National Health Service and chemists. Second in contribution to turnover was the sanitary protection business and third was the cosmetics and baby products section. About equal in size was the clothing business in 'Land o' Nod' infants' and girls' wear and 'Trimsona' nightwear. Fifth in importance was the growing line of industrial tapes, many of which were sold under the name 'Lasso', developed with know-how derived from Elastoplast manufacture. For nearly all these products the main raw material was textiles and the company was among the most vertically integrated firms in Lancashire. All the processes were undertaken within the group and costed without intercompany profits.[32]

Lilia Ltd were strong in the production of disposable towels; Dr White's, produced by Arthur Berton Ltd, was the most popular towel on the market; and Southalls possessed considerable technical developments to throw in. A plan gradually evolved which ultimately meant the closing of the two London factories of Arthur Berton, and the transfer of machinery and plant to Birmingham. The looms at Charford were scrapped, and cotton wool and surgical dressings production transferred to Lancashire, a move which enabled Smith & Nephew not only to bring in the London machinery, but to replan the whole of the factory and streamline the manufacture of each product.

Closing down the London factories and transferring production to Birmingham was a very difficult exercise. The success of this move was in no small way due to the loyalty and hard work of the people at the New River Mill and Old Street. It must have been a heavy blow to them, and especially to those Arthur Berton employees who had witnessed the growth of the company to realize that production of their popular towel was no longer to be carried out in London. They accepted the position in a magnificent way, and made a valuable contribution to the success of Smith & Nephew centralization plans.

Southalls' employees were heirs to a long tradition of loyal service and naturally did not take kindly to the prospect of working in a larger grouping. Little time was necessary, however, to convince them that the group intended to develop Charford Mills into one of the most modern factories of its kind in this country. The contribution of Southalls' employees during the very difficult years of 1958 and 1959 cannot be overemphasized. They accepted changes loyally, and the staff of the three merged companies developed into one of the strongest managerial teams in Smith & Nephew. Double-shift work came into operation very soon after the merger. In spite of a comparatively high turnover of labour in the initial stages, early problems were overcome and Charford Mills became a shift factory.

A new overall and turban scheme was put into operation, a system of good housekeeping instituted and every department was redecorated in modern colour schemes. More efficient running of existing plant, the installation of more modern methods of packing, conveyor feeding of raw materials, and automatic collection of finished work, together with a reduction of all forms of waste, all played their part in gradually establishing a modern production unit. Fibre loss in the production of cellulose wadding at Charford Mills was cut down from 22 per cent to 10 per cent.

Over the years 1955 to 1960, profitability increased markedly as factory unit costs were cut in nominal terms, helped by falling material prices, despite regular increases in wages and reductions in hours of work. Sales increased and prices remained steady even though national retail prices rose. The chief reasons for the improved performance were:

1.   Concentration in Birmingham and closing the London factories.
2.   Re-equipment, mechanization and production flow at Birmingham.
3.   Improved utilization of the assets available, in particular:

   - the large Birmingham factory with its high overhead cost,
   - the maximum capacity of the cotton wool bleaching plant,
   - the substantially increased speeds and output of the cellulose machines,
   - the mechanization of towel production by automatic stitching.

4.   The efficient utilization of raw materials, which meant:

   - reduction in fibre loss,
   - reduction in waste in towel production,
   - the substitution of mechanical cellulose wadding for bleached wadding in Southalls' towels,
   - the use of rayon waste and inexpensive pad mixes.

5.   Improved stock control, material usage control, and the introduction of budgets and standard costs.

Increased sales resulting in high factory activity to a great degree enabled the division to absorb continuous increases in:

1. Labour rates. There were four increases in labour rates and two reductions in working hours since 1955.
2. Salaries.
3. Overhead costs including increases in coal, electricity, maintenance and works engineering.

Selling Expenses

The concentration of production in Birmingham and the closing down of the London factories radically altered distribution costs, which include warehousing, stock movement, stock control, carriage and dispatch. From 1959 onwards a separate depot was necessary in London. All finished stock was moved from Birmingham and Nelson to London and also considerable quantities of materials were transferred between Birmingham and Nelson. The additional cost for this work was approximately 1.25 per cent on sales and was an offset to the reduced factory cost from concentration. There was a substantial increase in sales promotion and advertising, particularly on Lil-lets. By 1961 the budget expenditure on sales and promotion and advertising had risen to 3 per cent, nearly £170 000, of which £100 000 (2 per cent) was on Lil-lets and Golden Babe.

Automation

Cost reductions proceeded independently of post-merger rearrangements as well. How far automation had been taken at Southalls at the end of the 1950s was shown by the carousel. The carousel, run automatically and continuously on two central electric motors, was an overhead monorail type of conveyor. Starting in the number two shed of Charford Mills, the conveyor ran right through the mill, connecting all departments. Suspended from the conveyor rails at intervals of six feet were metal carriers which were reset to pick up the cartons of finished products at various points on their journey.

As the sanitary towels were made they were first packed into individual cardboard skillets, and then into larger cartons, after which they were automatically labelled and sealed, and passed on a ground-level conveyor belt to be picked up by the overhead conveyor. There was no danger of one carrier catching up another because they all travelled at a regulated speed. Some carriers were pre-set to pick up cartons of finished towels from one department, and some from another. From the mill the cartons passed to the two-storey warehouse, where they were dropped by the carriers on to various floors according to their type. All towels which were not Dr White's, such as Blue Star and Original, were stored on the top floor, whilst Dr White's travelled through a spiral chute to be stored on the second and ground floors.

The carriers returned to pick up more finished products, and sorting, loading and dispatch were performed manually.

The ground floor of the warehouse opened out on to four separate loading bays, a roller conveyor leading to each bay. When the products were labelled and ready for dispatch, they were pushed on the rollers out to the bays and into waiting vans. By an ingenious turntable system, the roller conveyors could be interconnected to carry the cartons to any or all of the four bays.[33] By speeding up the production and distribution process, the carousel and associated devices allowed a greater throughput at a lower unit cost. That this tradition of ingenious engineering was alive and well at the end of the 1970s is attested by the Price Commission, which reported:

> We were particularly impressed by the fact that [Smith & Nephew/Southalls] has designed and built the major portion of its production machinery and has engineered machine conversions resulting in substantial labour and materials cost savings…[34]

At a higher technological level the Birmingham plant forced down costs by becoming the home of the first electron–accelerator sterilizing unit in Europe. The problem the Van der Graaf generator posed was how to choose the energy level that would kill bacteria without degrading the product. Eventually a solution was found and the generator has remained in use until the time of writing as a cost-effective means of mass sterilization of bulky products, such as maternity pads.

Another piece of advanced technology introduced early into the Birmingham plant was the electronic computer. Southalls was one of the first buyers of Leo, the Lyons' Tea Shop computer of the 1950s. A replacement installed in 1963 possessed so much computational capacity that a computer service was made available to outside organizations. Even without those earnings the company saved £180 000 on work the computer was undertaking for the Smith & Nephew group. So successful was this venture that Smith & Nephew invested in another computer in 1970, a GE 615 costing £800 000. The new machine was capable of transmitting or receiving on telephone lines 31 separate sets of information simultaneously and was able to work on 96 different programmes at the same time.[35] Difficulties in gaining sufficient turnover from within the company dogged the new computer. External contracts were quite buoyant considering the power cuts associated with the miners' strike of 1972. The loss of £109 000 in the first 24 weeks of that year was nonetheless regarded seriously enough for the financial controller to take charge and the service was eventually closed down.[36]

Market Growth and Distribution

Mergers and cost reductions raised Smith & Nephew's market share, a tendency reinforced in 1962 when Johnson & Johnson sold the assets and facilities of their Wrexham sanitary protection factory to Smith & Nephew.[37] Curiously this market was showing faster growth than expected. Between 1957 and 1964 towel sales grew by 14 per cent although the female population aged 11–45 increased by only 4.25 per cent. The more expensive tampons doubled their market share over the same period. The bulk of advertising expenditure reinforced this trend, for tampons were the real competitor of towels, and in the UK that meant the tampon with the applicator, Tampax. Most towels (58 per cent) were sold through chemists and 21 per cent through Boots alone, but the growth of towels in the grocery trade was significant in 1965. It was obvious then that the food chain stores, amongst whom Sainsbury's, David Greig, Express Dairies and Home & Colonial were notable, would be where the market leaders in the 1970s would have to be established. Meanwhile in the early 1960s, Smith & Nephew's market success was critically dependent on their female representatives. How effective they were is indicated by Cuxson & Gerrard's belief that in 1962 Smith & Nephew employed 380 female representatives selling their 'personal products' around the country.[38] In fact the true figure was nearer 50. Sales were divided into two groups: the 'drug force' and the 'grocery force'. 'Grocery' was selling to wholesalers with all male personnel until 1970. 'Drugs' were women only selling to chemists, both small and wholesale, and to corner shops. Hats and gloves were compulsory for all these lady representatives in the 1960s.

The Educational Department may also be regarded as a form of sales force. At the beginning of the 1960s the department began with part-timers employed to talk to mothers in health and welfare clinics with a view to selling disposable nappies and tampons. Ten full-time nurses (SRNs or RGNs) now educate around 200 000 girls a year about anatomical changes. 'Sister Marion' or 'Marion Cooper', advertising her availability for advice on Lil-lets packets, was a member of the same group. How important her role has been and continues to be is shown by the massive correspondence she receives under one name or another.

These selling efforts were the more necessary because of the resistance to sanitary protection advertising on television. A test with Lil-lets in 1974 provoked so many objections that advertising on ITV was not permitted until 1986, although it was on Channel 4. Relatively few complaints were received by the Independent Television Commission during the following five years, but at the beginning of 1992 a demonstration of absorbency of a new sanitary towel threw up another barrage of objections.

By 1973 Lil-lets held 20 per cent of the tampon market and Dr Whites' alone, 29.1 per cent of the towel sector.[39] For Smith & Nephew these successes brought the penalty of a Monopolies and Mergers' Commission (1980) report on the supply of tampons in 1980. The Commission however concluded that the dominant position of the two competitor firms stemmed from being first in the field and having higher-quality products made with a high degree of manufacturing efficiency.

CONCLUSION

The thorough integration of Arthur Berton, Southalls and Smith & Nephew was a model of how mergers should be conducted if society was to benefit from them, and one that was still comparatively unusual in the British economy of the 1950s and 1960s.[40] Profits from reduced costs of production provided the financial basis for investment in other fields, and Arthur Berton supplied two subsequent chairmen of Smith & Nephew, Stephen Steen and Kenneth Kemp.

In a longer-term perspective the strategy of investing heavily in textiles raised a central question. Was the company going to remain primarily committed to health care or was it to diversify? Smith & Nephew had proved the British textile industry need not decline until it disappeared, but were textiles a suitable area of specialization for a high-income country and for a health care firm? Feminine hygiene was a slowly growing market in total and, after the merger with Arthur Berton and Southalls, Smith & Nephew could look for little growth from market share expansion. In all three product groups synthetic and paper-based materials were making inroads into the domain of cotton. If the company was to remain in health care, should not the bulk of investment be more focused on health care products such as pharmaceuticals?

NOTES

1. The company then consisted of Belle Vue, Fountain and Peel Mills, Blackburn and Oakenshaw, a small mill in Clayton. *Visit of Overseas Directors to Smith & Nephew Textiles Ltd, Brierfield, Lancashire, 15th July 1958.*
2. This claim, that competitiveness required high throughput, human and physical capital intensive production in vertically integrated organizations and an end to the flexible British horizontal system, is not universally accepted. The vertically integrated US industry suffered badly from foreign competition in the 1950s and 1960s. Jewkes (1946) is a long-standing proponent of the contrary view. For a forceful restatement of the virtues of verticalization see Mass and Lazonick (1990) pp. 9–65.
3. G. Whittaker, *A Handful of Shale*, 1979, unpublished ms.

4. Ibid., p. 178.
5. K. Bradshaw interview, May 1991.
6. *Smith & Nephew Annual Report, 1952.*
7. K. Bradshaw interview, May 1991.
8. Whittaker, op cit., note 3, pp. 190–92. Subsequently all surviving mills in Lancashire operated a similar system.
9. *Smith & Nephew Annual Report 1960.*
10. *Textiles: Report 9.10.1963*, Smith & Nephew Archives, London. Efficiency was measured by partial and total productivity indices. Efficiency or productivity is a relationship between what is produced (output) and what is needed to do the producing (inputs). Indices of efficiency or productivity are therefore constructed from ratios of output to inputs required. Since more than one input is necessary to produce yarn output, two partial indices can be presented, in which labour hours or spindle hours inputs appear in the denominator. Alternatively or additionally a total productivity index may be formed in which the labour and spindle hours are averaged in some way. Productivity or efficiency index numbers themselves only convey information when a base period or case can be used in comparison. The scheme to assess the Brierfield Mill productivity was obtained from the German textiles industry, and the standards used in the compilation of the figures were obtained from the German source. The implied weights used to average spindle and labour hour inputs were 7/12 and 5/12 respectively. Theoretically these weights should be the proportionate increase in yarn output from a given proportionate increase in one of the inputs, holding constant the other.
11. *Textiles: Report 9.10.1963*, Smith & Nephew Archives, London.
12. 'The Mill in the Dales', *Sanaco News*, Autumn 1957, pp. 18–20; 'Coral, the Mill of Contrasts', *Sanaco News*, Summer 1959, pp. 5–8.
13. *Smith & Nephew Annual Report, 1957.*
14. Weft is the thread running from east to west. Weft yarn has fewer twists or turns to the inch than warp.
15. *Investors' Chronicle*, 3 October 1958, pp. 12–13.
16. *Smith & Nephew Annual Report, 1959.*
17. 'The Finishing Touch', *Sanaco News*, Summer 1958.
18. For two years a printing operation was run from Glen Mills to supply the Manchester clothing company, but results were unsatisfactory and the project was scrapped. 'Glen Mills Starts to Print', *Sanaco News* Autumn 1959; K. Bradshaw, interview.
19. 'The Newer Factory at Hollinwood', *Sanaco News*, Christmas 1956, pp. 12–14.
20. 'Made in a Minute', *Sanaco News*, Spring 1959, pp. 19–21; 'It Follows You Through Life', *Sanaco News*, Summer 1959, pp. 40–42.
21. P. Wilsher, 'Big Name in Bandages' *Sunday Times*, 16 June 1963, City Section p.9.
22. Whittaker (op. cit., note 3) was characteristically more blunt.
23. *Chemist and Druggist*, 30 December 1957, p. 592.
24. P. Wilsher op. cit., note 21.
25. *Smith & Nephew Company Report 1956 or 1957.*
26. Dickinson (1945), p. 490. For some medical reactions see the correspondence in response to Mary Barton's 'Review of the Sanitary Appliance with a Discussion on Intra-Vaginal Packs', *British Medical Journal*, 25 April 1942, p. 524; 31 January 1942, p. 164; 4 April 1942, p. 452; 25 April 1942, p. 537; 23 May 1942, p. 654.
27. G. Whittaker op. cit., note 3, p. 195.
28. *Smith & Nephew Board Minutes*, Smith & Nephew Archives, London.
29. Arthur Berton Centenary leaflet 1950 (courtesy of Alan Berton); K. Bradshaw interview, 1991.
30. Seymour interview, 1991. C.F. later Lord, Kearton joined Courtaulds from ICI in 1946. Six years later he was on the board and in 1964 he became chairman. See Coleman (1980) p. 20.
31. *A Review of the Merger Between S & N (Lilia) Southalls & A B*, 26.3.61 by G.A. Hazlitt, C.W. Crouch, and J. Hargreaves, Smith & Nephew Archives, London.
32. *Investors' Chronicle*, 3 October 1958.

33. 'The Charford Carousel', *Sanaco News*, Autumn 1959, pp. 22–3.
34. Department of Prices and Consumer Protection, *Southalls (Birmingham) Ltd Sanitary Protection and Other Hygiene Products*, HMSO 1978, p. 2. The same source also noted it was '... a well-managed company with strong budgetary controls. Southalls has responded to all product developments ...'.
35. 'Midland Firm to Install Britain's First Bureau Service Computer', *Birmingham Post*, 8 January 1970.
36. *Report on the Operations for the the First 24 Weeks 1972*, minute no. 702, *Smith & Nephew Board Minutes*, 15 August 1972.
37. Johnson & Johnson (GB) Ltd circular letter 23 February 1962, Smith & Nephew/Southall Archives, Birmingham.
38. Note from A.D. Gerrard, 27 February 1962, Cuxon & Gerrard File, Smith & Nephew Archives, Hull.
39. 'Personal Hygiene', *Chemist & Druggist*, 27 April 1974, p. 503.
40. The British Motor Holdings and British Leyland mergers in the motor industry are among the more often cited cases of groupings that were too slow to reduce their product range and integrate production units.

9.   Research, pharmaceuticals and plastics

Before the Second World War Smith & Nephew licensed new products developed elsewhere. The company therefore had not been obliged to address the problem of meshing research with broader company objectives. As experience with Cellona showed in Chapter 4, the strategy could lead to difficulties guaranteeing a continuing transfer of technology. In resolving these problems a research department, familiar with the relevant literature and techniques, would have been valuable. A potential world class company could not continue to be almost completely dependent on buying other firms' technology. For one thing, as products became more complicated, the search and evaluation processes themselves became more complex, requiring skilled research staff (Rosenberg 1990; Griliches 1986; Mansfield 1980).

Chairman George Leavey recognized this deficiency in the company and so acquired Herts Pharmaceuticals in 1951, in part for the research department. But pharmaceutical research fitted rather uncomfortably with Smith & Nephew's established patterns. The bulk of management effort in the 1950s was directed to rationalization of and investment in textiles, dressings and feminine hygiene. There was little time, understanding or resources for pharmaceutical research. Research objectives varied over time and few effective products were brought to the marketing stage. Then the adverse publicity associated with an antidepressant drug provided a reminder of the complexity, as well as the size, of risks associated with pharmaceutical investment. Fitting an outside research department of any sort into a company with little or no research tradition was bound to be difficult, as an early company statement perhaps unconsciously revealed:

> In strictly commercial terms, [research's] rewards are rarely commensurate with the cost, time and effort that goes into [new drug] production, but we feel we should be failing in our duty not to continue to make the effort.[1]

With minimal experience in pharmaceuticals, and very little in the way of a pharmaceutical sales force at first, Smith & Nephew were handicapped in diversifying the product range beyond the path-breaking TB drug expertise they had acquired with Herts, by a rather small research effort. They were much more successful in that component of R & D devoted to their core product areas, which gave rise to Airstrip, Net 909 and OpSite. And that is the direction in which resources shifted in the 1960s. Plastics and polymer[2] science offered more effective ways of developing Smith & Nephew's traditional health care products. At the same time they indicated a long-term shift away from textiles.

A TREATMENT FOR TB

Most of the wartime work at Herts was developmental and focused on cosmetic emulsions and industrial adhesive tapes. Although the staff then consisted of only two organic chemists, a pharmacist and an analyst, some research was undertaken and published on emulsions and new drugs. Shortly after the end of the war the team made their breakthrough with a TB drug, PAS.

The conquest of tuberculosis (earlier known as phthisis or consumption) was one of the more remarkable achievements of the pharmaceutical industry in the generation after the ending of the Second World War. At the beginning of the century about 12 per cent of mankind died of some form of TB and 40 per cent of the cows in Britain were infected. That meant children in particular were at risk from milk until it was 'Pasteurized'. A German scientist, Robert Koch, identified the cause of TB, the tubercle bacillus, in 1882. Two French scientists, Albert Calmette and Camille Guérin, cultivated the bacilli and developed BCG vaccine, first used on human beings in 1921. BCG was an attenuated strain of TB, and therefore fears that the strain might become virulent were hard to quell. This was especially true after the Lübeck tragedy of 1930 when, of 249 babies vaccinated, 67 soon died of TB. The problem was that, mistakenly, they had not been given the BCG vaccine but a culture of virulent bacilli. Chemically based *treatment* began with the discovery of streptomycin in 1944 by the American Dr S.A. Waksman. Streptomycin was available to the public in small quantities during 1947. That year the Medical Research Council organized a successful trial, the results of which were reported in 1948. British supplies of streptomycin were not available until the following year, by which time almost £1m of scarce dollar reserves had been spent on imports (Dubos and Dubos 1953, pp. 160–62; Caldwell 1988, pp. 261–4; Smith 1988, p. 246; Bryder 1990, pp. 253–7).

A 1946 report in the *Lancet* by the Swedish Professor Lehmann of Gothenberg announced the effectiveness of para-aminosalicylic acid in the treatment of the TB bacilli. Lehmann had noted that the action of the bacilli was accelerated by salicylic acid. He therefore asked a colleague to identify a compound with exactly the opposite composition. It turned out that such a substance had been synthesized at the beginning of the century, but the production process was long and low-yielding.[3] D.E. Seymour, C.W. Picard and colleagues at Herts Pharmaceuticals together with F.S. Spring (by now at Glasgow University) found a more effective process for synthesizing the drug. After six months they had made only five grammes, but by October enough was available for Dr T.G. Dempsey of Grove Park Hospital to begin trials, with dramatic results. Given only a few weeks' treatment of PAS, patients who were thought to have no hope of recovery began to put on weight and cease to be infectious. Dempsey and Logg published the results of their trials in the *Lancet* and hospitals and sanatoria all over the world began demanding PAS. Although the discovery of PAS did not receive as much publicity as streptomycin, specialists called urgently upon Herts for their precious supplies of PAS. One afternoon Seymour arranged a flight from the adjacent De Havilland works by the test pilot in a Mosquito to deliver PAS for a desperate tubercular meningitis case at Bristol (Spriggs 1948, pp. 4–5; Martin *et al.* 1948, pp. 161, 435; Bavin 1965, pp. 820–25; Lehmann 1946, pp. 15–16; Waksman 1965, pp. 138, 184–7; Sneader 1985, pp. 292–5).

PAS was the only oral treatment for TB at the time, but Herts had no money to develop it. Acquisition by Smith & Nephew was therefore sensible, since the company was comparatively secure financially.[4] Seymour later wrote:

> Though these developments turned out to be commercially important, they were the result of 'skilful opportunism' and the amount of classical pharmaceutical research required to make the 'break through' would, on [early 1960s] standards, be considered very small.

Like cod liver oil in the early days of T.J. Smith's business, PAS tasted unpleasant. The Herts team contributed towards the solution of this problem by the synthesis of calcium benzaminosalicylate (Therapas), a comparatively tasteless substance which liberates PAS in the body. A more active substance, isoniazid, was discovered independently by three companies, Bayer, Hoffman La Roche and E.R. Squibb & Son in 1951. The Herts team quickly found a way of manufacturing isoniazid which turned out to be the ideal companion drug to PAS. At least two drugs were needed because the bacilli quickly became resistant to one given alone. Smith & Nephew's Inapasade, which combined PAS and isoniazid in 'adegrate' granules, and needed only one or two granules daily dose, was among the simplest and most pleasant therapies available. A curious sidelight on TB treatment was the resurrection of rice-paper cachets. These had almost disappeared until they became popular for administering the bulky powders of tuberculo-therapy.

Despite the success of TB treatment, at the end of the 1960s there were still 15 million TB sufferers throughout the world and 3 million deaths annually. These were concentrated in poor countries which often either lacked the money for the drugs or the organization to provide treatment.[5] Smith &

Nephew's Ethiopian joint venture (Chapter 10), an attempt to transfer the benefits of Western TB treatment, failed because of general political and organizational difficulties in that country.

RESEARCH AND DEVELOPMENT

The research department of Herts Pharmaceuticals in Welwyn and the technical staff of T.J. Smith & Nephew were merged in a research company in late 1952 at Hunsdon, seven miles from Hertford.[6] D.E. Seymour, former research manager of Herts Pharmaceuticals, became director.[7] Of the staff of 81 about 30 were science graduates and other technically qualified personnel. The company was organized so that a new product could be developed from the idea through to clinical trial or pilot marketing. The technological division studied textiles, surgical plasters, industrial tapes, surgical dressings and packaging. The division included the analytical laboratories. When a new drug or product was marketed, these laboratories were responsible for devising assay methods. The biological division included the pharmacological laboratory studying new drug problems such as dosage, patient safety and efficacy. Pharmacy was concerned with the presentation of new drugs and the formulation of cosmetics. New drugs, such as tuberculosis treatments, passed through the first stage of testing at the bacteriological laboratories. The chemical division made, on a small scale, many compounds to be tested. After satisfactory testing larger quantities were prepared in the chemical development laboratory for hospital clinical trials.

By 1958 staff numbers had risen to 140, of whom one-third were university graduates. New adhesive materials resistant to heat and light were researched in the physical chemistry division. Production teething troubles required the process development division head liaise extensively with Hull. The development engineering section played a leading role in the process of manufacture of Elastoplast Airstrip (Chapter 7) and pilot plants for splinting bandages, fine chemicals and plasters were established.

For the first year at Hunsdon much of the research work was concerned with the backlog of technical problems that had built up in the manufacturing units and automatic plants, recently installed in the main production centres. The technology division dealt with process development work on the production of a wide range of pressure-sensitive adhesive products, plaster of Paris bandages and polymer films. Longer-term development was undertaken in association with the Royal National Orthopaedic Hospital on a new first aid dressing that for the first time employed a semi-permeable plastic material which allowed moisture vapour to escape from the skin, but which did not permit entry of bacteria or fluids.[8]

Pharmacological and microbiological screening facilities were extended and employed to investigate a wide range of new compounds synthesized by the organic chemistry department. There was little theoretical guidance as to which compound influenced what biological activity. An example was provided by Dilacol, a treatment for the common cold. Dilatal (the active ingredient in Dilacol) was being given to hospital patients in an attempt to increase the blood supply to certain parts of the body. By chance it was noted that patients who were suffering from colds and who were being given aspirins simultaneously with Dilatal found their colds quickly eased.

Screening tests, however, aimed to identify potential anti-inflammatory, oral antidiabetic, hypotensive and psychotropic drugs. Work in the last field brought into medicine phenoxypropazine, a new and more active monoamine oxidase inhibitor. TB drug research also continued.

MENTAL ILLNESS RESEARCH

As the list indicates, the declared, albeit largely unsuccessful, policy in the early 1950s was to enter commercially fields additional to TB drugs. During the first five years, 1953–58, limited sorties were made into various areas, the most important being rheumatism, and the search for a new oral antidiabetic drug. Some progress was achieved in both fields but a decision was taken by the pharmaceutical company board not to pursue the research. In 1958 research into mental disease began. Forty per cent of hospital cases suffered from such ailments and some strides had been taken in brain biochemistry. The team was, therefore, directed to the study and design of substances which might correct the abnormal brain processes which cause failure in mental health.

Drazine emerged from this work. Regrettably, in spite of its undoubted effectiveness in the treatment of depression, it exhibited the experimentally unrecognizable and unpredictable side-effect of human liver toxicity. After Drazine's discovery in 1959, work on brain biochemistry continued and the research group received recognition from world authorities.[9]

In the summer of 1963, Drazine received adverse lay press publicity following the deaths of two patients. Smith & Nephew therefore decided to withdraw the drug from general medical distribution and obtain the opinion of the Adverse Drug Reactions Committee, established under the auspices of the Ministry of Health. The official statement of that opinion was that Drazine and other members of this class of drug should not be discontinued, but the company decided that availability of Drazine should be restricted to hospitals.[10] The Drazine episode was a reminder of the risks which are associated with any effective therapy, whether it be a drug, manipulation or surgery.

Mental disease patients present special problems in this respect for although these conditions cause great misery, they do not directly cause death (other than by suicide), and in their early stages are often regarded as minor ailments and even a nuisance to the general practitioner. Lack of discrimination in the use of such drugs resulted in some very effective and valuable substances being thrown into disrepute and being classified as 'pep pills' or 'tranquillizers'.

RESEARCH AND THE PHARMACEUTICAL BUSINESS

The small research unit Herts brought into Smith & Nephew created numerous opportunities for the group, while at the same time fitted fairly snugly with its corporate image. Having acquired the keystone, there was a real possibility of building up a pharmaceutical company in 1951. However, only 12 years later, the position had deteriorated to the extent that in 1963 the board requested a report into the viability of retaining their pharmaceutical interests (Smith 1963 see Chapter 6, note 9). Over-reliance on antitubercular drugs, the price of which had fallen dramatically, and considerable increases in the cost of selling and research were the symptoms, but not the underlying cause, of the problem. Although 1962 had been a record year for sales revenue (£727 000), the balance sheet showed a loss, for the first time, of £24 000.

From an early peak in turnover of £660 000 in 1951, sales fell by almost two-thirds over the next three years. The principal cause of the drop in revenue was the fall in price of antitubercular drugs, in turn due to entry of large American pharmaceutical companies. ICI's pharmaceutical division which spent more on research and development (£493 000) than Smith & Nephew's entire pharmaceutical turnover in 1952 (Reader 1975), suffered a similar fate. Largely because of their overcommitment to penicillin and its falling price, ICI lost more than £0.25m in 1953. By 1958 Smith & Nephew's pharmaceutical turnover had returned to a figure similar to that at the beginning of the decade, £623 000, but at the same time the percentage of revenue gained through the sale of antitubercular drugs had risen from 90 per cent to 96 per cent. There had been no diversification into other types of drugs to reduce vulnerability to market fluctuations. In 1956 a sub-committee was formed to address pharmaceutical policy. The findings were clear: to specialize in antitubercular drugs was risky. Recommendations included a detailed proposal of the sales organization necessary to increase turnover. Twenty-four exclusively pharmaceutical representatives were to be appointed in a relatively short time. To be successful the company required additional annual expenditure of £75 000, which it was thought could be covered by an increase in turnover of £180 000; initial capital requirements were estimated at £100 000. The additional turnover was to be earned by 13 product groups; it was suggested that the existing range of products outside the TB field could within a short time produce a turnover of £50 000.

Although some of the recommendations of the sub-committee, with hindsight, were rather optimistic (the figure of £180 000 increased turnover to cover additional expenditure proved to be far too low), the correct policy had been laid down, so long as Smith & Nephew was not to develop ethical pharmaceuticals. However by 1963 their recommendations to widen the product range and the proposed selling organization had been far from fully implemented, and action that had been taken was too slow. Furthermore, emphasis had been laid only on ethical products. What finally tipped the operation into the red in 1962 was the partial implementation of the recommendation to increase the selling force. The number of ethical representatives rose from 14 to 30, but sales were not high enough to compensate for the additional expense. The highest ever gross margin was achieved in this year, £320 000. Unfortunately the figure was converted to a final loss of £24 000 by selling expenses of £260 000 and long-term research costs of £84 000.

In the same year the percentage of TB drugs in total sales had at last fallen to 72 per cent. The urgency of such a cut was emphasized by the Ministry of Health enforcing price reductions in TB drugs, causing a potential loss for the pharmaceutical company of £28 000. Of the non-TB products, the prescription hypnotic 'Welldorm' accounted for almost half the turnover.[11] Next in importance were ophthalmics with a sales volume of £34 000 in their second year of manufacture. Exports steadily increased relative to home sales, and from 1961 to 1962 export figures rose by over one-half to 28 per cent of total sales.

The real problem behind the disappointing sales figures was still the inadequate range of products, though, which in turn reflected the effectiveness and magnitude of R & D effort. The company possessed expertise in the TB field which in some respects it made sense to maintain. Unfortunately, in addition to problems with the principal buyer, the big pharmaceutical companies had quickly moved into TB drugs. Lazell at Beecham's was unwilling to pursue research in this field for that reason, even though he was prepared to commit substantial sums to research (ultimately very successfully) into antibiotics (Lazell 1975, pp. 136–41).

Expenditure on research alone over the nine years from 1954 to 1962 averaged £52 000 per annum. However research spending had risen to £96 000 in 1962. This figure may be further qualified by the fact that expenditure as a proportion of pharmaceutical sales remained fairly constant at 10 per cent, with the exception of the years 1961 and 1962, when it crept up to 11.6 per cent.[19] Since sales were down to less than a £0.25m in 1954, R & D at that date was correspondingly low. In total, over £600 000 had been spent on research, development and standards in the nine-year period. (Standards had been operating since 1960 and cost £4 000 per annum.)

The parent board maintained in 1963 that such expenditure should have produced more marketable products, sales of which could have generated an adequate turnover to support the rising costs of research. Research was not sufficiently successful in areas outside the TB field, although the pharmaceutical company was recognized to have made valuable contributions to development work initiated from outside. Welldorm, a modestly successful line, although not discovered by the company, owed its process of manufacture entirely to Smith & Nephew chemists. Research had also contributed valuably by improving chemical manufacturing processes.

Either the company could continue to concentrate on original research and the development of royaltied products; or it should go into proprietary products. The pharmaceutical interests of the group added to its prestige, 'but ... prestige without profit is not much of an asset'. The main recommendation to the board in 1963, echoing Sir Thomas Barclay's proposal for a health food half a century earlier (Chapter 2), was that immediate effort should be directed toward public lines, although ethical products were not to be neglected; acquisition of complementary concerns was also recommended, but opportunities for this type of activity were very limited.

The pharmaceutical company's management considered proprietary products the previous year and developed several of them. They were reasonably simple in formulation, they were safe (a bonus considering the recent Drazine incident), and they were in fields where there was a substantial turnover. The lines were expected to generate a gross revenue of £250 000 in their first full year of marketing, which was to be 1965. This would push the total turnover of the pharmaceutical company to over £1m, and it was estimated that profit before research would be in the region of £150 000.

Because of the considerable expense of advertising and display aids necessary to launch the new products, and the poor performance of the company to date, it was recommended that long-term research spending should be restricted to £60 000 per annum for several years. That could be expected to exacerbate the problem in the hi-tech sector. The company therefore ceased drug synthesis in 1966. Smith & Nephew was lucky to develop products which had tended to be resilient to both competition and disease. By the early 1960s it was recognized that such conditions would not last much longer.

Leading authorities saw that there was a minimum size for a pharmaceutical research and development group, below which its chances of success rapidly declined. Glaxo's view was that:

> Excluding all considerations of capital cost of buildings and equipment, a graduate operating in this field is likely to cost, with supporting services and technical

help, £5,000 to £6,000 per annum, a cost which has steadily increased over the last decade and shows no signs of stabilization. For an annual expenditure of between £150,000 and £200,000 a company may reasonably hope to build up valuable research and development capacity in a restricted field that its tradition or its own initiative has indicated as worth while and relevant to its business future.[13]

The management of the research company verified these figures and stressed that the annual expenditure of Smith & Nephew was the minimum effective level of investment. In 1963 Smith & Nephew's expenditure on pharmaceutical research, development and standards ran at approximately £100 000 (38 per cent of the total research company budget) per annum, over 80 per cent of which was related to long-term studies. Taking the Glaxo figures at face value in fact suggests that Smith & Nephew's pharmaceutical effort was too small, and that, in the absence of a stronger corporate commitment to the sector, what R & D funds were available might be better directed to other fields, such as plastics. On the other hand, for a health care company, greater commitment in the crucial 1950s and early 1960s to new pharmaceutical products would probably have been more appropriate than commitment to textiles, if not to plastics.

PLASTICS

The plastics industry in the UK before the Second World War was mainly restricted to resins similar to bakelite. The advent of polyethylene, polyvinyl chloride (PVC) and a large number of other synthetic polymers made plastics a household word, and by the early 1960s they played a part in all aspects of everyday life. Smith & Nephew clearly had an interest in applications of plastics to dressings, containers, and other health care utensils such as gloves and syringes. The industry was still young and growing very rapidly. New resins were being innovated, requiring new techniques in processing, and invading markets previously untouched by plastics. The research work, development and production of the new products involved the expenditure of large sums of money.

Since one of the main raw materials was crude oil, the oil companies, in conjunction with the chemical companies, played a significant role. Many of the plants were large and involved high capital costs, committing manufacturers to selling their entire outputs in order to recover the money invested. The polymerization units necessary for the production of these materials were costly and thus the minimum economic unit was large, about 15 000 tons per annum.

The original agreements between oil firms and polymer manufacturers were intended to safeguard the sale of raw materials on one side and the supply of raw materials on the other. Further extension of this principle to the conversion field brought the polymer manufacturers into the manufacturing and processing of polythene films. The polymer film industry absorbed nearly one-third of the UK's production of resin in 1963. Production of other resins such as polystyrene and PVC did not require the installation of such large and expensive units, and in part this accounted for the absence of overproduction in these fields.

Smith & Nephew's direct involvement with plastics dates from Seymour's introduction of Whittaker in 1958 to Bud Krohn of the Clopay Corporation, Cincinnati. Krohn had a fingernail covering that substituted for nail varnish. Whittaker visited the American plant and there saw for the first time extruded polythene and other polymers, as well as injection moulding. Smith & Nephew duly launched Clopay's nail product as 'Tip Tops'. They sold well but unfortunately nails covered in Tip Tops cracked, and the product had to be quickly withdrawn. Other lines were more successful although Smith & Nephew Plastics did experience teething troubles. In 1960 these prompted Leavey to send a letter to Whittaker, then in South Africa, to terminate the experiment. Whittaker decided that diplomacy required him never to have received the letter and plastics survived in the group.[14]

Net 909

Closure of plastics operations would have been singularly inept in the year of the first large-scale Smith & Nephew research success in polymer technology with the Net 909 patent (see Table 9.1). Net 909, the origin of polymer melt technology, derived from the accidental discovery, during work on film for Airstrip dressings, that polypropylene[15] with embossed patterns, when pulled, made a net pattern, instead of breaking. The resulting soft structure, full of holes, was useful for clothing, dressings, horticulture and sanitary towels (see Figures 9.1 and 9.2). The special plastic properties and different mesh structures allow the 909 range of high-density and polypropylene nets to act as a hot-melt adhesive for fabric lamination and stiffening processes. Second generation nets came to be used in biomedical filters, furniture and in Smith & Nephew's own surgical dressings. Continuous production of nets required great engineering ingenuity, a challenge to which engineering staff rose.

The company received the Queen's Award for Technology in 1968 for Net 909. No less gratifying was the licensing of the technology to the Hercules company of Wilmington, USA for an annual fee of $120 000. The pleasure was only slightly diminished when the alacrity with which Hercules accepted the terms first offered made Smith & Nephew realize they had probably underpriced the licence.

Table 9.1   Polymer technology at Smith & Nephew Research until 1976

Date	Event	Significance
1951	Herts Pharmaceuticals acquired	Technical base became Smith & Nephew Research
1952	Airstrip patent	First Smith & Nephew breathable plastic film
1956	PVC cast film process (Clopay Inc.)	Polymer cast film technology
1960	Net 909 patent	Beginning of polymer melt technology
1962	Smith & Nephew Research moved to Gilston Park	
1966	Drug synthesis ceased at Smith & Nephew Research	
1967	Visit to Prof. Wichterle, Prague	Beginning of hydrophilic polymer technology
1969	OpSite patent	Breathable PU film technology
1973	Haemocol patent	First truly multidisciplinary project
1974	Contact lens polymer patent	Acrylic hydrogel polymer chemistry well established
1976	Crystona patent	Polyacrylate chemistry for splints

Note: This is not an exhaustive list – only significant jumps in polymer technology are shown.

Source: J. Fennimore, Smith & Nephew.

Figure 9.1   Polymer melt technology

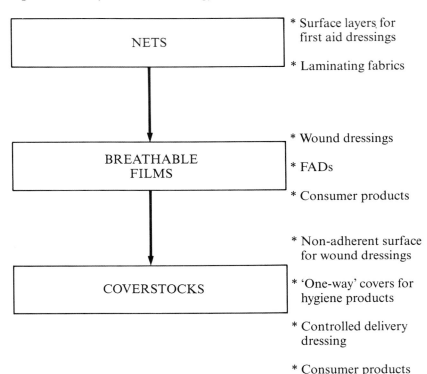

NETS

* Surface layers for
  first aid dressings

* Laminating fabrics

BREATHABLE
FILMS

* Wound dressings

* FADs

* Consumer products

COVERSTOCKS

* Non-adherent surface
  for wound dressings

* 'One-way' covers for
  hygiene products

* Controlled delivery
  dressing

* Consumer products

Advances in Plastics Production

From the formation of Smith & Nephew Plastics in 1958, output of extruded film increased from 225 000 lbs in 1958, to 1.7m lbs in 1962.[16] The quality of Smith & Nephew film improved almost every year in order to keep abreast of technical advances in this field by competitors. Film which was produced and sold in 1958 would not have found a market five years later.

Because large plastics producers acquired a considerable number of independent converters to whom Smith & Nephew had been selling, the company was compelled to enter printing and conversion as rapidly as possible at short notice. Smith & Nephew therefore bought the entire plant of Messrs P.P. Payne of Nottingham and achieved the ability to print and produce bags, after training the operatives. The acquired plant was not the most modern, but nevertheless it could cope with a considerable proportion of Smith & Nephew's business. Entirely thanks to the skill of Smith & Nephew technicians,

Figure 9.2   Polymer melt technology at Smith & Nephew Research

1960	NET 1 PATENT *Nets in HDPE only
1963	CAVITY NET PATENT *Nets in HDPE and PP
1968	MULTIFILAMENT YARN PATENT *Highest-tenacity PP yarn available
1972	'SOFT' NET PATENTS * Polymer blends used for nets and breathable films
1981	ELASTIC NET PATENTS * Truly elastic nets in PU, EVA and PIBD
1983	3D COVERSTOCK PATENT * Wide range of nets suitable for medical and consumer products * Fluid transmission and adherence control
1988	NET '2000' MARKETED * Polymer blend nets using special high- temperature post-treatment

the company was able to develop the cast film process so that the whole of waterproof and invisible dressings production was eventually made in this plant.[17] At the same time in-house production improved the quality of Smith & Nephew waterproof films and lowered their cost. If the company had been obliged to purchase this film from outside they would have found difficulties. There was no known manufacturer of cast surgical films in England and, therefore, Smith & Nephew would probably have sought supplies from the US. In 1963 saving on own production against US supply was £27 000.

Smith & Nephew bought a bottle-blowing plant for producing their own pharmaceutical and cosmetic containers. All the bottles required by the pharmaceutical company for Transol and Soquette were being produced by 1963. Plastic bottles for Nivea were also made in this year, employing the plant for about two shifts a week. The company gained considerable knowledge of this technique and became able to blow bottles in most of the known resins.

The plastics company also developed machines for use with their film. Sales of these machines were very satisfactory; in the first six months of 1963, together with spares revenues, totalled £14 818. In the second half of 1963 Smith & Nephew began production of plastic gloves for domestic use. There were start-up problems but production soon reached 10 000 pairs a week and sales mirrored production.

Injection Moulding

Plastic syringes were beginning to replace the glass product sold by Smith & Nephew through their ownership of Everetts at the beginning of the 1960s. The Plastic Box company was therefore bought in 1962 to enable Smith & Nephew to manufacture plastic disposable syringes. Very early on it had been decided to use polypropylene resin for syringe manufacture but several initial problems had to be overcome before production started in August/September 1963. The main business of the Plastic Box company was the manufacture of plastic containers and this side of the business continued to flourish. The total turnover of this particular unit was £150 000 in 1962.

Smith & Nephew needed to look to fields outside its core areas and traditional technologies for large-scale expansion. The plastics field had an obvious appeal because it was growing strongly and encroaching on all industries. However, plastics technology was changing rapidly and any manufacturer wishing to become successful in plastics had to be able to adapt quickly.

The plastics company of 1963 was based broadly in two different fields: packaging film and injection moulding. Because of the marked differences between these two activities (due to the differences in their raw materials and production methods) their development and expansion needed different treatments.

The injection moulding venture yielded a good return on capital. Smith & Nephew's 1963 scope of operations in the polythene packaging field was very vulnerable and unlikely to continue to yield reasonable returns unless the plastics company reached an agreement with a resin manufacturer, such as the American Monsanto company, on competitive raw material prices. It would be very difficult for the plastics company to compete with converters already linked with resin manufacturers: Visqueen and ICI, Metal Box and Shell, and BX Plastics and Union Carbide. Alternatively a policy of ensuring that Smith & Nephew were in the van of new developments would involve capital investment in countries such as Germany and Japan, which were already in plastics technically more advanced than Britain.

Assuming a reasonable proportion of plastics development projects came to fruition, investment would be needed at the average rate of about £100 000 per year, excluding any acquisitions. Investment of £252 500 over the next two years was expected to yield a return to the group of about £68 000 per annum. Research and development would require the expenditure of about £20 000 per year on capital equipment over the following five years, as well as a revenue expenditure in the first year of £45 000 rising to approximately £100 000 per annum. By comparison with past pharmaceutical research these sums were rather large but plastics had achieved the Net 909 patent success, which pharmaceuticals could not match. If supporting both lines of research was too expensive, which one would be dropped was becoming obvious.

HYDRON AND OPSITE

Plastics converged with traditional health care products in Hydron and related developments. Smith & Nephew acquired their interest in Hydron through Seymour and the National Patent and Development Corporation (NPDC) in New York. The Corporation was established by two lawyers, Martin M. Pollak and J.I. Feldman to bring 'iron curtain' inventions to the US. The lawyers visited Kruschev himself to set the business up. One of their deals was apparently with Professor Wichterle of Prague Institute of Macro-Molecular Chemistry in 1967. In February of that year, Seymour met Pollak who showed him materials of possible interest to Smith & Nephew.[18] Further visits, by Suddaby and Howes of Smith & Nephew Research to the Czechoslovak Academy of Science in Prague, and to NPDC in New York and London, culminated in a joint operation between Smith & Nephew and NPDC, Hydron Ltd, to exploit Hydron.

Hydron was the registered trade mark coined by NPDC to describe a range of new plastics or polymers which are able to absorb water into their structure or transmit moisture vapour and/or form gels with water. This overall property of plastics can be described as 'hydrophilic'. Seymour discussed with Pollak the advantages of such material for contact lenses, then made from hard glass-like material.[19] These lenses needed to be made from biologically compatible polymers, that is they should have no body reactions. Perspex, the obvious lens material, did not absorb water, but the hydroxyl group of acrylates will.[20] So hydroxylated perspex was a jelly-like substance that shaped itself to match the eye.

The British joint company, Hydron Ltd, formed to exploit the medical uses of the Hydron polymer, was independent of pharmaceuticals and was to direct development towards wound dressings. Hydron itself was not quite suitable.[21] Research was needed to find a water vapour-permeable adhesive, so that the dressing could 'breathe' (lose water) like skin. Plastic dressings lack this property while cloth dressings have it. Twenty Smith & Nephew researchers worked on these problems and came up with the new material OpSite, a polyurethane, on which patents were taken out throughout the world.

Just as PAS was directed at the same target as T.J. Smith's cod liver oil, so OpSite was an equally revolutionary step in surgical dressings to aid wound healing processes that had concerned Gamgee, Lister and Southall. The revolution was based on 'moist-wound healing', fathered by George Winter. At the end of the 1950s the conventional wisdom was that wounds heal most quickly when kept free of infection, protected from physical damage and when exposed to air (hence Airstrip Elastoplast). Subsequently George Winter's papers in *Nature* in 1962 and 1963 showed that wounds healed most quickly when kept moist (Chapter 6). The challenge was to create a dressing that would allow a wound to stay moist and yet free of infection.

The Origins of OpSite

David Drain (head of pharmaceutical research) and John Howes met Pollak in the Summer of 1967. His 'Hydron' (polyHEMA) samples included soft lens samples, sponge, encapsulated flavours and various types of tubing, which they thought might prove to be successful vascular prostheses (a 'Holy Grail' of medical prosthetics, still to this day undiscovered). As a potential material for permeable film, however, polyHEMA is self-evidently unsuitable, being bulk-cast. It is therefore not appropriate for large-scale film manufacture, and in the dry state, is exceedingly brittle. After having visited Wichterle in 1967, and again in early 1968, Howes and his colleagues were convinced the material had a future, but especially in the area of the soft contact lens, sponge breast implants, and small-bore vascular prostheses. Projects in all three areas were set up. For various technical reasons only the first area proved commercially exploitable[22]

The Hydron project, indirectly, played an important part in the birth of OpSite which, at least in its current main use as a wound dressing, can truly be described as a happy accident. Because of the wide range of interests in Smith & Nephew research in the 1950s and 1960s, there were fairly broad areas of expertise, appropriate parts of which could be combined in product development. This diversity was maintained throughout the 1970s and 1980s, and was repeatedly beneficial in development of recent products. 'OpSite' was probably the first example.

The areas involved in the OpSite case were:

1. The original Clopay 'Tip Tops' project (1958).
2. Airstrip development (1952).
3. Film technology development (1958).

4.   The Hydron project (1967).
5.   Polyethylene drape project (1965–67).

The original 'Tip Tops' project had shown that, in body surface applications, polymer films needed permeability to both oxygen and moisture to be successful. The development of Airstrip (and consideration of Winter's publications of 1962 and 1963) had led to attempts to increase permeability of surgical adhesives, and to study other products, which included the polyvinyl ether adhesive formulation B6, used on early OpSite. The drape project demonstrated the technical shortcomings of impermeable polyolefin films on long-term application to large body areas, as is required during surgery. (Surgical drapes cover the patient's body at the site of the operation before an incision is made. The cut is made through the drape and the drape ensures bacteria from the body do not enter the incision.)

In its early stages, the Hydron project concentrated entirely on converting the academic technology derived from Czechoslovakia to practical larger-scale technology using industrially available HEMA monomers. This required considerable chemical effort, and an investigation was therefore launched into the factors that gave polyHEMA its, at that time, unique properties. As part of this effort, two monomers EEMA and MEMA, related to HEMA, were prepared. They were designed to be combined with HEMA, to give EEMA/HEMA and MEMA/HEMA polymers with undefined properties.[23]

Because these monomers were available, one of the chemistry team, who liked dabbling in new materials, prepared MEMA/EEMA polymers. Suprisingly the new polymers proved not to absorb water (like HEMA), but nevertheless they could be made into flexible film (rather like polyethylene), which was highly permeable to oxygen/water vapour, and was quite strong (in marked contrast to HEMA itself).

Mr Suddaby, a senior director of Smith & Nephew research, who had been assigned the overall board responsibility for the project, and whom Howes had accompanied to Prague on the first visit in mid-1967, was the first person to spot the potential of this material. Recollecting the Clopay work of 1958, Suddaby suggested that new 'Hydron Tip Top' would overcome the original product disadvantages. When combined with the B6 adhesives, available from the Airstrip development team, Hydron Tip Tops (MEMA/EEMA film/ B6 adhesive) were successfully clinically tested.[24]

Because of the interest in surgical drapes (from 1965), and the obvious similarities in requirements for this product and nail covers, development of Hydron surgical drapes from the same formulation was virtually contemporaneous with the nail covers.[25] Much of the success of OpSite can be ascribed to the enthusiasm of Hull technical personnel who obtained the feedback from the medical profession that expanded its uses into the field of wound and bedsore dressings.[26]

For a short time EEMA/MEMA film was the standard (and still is for a spray-on version, 'OpSite Spray' which is a current product). But a survey of other films, obtained from products studied by the film technology group, showed a polyurethane ('Estane') film possessed reasonable permeability and better physical properties than EEMA/MEMA. After experimental samples of 'Estane OpSite' had been successfully evaluated, it became the standard product from about 1971. This material was replaced only after 1989, when 'No.8' adhesive, an in-house product, took over from the original B6.

The OpSite story is typical of the way most products ultimately were developed. A special strength of Smith & Nephew research was that there were a number of disparate disciplines, all of which contributed in the medical device field.

OpSite became the basis of Smith & Nephew's claim to be a world leader in surgical dressings. But subsequent work on burn dressings was also highly regarded. Burns are most demanding of their dressings. A burn dressing must control infection, usually over a large area; it must offset the otherwise compromised nutritional balance of the body (salt and fluid retention is affected by the absence of tissue); and it requires great absorbency because burns leak a great deal of fluid. In 1973 Smith & Nephew introduced their burns dressing Flamazine, employing as an active agent silver sulphadiazine.

THE ORIGINS OF HAEMOCOL[27]

Smith & Nephew research was known in the late 1960s and early 1970s for its interest in hydrogels and also in renal dialysis (through sponsorship of the Leeds Dialysis Unit). This project (1969–71) was ultimately unsuccessful.

In late 1971, Smith & Nephew were approached by Dr Roger Williams for the King's College Hospital Liver Unit, with a request for a collaborative venture to develop a film suitable for dialysis from the blood of the 'middle molecules', believed to be responsible for the lethal toxicity associated with acute liver failure. After consideration, a project was initiated which ran from 1973 to 1980. The original 'dialysis' approach was deemed impractical, but there was some evidence in the literature that direct passage of blood over an absorbent (so-called 'haemoperfusion') was more promising. Early evidence suggested activated charcoal would work, but that extensive damage to the cellular components of the blood resulted.

Eventually a specially purified form of activated charcoal was developed, coated with a biocompatible polymer film, permeable to 'middle molecules', which minimized blood damage, in a carefully designed housing to give maximum absorptive area for a minimum of extracorporeal blood volume.

The team developed for this project was genuinely multidisciplinary, and the first of its kind (such teams, in 1980s projects, were the norm). In-house expertise, which led to the final product, was from:

- the Hydron project – protective film formulation;
- chemical engineering – contributed to device housing design;
- expertise in activated charcoal technology from the earlier chemical development project;
- the dialysis project – design of ancillary tubing and pumps.

Jack Fennimore, a chemical engineer and later director, led the project. The columns of activated charcoal were very effective, and several spectacular results were obtained in liver failure induced by drug overdose. Later collaboration with Dr Roy Goulding at the Guy's Hospital Poisons Unit was most fruitful. Goulding subsequently became toxicological consultant to Smith & Nephew.

Haemocol was a technical achievement of considerable merit, and was later copied by others. It certainly helped to put Smith & Nephew in the limelight as an innovative health care company. Unfortunately, high unit costs and limited market potential rendered Haemocol financially unviable for Smith & Nephew and it was discontinued.

OPHTHALMICS

The decision to opt out of 'new molecule' drug research led to confusion and uncertainty among Smith & Nephew researchers for a considerable time. PolyHEMA appeared in mid-1967 as a saviour for the chemistry department. With the other departments, such as pharmacology, pharmacy and biochemistry, the flux lasted rather longer. However, by 1968, it had been decided to retain these disciplines (to the advantage of later work, when wide multidisciplinary knowledge and facilities proved essential), and to concentrate on the ophthalmic sector of pharmaceutical development.

The main fields largely influenced by Smith & Nephew's new interests in contact lenses through HEMA were glaucoma drugs (preferably formulations of existing drugs used in other areas, thus reducing safety testing costs), lens accessory solutions, and novel methods of eye dosage. Glaucoma was a 'Cinderella' condition as far as research investment by the large companies was concerned and was therefore deemed a viable area for Smith & Nephew.[28]

Reasonably high levels of work in these areas were maintained up to the mid-1980s, since when it tailed off.

First, improvements were made to the adrenalin-based EPPY products originally from Barnes–Hinds. Eppy is a stable non-irritant form of adrenaline (epinephrine). Second, a significant advance on adrenalin-based glaucoma treatments was made in the form of 'Ganda', a current project in 1991. This is a combination of adrenaline and Guanethidine, which allowed use of much lower doses of adrenaline, avoiding the main side effects, and developed from ideas generated within Smith & Nephew Research. Third, new dosage forms for the eye, Minims, unit/dose sterile disposable eye drop applicators designed to eliminate the risk of contamination by bacteria. All common diagnostic ophthalmic solutions are available in Minims form. Minims preparations avoided use of preservatives, were widely sold, and were trail-blazers in ophthalmic single dose treatment. More recently, a solid single dose system ('NODS') was developed – a unique product in 1991 still to reach the market. In both instances, the products needed a combination of pharmaceutical and polymer chemistry technology. Finally, several new systems for wet sterilization of contact lenses were developed. One, 'Prymecare', has been on the market for several years.

Although this area was of diminishing importance later in the 1980s, having peaked in the late 1970s, Smith & Nephew acquired a considerable reputation in the field of ocular pharmacology.

Hydrogel Projects

After solving the initial problems of HEMA technology, the soft contact lens was marketed jointly with National Patent from 1970. Because of Hydron, Smith & Nephew was the first to manufacture and sell soft contact lenses in the UK. The five-year plan for Smith & Nephew Pharmaceuticals involved the expansion of ophthalmics and contact lens solutions. Acquisition of Obrig, the contact lens group, in June 1970 was the first leg of this policy.[29] Obrig gave Smith & Nephew access to clinics but larger manufacturing facilities were wanted as well.

From 1973 to 1977–78, the range of materials was enlarged, and 'Snoflex50' and 'Polymer 407', high water uptake soft lenses were made; the former are still in production. In the early and mid-1980s other materials, a so-called 'permanent wear lens', and a 'gas-permeable hard lens', were also developed. Smith & Nephew no longer make lenses, but production of the basic lens materials has continued, supplying other lens manufacturers with polymer buttons.

CONCLUSION

During the 1950s and 1960s, Smith & Nephew made the transition to a research-based health care firm. It also entered and left the mainstream pharmaceutical industry. Perhaps the culmination of that episode was the 1967 World Tuberculosis Symposium held at the Royal College of Surgeons. In the 1960s Smith & Nephew made great improvements in the manufacture of Thiacetazone which in certain forms discussed at the symposium could be a still more effective treatment for TB. Thiazina, the combination of Isoniazid and Thiacetazone, which the Medical Research Council found most efficacious, with very few toxic effects, was marketed by Smith & Nephew especially in poorer countries where TB was still rife. The simplicity of dosage of the new treatment was particularly attractive, for the patient needed to take only one tablet the size of an aspirin.

A year before the symposium, Smith & Nephew withdrew from drug synthesis. By then the plastics and polymer research programme was well established and promised a more acceptable combination of risk and return. Net 909 and OpSite were innovative and very profitable, Haemocol was innovative but unprofitable, and ophthalmics maintained a foothold in pharmaceuticals that meshed conveniently with the company's polymer and plastics interests.

Research teams built up over the period of traditional pharmaceutical investigation proved their worth in the face of the multidisciplinary demands made by new medical devices. Their experience also showed the often unexpected scientific or technological connections between earlier failed projects (such as Tip Tops) and later successful work (such as OpSite). Interrelationships of this nature create difficulties for individual research project costing. They indicated the need for a long-term corporate commitment to research in the fields where the company saw its principal markets, independently of the profitability of individual projects.

NOTES

1. *Smith & Nephew Annual Report*, 1959.
2. Polymers are substances that consist of many monomers (small molecules) bonded together in a repeating sequence. For example ethene molecules (C_2H_4) are monomers that react together to form polythene. Polythene is a homopolymer, being a polymer made from a single type of monomer (under high pressure at 200C). It is formed by addition polymerization, reactions in which monomers bond together without losing any atoms. The polymer is the only product and has the same empirical formula as the monomer.
3. His acid was prepared for him by the Ferrosan Company of Malmo.
4. Seymour interview, June 1991. The quotation is from D.E. Seymour, *R & D Policy: Pharmaceuticals*, 1963, Smith & Nephew Archives, London.

5. *Tubercle*, March 1968.
6. Donald Burley was Hull's chief chemist and Peter Bricklebank, who played a major role in plastics developments such as Net 909, was his assistant. Victor Hammond was the Hull pharmacist.
7. Seymour had been elected a Fellow of the Royal Institute of Chemistry in 1946.
8. *Sanaco News*, Spring 1954; *Sanaco News*, summer 1958; Bavin (1965).
9. Joint publications were made with scientists at the National Institute of Health in Washington, USA. At the International Pharmacological Congress held in 1963 in Prague, related substances derived by the team were discussed and agreed to be among the first drugs to have potential in the treatment of certain types of hitherto irretrievable mental disorders.
10. *Smith & Nephew Annual Report, 1963*; Committee on Safety of Drugs, *Adverse Reaction Series, No. 1*, February 1964, HMSO.
11. Unlike barbiturates, Welldorm is a sedative that was rarely habit-forming or cumulative in effect; nor did it give rise to hangovers.
12. ICI's pharmaceutical division in 1952 spent 11.5 per cent of turnover on research and development but with sales almost ten times those of Smith & Nephew's pharmaceutical division.
13. H.W. Pakmer, Glaxo group, Address to the Royal Society of Medicine, 1963.
14. G. Whittaker *A Handful of Shale* unpublished ms, pp. 196–7.
15. The monomer propene (C_3H_6) is a colourless gas. Some kitchen tools are made from polypropylene.
16. S. Clarke *Plastics Report*, September 1963, Smith & Nephew Archives, London.
17. *Smith & Nephew Annual Report 1958 and 1959*: '...advantages failed to materialise..and it became necessary to terminate the contract with the American company...'.
18. D.E. Seymour, *Memo on Hydron to SANACO Executive Committee* Minute no. 370–(2), Smith & Nephew Board Meeting, 11 July 1967.
19. Seymour interview, June 1991.
20. Acrylic is a polymer formed from the methyl methacrylate monomer,

$$H-C=C-CH_3$$
$$H \diagdown \quad \diagup \diagdown COOCH_3$$

Hydroxyls have OH functional groups.
21. Nonetheless there was press speculation about the wonder material that encouraged an excessive bidding up of Smith & Nephew share prices. Quaestor, 'Smith & Nephew All Set for a Leap Ahead', *Daily Telegraph*, 26 April 1971. The earlier, T. Johnson, 'Breathing Plastic Comes To Life', *Sunday Times*, 27 July 1969, appearing in the technology column rather than as a share tip, had no such impact. This is an indication of the information used by the stock market in appraising corporate prospects. The board felt obliged to issue a statement to calm the speculators.
22. J. Howes, 'Notes on Research at Gilston Park', unpublished ms, 1991.
23. The HEMA monomer is hydroxyethylmethacrylate, the EEMA monomer is ethoxyethylmethacrylate and MEMA is methoxyethylmethacrylate.
24. Although very well received on test marketing, a management decision was taken not to proceed with the project.
25. These projects began in 1968–69 but the OpSite patent is also dated 1969. This does not mean that the projects were short-term. It is quite normal for patents to be applied for at the idea stage and, when 'completed' two to three years later, to contain the technical information obtained in the interim.
26. John Colville and Brian Sanderson made particularly significant contributions.
27. Howes, op. cit., note 21.
28. Ibid.
29. J. Hargreaves, *Contact Lens Group*, Memo to K.R. Kemp and D.E. Seymour, 11 June 1971, Smith & Nephew Archives, London.

Plate 18   Temple Place, London, the headquarters of Smith & Nephew plc.

Plate 19   The purpose-built Group Research Centre at York University Science Park was completed in 1992.

Plate 20 During a period of intense acquisition activity during the 1980s, particularly in the US, Richards Medical Company, Memphis was purchased in 1986, a leader in orthopaedic trauma and implant products.

Plate 21 Rolyan, based at Menomonee Falls, Wisconsin, specializing in casting and rehabilitation products, was purchased in 1983.

Plate 22 Perry Gloves were purchased as part of Affiliated Hospital Products in 1985. Highly efficient production of surgeons' and speciality gloves takes place at Massillon, Ohio.

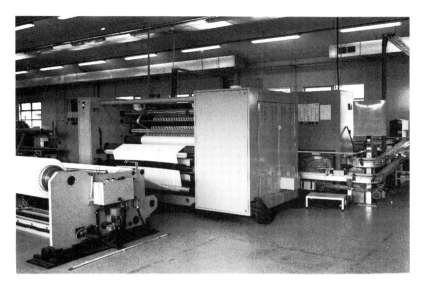

Plate 23   The 1980s and early 1990s was a period of development and expansion throughout mainland Europe including the commissioning of a new surgical tapes plant in France, by Smith & Nephew Laboratoires Fisch.

Plate 24   The potential of the world's largest health care market, Japan, is a key to growth in the 1990s.

Plate 25   Allevyn cavity wound dressings form part of a team of products which treat chronic wounds such as leg ulcers and pressure sores.

Plate 26   Smith & Newphew's advanced wound management products contribute to faster patient healing and reduced hospitalization. Their efficiency and simplicity of use support the trend towards health care in the community. (Photograph by David Partner)

Plate 27   Dynacast Pro is an advanced polypropylene casting tape.

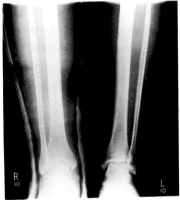

Plate 28   Dynacast Pro has the property of excellent X ray translucency which reduces the need to remove casts to monitor healing progress.

Plate 29   Smith & Nephew Donjoy are world leaders in the knee brace market. The Donjoy Defiance knee brace is one of their latest developments.

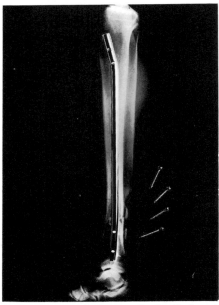

Plate 30 Russell Taylor intramedullary nails for limbs with difficult breaks were developed in close consultation with two leading orthopaedic surgeons in the US.

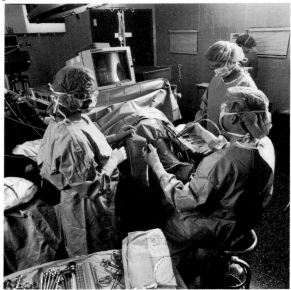

Plate 31 The current trend is towards minimally invasive surgery or 'keyhole' surgery. Arthroscopy is the orthopaedic side of this type of surgery where Smith & Nephew Dyonics is the world leader.

Plate 32   Precision manufacturing is a feature of the production process for orthopaedic implants. Hip stems are checked on a comparator which superimposes an accurate image of the product on to specification drawings. (Photography by David Partner)

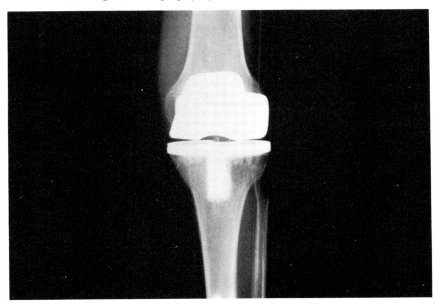

Plate 33   Genesis knee implants provide great flexibility for the surgeon and improved quality of life for the patient.

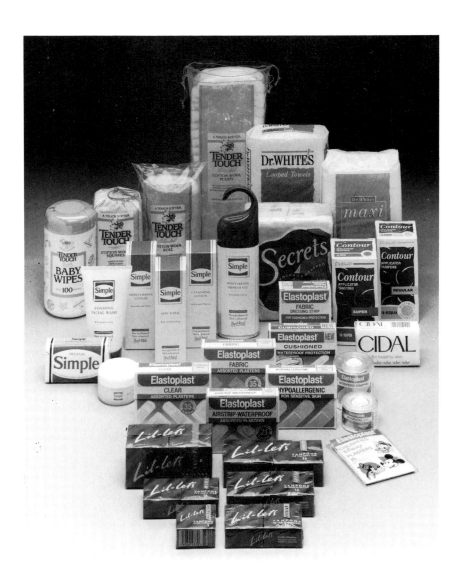

Plate 34   A modern range of consumer health care products featuring additive-free toiletries, a comprehensive range of first aid dressings, high-performance feminine hygiene products and high-quality cotton wool.

10. Smith & Nephew overseas, 1906–80

From the beginning Smith & Nephew's business depended on overseas trade, although at first primarily as an importer of materials and techniques. In the twentieth century overseas markets came to account for more and more of the company's sales. The pattern of expansion abroad was first to establish agency agreements for selling exports and later, sales branches. Dating from 1955, the third stage was calculated to reduce transport costs, and avoid trade restrictions, by building manufacturing plants (cf. Nicholas 1983).

Commonwealth sales branches were sporadically profitable in the interwar period, thanks to Smith & Nephew's early development of professional management and popular brands. But these were not prosperous years for economies such as Canada, Australia and New Zealand, earning a substantial proportion of their incomes from exporting food and raw materials. In consequence profits were hard to earn for new market entrants. South African industrial production grew faster than that of almost any other country between the world wars and therefore South Africa provided a relatively prosperous market in the 1930s. The company preference for these countries may be explained by the enormous British overseas migration during the nineteenth century to the US or to Empire countries. Empire migrants established overseas markets with tastes and incomes similar to those in Britain in countries with similar legal and cultural backgrounds.

Political and cultural differences required a new style of expansion into continental Europe, initially a phenomenon of the 1960s. Under stimulus of what was expected to be imminent entry to the Common Market, and despite Treasury restrictions on capital exports, Smith & Nephew began buying equity stakes in family health care enterprises. As founders or their families decided they wanted more security and less management, Smith & Nephew bought the remaining shares. Although attempted on a number of occasions from early in the twentieth century, expansion into the US proved more difficult. The principal problem was traditionally that Smith & Nephew's best selling products were licensed for the British Commonwealth only and not for the US. Smith & Nephew interests there remained comparatively small until the 1980s. The 1980s also saw a new wave of manufacturing investment in the newly industrializing countries (NICs).

THE HEROIC AGE OF SALESMANSHIP: SOUTH AFRICA AND CANADA

H.N. Smith's love of travelling and, in particular, his interest in North America, ensured that Smith & Nephew would quickly enter export markets. His earliest overseas orders, from Canadian hospitals for surgical dressings, probably date from 1906, when he first crossed the Atlantic and, with typical entrepreneurial nerve, only established the means of fulfilling the contracts once he had returned to Hull.[1] Seven years later, two Hull employees were sent to Montreal with a view to boosting exports.[2] A sales agency agreement was concluded in New Zealand in 1909.[4] H.N. visited South Africa at the beginning of the 1920s to develop that market. The pattern in all the overseas branches, as with other companies, was that once sales volumes were sufficient, a separate sales company was formed and a member of the UK company was eventually sent out to run it. The Canadian company was established in 1921 to import surgical dressings manufactured in the UK. Previously the Wingate Chemical Company managed Smith & Nephew sales, and the connection was maintained by locating the office on the second floor of a Wingate Chemical drugstore. In 1923 H.N. Smith twice visited Montreal. Although small profits were earned in the first full year of operation, 1922/3, most of the remainder of the 1920s showed losses, following the move to 378 St Paul Street West, Old Montreal, in 1926. There the company began converting absorbent gauze and cotton into surgical dressings and sanitary protection products. Competition from the two largest surgical dressing firms in the world, located in the US, proved stiff.[4]

A key man in overseas operations for four decades was Fred Medhurst. Because he could speak French, when he arrived back from the war in 1918 and walked into the Hull office of Smith & Nephew, he came out with the job of export manager.[5] Two other characters played central roles, Vernon Wisby and H. Stanley Dagger. Wisby joined the Hull export department in 1922 as a junior. Although he left the next year to study languages, literature and philosophy in Spain, he returned to the Smith & Nephew fold, for in 1927 he was sent out to improve the Canadian company fortunes.[6] Losses in Canada continued during the world depression that began in 1929; profits were not restored until 1936.[7] Almost certainly the turn-around occurred because the previous year the subsidiary was reorganized as the brands Elastoplast and Cellona were introduced.[8]

A decade after the Canadian subsidiary, the South African company was formed in 1931 at Commissioner Street, Johannesburg, with H.N. Smith, his son Alister, John McLaren (of SASHENA) and McLaren senior, as directors. Initially the business was managed by the South African associate of the British Sanitas Trust, Oppenheimer and Co.'s managing director, but staff and financial problems were compounded by inadequate liaison with the British headquarters. Smith & Nephew therefore sent Wisby from Canada in 1933 to join Medhurst from Hull in sorting out South African affairs. They travelled throughout the country building up a chain of agents. Then Medhurst returned to Hull, leaving Wisby to eliminate the operating loss and raise sales with the help of Transvaal branded line distributors B. Owen Jones Ltd.[9] At the end of 1934, Wisby returned to Canada and Dagger, who had joined Smith & Nephew as a sales assistant in Manchester in 1928 (and gained early experience with 'Phyllis', see Chapter 5), took his place at the beginning of the following year.

In South Africa, as in Canada and the home market, the opportunities in the 1930s were primarily created by the branded goods, Elastoplast and Cellona. Dagger concentrated on selling Elastoplast to the mines and converting orthopaedic surgeons to use factory-made Cellona plaster of Paris bandages. The area Dagger was obliged to cover was enormous; he might have to spend three days driving on very poor roads from Durban to Johannesburg, for there were no air services. For 14 years he covered 14 000 miles a year handling sales from the Transvaal. In confronting this enormous task he had one assistant. When the Natal agent retired in 1948, Dagger took over the territory and moved the head office to Durban. H. Canard & Co. were appointed sales agents in the 1930s, a position they held until 1981 when Smith & Nephew established their own depot in Cape Town.

ORGANIZATION FOR OVERSEAS EXPANSION

A successful international company needs an organization capable of coordinating operations around the world, a task eased by progress in communications technology. Without international telephones and air travel, a head office was likely to function as a holding company, allowing almost complete autonomy to overseas businesses, merely because of the difficulty of doing much else. True, the telegraph, the post and the railway made coordination possible but administrative costs were high. From 1927 a transatlantic telephone link was available and radio soon extended the facility, albeit at considerable cost per call, to Australia and South Africa.

During the generation after the Second World War multinational activity boomed, facilitated by increasingly cheap, rapid and reliable long-distance air travel. Greater contributors to the spread of multinational business were political and economic conditions more favourable than they had been since 1914. Unprecedented economic growth and increasing liberalization of international trade encouraged sales, but transport costs, the peculiarities of local marketing and economic nationalism placed a premium on production in the country of sale, if it constituted a large enough market.

Table 10.1   Smith & Nephew overseas sales, 1955 (£'000)

(A) Overseas companies		
Australia	Public	
	Elastoplast dressings etc.	196
	Nivea preparations	24
	Industrial tapes	7
	Medical	
	Elastoplast Bandages etc.	199
	Pharmaceuticals	2
	TOTAL	428
Canada	Public	
	Elastoplast dressings etc.	88
	Nivea preparations	152
	Medical	
	Elastoplast bandages etc.	260
	Pharmaceuticals	–
	TOTAL	500
New Zealand	Public	
	Elastoplast dressings etc.	61
	Nivea preparations	17
	Industrial tapes	5
	Medical	
	Elastoplast bandages	40
	Pharmaceuticals	16
	TOTAL	139
South Africa	Public	
	Elastoplast dressings etc.	171
	Nivea preparations	47
	Medical	
	Elastoplast bandages	190
	TOTAL	408
(B) Other export markets (paid for in the market)		
Belgium	Public	
	Tensoplast dressings etc.	63
	Medical	
	Tensoplast bandages etc.	15
	TOTAL	78

Table 10.1   continued

(C) Export markets (paid for in the UK)	
Public	
Elastoplast etc.	110
Nivea etc.	20
Industrial tapes	42
Medical	
Elastoplast, Gypsona, Jellonet	227
Pharmaceuticals	17
Surgical dressings	300
TOTAL	716
TOTAL overseas markets	2269
TOTAL home + overseas (excl. US)	5748
Percentage of overseas to total sales	39.5

When Smith & Nephew went public in 1937 there were three overseas subsidiaries, in Canada, South Africa and the US. By 1954 fully owned overseas subsidiaries had increased to include those in Australia and New Zealand. Measured by turnover, the three major subsidiaries, in Canada, Australia and South Africa, were roughly comparable in size, although the Canadian company was the largest (Table 10.1). Each of the three divided sales approximately equally between medical and public users, but Nivea sales in Canada were far greater than in other Dominions. Other export markets in total turned over less that two of the three big Dominion subsidiaries taken together. Almost 40 per cent of total company revenue was generated overseas.

Cheaper and safer air travel allowed the introduction in 1957 of the policy of annual meetings of the managing directors of all overseas companies so that they could see for themselves changes in UK production technology and appreciate difficulties and opportunities in the Commonwealth. In 1958 Smith & Nephew (Overseas) was formed. The company was by now firmly committed to extending overseas production even though they expected that exports from Britain would suffer. Economics and politics conspired to make this inevitable.

The two prongs of Smith & Nephew's overseas policy were made explicit in the divisional reorganization of the company in 1960, in which separate overseas divisions were established for the Commonwealth and Europe. Two years later the thrust of policy was reinforced by the vesting of the day-to-day activities of the company in three executive boards, each under the chairmanship of the managing director, responsible for

- the UK
- Europe excluding the UK
- the Commonwealth and other overseas countries.

Centralized control over major matters of policy and finance was retained by the parent board. Returns from overseas activities showed how justified the focus on overseas markets had been. Profits reached record levels in 1962; especially notable were those in South Africa, Australia and New Zealand. Factories then under construction in Canada, Australia, India and Pakistan in due course were to replicate the success of the 1955 South African plant.

Overseas activities contributed 14 per cent of the group's profits in 1964. Despite the growing proportion of sales originating from local manufacturing units, exports from the UK continued to rise. In 1964 these increased by some 8 per cent as compared with the national average of 4.25 per cent.

A broader overseas strategy was inaugurated at the end of the 1960s when each of the chairmen of the UK divisions was also given area responsibilities, for Africa, Australasia, Europe and the Americas. Recognition of the trend towards internationalization of the company was the tour of UK plants and facilities on which the entire Canadian sales team was taken in 1974. In that year overseas companies provided most of the increase in profits and over half of Smith & Nephew's total profits were generated by exports or overseas subsidiaries.

A continuing element of Smith & Nephew strategy has been to employ the human capital of acquired companies at least as intensively as the physical and marketing assets. In the management of overseas subsidiaries this is particularly apparent in the case of Herts Pharmaceuticals. Don Seymour (see Chapter 8) from Herts was Canadian chairman from 1974 to 1981. Sid Mitchell joined Herts in Welwyn in 1941. He was sent to establish a manufacturing plant for Herts in Calcutta and then to South Africa in 1954 as production director for the Pinetown factory, which he was also to set up.[10] C.B. Worsley arrived back in New Zealand in 1946 as a Herts representative having worked for Herts in many other parts of the world.[11] In 1957 he also became managing director of the Australian subsidiary.

Some overseas management continued to originate from Hull, of course. Kenneth Lunn joined Smith & Nephew at Hull in 1951 and the next year transferred to South Africa as sales representative. He became managing director of Smith & Nephew South Africa in 1971, and later a board member of the parent company. Terry Winter followed a similar pattern but through Smith & Nephew Canada, joining Smith & Nephew Research in 1960 before moving to Montreal as technical manager in 1965, and becoming president in 1975. On his retirement in 1989 he was president of Smith & Nephew Inc. in the US and chairman of the Canadian company, as well as a main board associate director.[12] Bill Bygott, first production manager of the Australian manufacturing operation from 1962, trained in Hull under the cadet training scheme, eventually becoming a board member of the Australian company.

Other management originated with overseas acquisitions. M.J. Kiely was accountant for Camille de Stoop when Smith & Nephew Australia bought it. At the time of the purchase, the asset valuation was agreed except for the stock, over which the two parties differed by about A$100 000. L.G. Long for Smith & Nephew and Kiely for Camille decided to choose one of the valuations by tossing a coin. Kiely won the toss and it was therefore only right that he should go on to become managing director of Smith & Nephew Australia and a board member of the parent company.

THE FIRST COMMONWEALTH MANUFACTURING SUBSIDIARIES

The big three Commonwealth subsidiaries, in Canada, South Africa and Australia, confronted broadly similar problems and adopted approximately similar growth strategies. They each acquired Nivea subsidiaries, considered setting up or bought textile manufacturing facilities, investigated plastics production and faced roughly comparable marketing environments. Economic nationalism was a fact of life, as was dependence of the national economies upon primary product exports.

The 1950s

Because of foreign exchange shortages, Australian import licensing began in March 1952, based on imports in the year ended June 1951. The scheme was abandoned in 1954 but reintroduced at the beginning of 1955. Smith & Nephew branded lines had been handled by Drug Houses of Australia (DHA) since long before the Second World War.[13] DHA therefore held the import licences but were scrupulously fair in their allocation to Smith & Nephew products. The two organizations' views diverged particularly over the granting of wholesale terms, however. In 1953 the Minister for Trade and Customs had made it very clear to Smith & Nephew's Fred Medhurst that the Australian government intended to establish industries 'to support the Australian economy' and if necessary to protect them by tariffs. Australia was heavily dependent on exports of wool and cereals: other industries were believed essential to insulate the Australian economy from swings in world commodity prices. Johnson & Johnson were already strongly established in Australia and were likely to press for tariff protection. That and the import licensing system pointed to domestic manufacture by Smith & Nephew, Medhurst reported in 1956, even though, since Australia had a high standard of living, production would be more expensive than in South Africa.

In the same year the subsidiary ran into difficulties with the Australian Chemists' Guild who were hostile to direct selling and asked members not to stock company products. In developing alternative outlets Worsley was helped by the Australian director O.V. Fyfe.[14] Perhaps because of these difficulties, not until 1959 did Smith & Nephew buy the land for the manufacturing plant.

Nivea/Herts sales were produced locally in Canada and Australia unlike other Smith & Nephew products during the 1950s because of a tariff incentive. When owned by Beiersdorf during the 1930s, Nivea imports did not benefit from the lower Empire tariff to which imports from Britain were subject. In Australia, not only Nivea Creme and Skin Oil production, but also the cutting and packing of Sleek Plasters, were undertaken locally. Other Smith & Nephew products were imported direct from the UK and distributed to wholesalers and hospitals across the continent. Elastoplast had just been introduced in restricted range to all non-pharmacy wholesalers and retailers. In 1951 the sales organizations of Nivea Pharmaceuticals Ltd and Smith & Nephew Ltd in Canada were integrated, though Nivea continued to operate from their Toronto factory at 253 Spadina Avenue.[15] Even New Zealand manufactured (only) Nivea Creme and Skin Oil (under licence). The rest of Smith & Nephew's products were shipped 13 000 miles to a New Zealand port from the UK. Sales strategy and stock holding had to take into account the four-month delivery period.[16] In South Africa Nivea was handled by Hill & Murray on an agency basis even when the Pinetown factory began producing Elastoplast, Gypsona and Jellonet in 1955.

South Africa gained the first original Smith & Nephew manufacturing facility. At the time that 'Elastoplast House', 467 Smith Street was acquired in 1950, when H.N. Smith visited Durban, Dagger saw that growing sales in South Africa warranted considerably more expansion. In 1953 he persuaded the board of Smith & Nephew to acquire a 23-acre site at Pinetown for £17 000. Pinetown was selected for its proximity to the port of Durban and for the less expensive land.

In view of the company achievements in textiles in the UK it was natural that these should be extended overseas, especially when tariff protection was taken into consideration. Plans for the South African textile plant for spinning, weaving and bleaching were completed in 1959. The following year the factory was opened by the then finance minister and soon captured almost all surgical dressing business at profitable prices.[17]

Australia in the 1960s and 1970s

Australia was already operating unprofitable small spinning and weaving companies, when a large area of land was bought in Melbourne during 1959 for a grandiose conversion unit. The outline plan to provide the capacity required for the production of the majority of Smith & Nephew products advanced slowly. It was held back because various British companies, with whom Smith & Nephew were associated, wanted to participate and the Board of the overseas division spent time exploring the possibilities. In the meanwhile the site considerably increased in value.

The Australian company adopted a similar structure to that of the parent in 1963, with a holding company controlling a number of Australian businesses and reporting to the parent board in London. The first two acquisitions under this structure came the same year. Two textile companies, Camille de Stoop and Wonthaggi, were bought to supply the cloth for Elastoplast in 1965. The Australian company went on to buy into surgical instruments, first aid items for industry and hair care. Divisionalization of corporate structure followed in 1968.[18]

In 1970 the Australian subsidiary diversified into plastic injection moulding and film extrusion by acquiring an interest in Vinyl Clad Pty. Vinyl Clad were estimated to have 70 per cent of the ice cream container market in Australia. Smith & Nephew saw an opportunity to source plastic film for Elastoplast from Vinyl's plant, making Nivea containers, Elastoplast plaster spools and disposable plastic syringes, as well as utilizing the exceptional entrepreneurial qualities of one of the founders, W. Vautin.[19]

Between 1972 and 1977 the Australian businesses almost doubled their turnover and nearly trebled their profits. Their main strength lay on the medical side where they held a large share of hospital dressings, plaster of Paris, and elastic adhesive bandages markets.[20] Lack of significant market share in feminine hygiene was a continuing painful reminder of earlier missed opportunities. Experience with disposable hypodermic needles, originating with Everetts, was similar to that of the parent company. By 1975 intense Japanese competition rendered the operation unprofitable. Textile operations were slimmed down from 1976 when steps began to be taken to concentrate all textile production at Wonthaggi and only to supply within Smith & Nephew's own requirements.

Smith & Nephew Australia gained more independence from the parent company in 1970, when they were permitted to export to Indonesia. This radical change in Smith & Nephew policy culminated in 1988, from which year all Smith & Nephew's South East Asian interests reported to Australia. A second step along this road was investment in an Indonesian subsidiary in 1977/8. A third step, eventually retracted, was new product introduction.

Snoflex soft contact lens material was made by Smith & Nephew Pharmaceuticals in the UK and in the three years after 1978, lenses were manufactured and sold in Australia. The new optics division also was intended to promote a new soft lens cleaning solution. When the product failed clinical trials, the Australian company decided to sell the Optics division.[21]

Economic Nationalism in New Zealand

During his 1959 world tour, Smith & Nephew Chairman, George Leavey, identified New Zealand, a small market with a population of 3 million, as worthy of further investigation. There was no textile industry and the Labour government were interested in establishing one. Smith & Nephew confirmed that the leader of the opposition also approved of the project in principle. The 1960 agreement reached with the New Zealand government was that Smith & Nephew would be permitted a monopoly and imports would be controlled, in exchange for a guarantee never to exceed the imported price, except when warranted by material and wage costs. The new textile factory was financed by the creation of a New Zealand public company under the name of Commonwealth Fabric Corporation Ltd, with a nominal capital of £5 000 000. Smith & Nephew subscribed £500 000 so that first stage could begin without delay. Limited production was planned to start towards the end of 1962.

By the time the building, at Nelson, South Island, was half constructed, vocal opposition from farmers, who did not want competition for labour, and from clothing manufacturers, worried about restrictions of supplies, persuaded the now national government to withdraw from the project in 1961, after compensating Smith & Nephew.[22] However in 1965 a new and larger factory was opened in Auckland to make Nivea Creme, Elastoplast, Gypsona, hospital disposable products, and cotton wool.

South Africa in the 1960s and 1970s

South Africa overtook Canada as the largest subsidiary between the mid-1950s and the mid-1960s (Table 10.2). The South African company successfully emulated the parent with its textile operation. It therefore tried to replicate another achievement of Smith & Nephew in Britain during the 1950s, the merger with Southalls and Arthur Berton. Dagger, and George Whittaker for Smith & Nephew (Overseas), proposed a merger with Partex, the principal South African rival in sanitary protection and cotton wool, but were turned down by the main board. However a Johannesburg surgical dressings company, Natpha (Pty) Ltd, using imported cloth, was acquired in 1961. The Physical Planning Act rendered labour-intensive operations in Johannesburg uneconomic and in 1964 Natpha was integrated with the Pinetown operation.

Table 10.2   Sales and profits of overseas subsidiaries in 1964 (£'000s)

	Sales	Profit
Canada	1 072	183
South Africa	1 613	218
Australia S&N	611	72
Camille	395	12
Wonthaggi	33	8
Everetts	66	10
New Zealand	365	34
India	302	12
Pakistan	14	−2
Malaya	155	0
Total overseas	4 626	487
Ireland S&N–Southalls	380	55
W. Cameron	20	1
Belgium S&N	155	9
Italy	80	−14
Scandinavia	50	−1
Total international	685	3
(Partnerships)	1 458	−36
Total net group	28 299	2 998
Internat. + overseas (%)	19	14.8
UK non-group exports	2 453	
Overseas markets sales (%)	32	

Note: some 1964 figures are estimates.

Sources: S.N. Steen to Sanaco Board, Minute no. 224, Meeting 13 July 1965, *SANACO in the 1960s*.

When Dagger retired in 1968, 61 per cent of all South African first aid dressings sold in the last two months of the year were Elastoplast. Personal hygiene products were late arrivals in Smith & Nephew South Africa's portfolio, only beginning to be added when the textile factory was manufacturing from 1960. They proved very profitable and brand shares continued to rise. Lil-lets, launched in 1966, 12 years after their arrival in the UK, achieved 39 per cent in 1978, 46 per cent 1979 and 48 per cent in 1985. Lasso industrial tapes were partly manufactured in South Africa between 1960 and 1966. In that last year Smith & Nephew were able to buy PVC so that the entire process could be undertaken locally. The management transition after Dagger was not altogether smooth. During their visit to South Africa in September 1969 Kenneth Kemp, Chief Executive, and Stephen Steen, Chairman, introduced a number of changes which they had not originally anticipated.[23]

Good industrial relations are notable for the attention they do not attract, although they are essential to a strong business performance. In South Africa they presented unique challenges to which Smith & Nephew rose. In June 1974 Smith & Nephew became the first company in South Africa to sign an agreement with a black unregistered trade union, the National Union of Textile Workers. The previous year Peter Masondo became the first black employee promoted to a supervisory position.

Staff turnover can often be a measure of personnel satisfaction with a company. Judged by this criterion the company performed well, for almost one-fifth of South African employees in 1977 had accumulated more than ten years' service. Smith & Nephew pioneered works committees and works councils to cover issues outside the union's sphere of interest. In particular council schemes for the education of employees' children and housing were implemented in 1979. Interest-free school loans for children of weekly paid employees were introduced (with nine months to repay) as were high school and tertiary education bursaries and loans. A 20-house scheme for black employees was also begun at KwaNdengezi.

H.N. Smith would have been delighted by the corporate encouragement of sport in South Africa. Dagger began annual presentations in 1960 to employees who finished in the Comrades' Marathon. Two years later Nivard Mthethwa, of the Gypsona Department, started the Smith & Nephew football club.

Canada in the 1960s and 1970s

The 1960s and 1970s saw the Canadian subsidiary transformed from an importer and distributor of products designed primarily for the UK market and packaged to resist the most adverse export conditions, to a manufacturer and marketer of products more appropriate to the largely US-influenced Canadian market.[24] Canadian manufacture began in a newly built factory/office complex on an 11-acre site acquired in 1960. As is frequently the case with manufacturing start-up, there were quality problems, many related to the extremes of the Montreal climate, unique among Smith & Nephew's production locations. The simultaneous change from over-engineered and expensive export packaging gave prestigious and influential surgeons a signal to impede change. For the sales force in particular at that time, local manufacture was therefore very much a mixed blessing.[25]

As the challenge of local production diminished, and product design and logistics were brought under local control, attention turned more and more to marketing. By the late 1960s and early 1970s the marketing organization was the principal influence on the Canadian company's activities, rather than production, as hitherto. Until 1958 all Canadian sales reps sold Elastoplast and Nivea, as well as the imported medical products, direct to hospitals. Thereafter two exclusively medical sales reps were appointed. Sales specialization was taken another step in the middle of the 1960s when all sales areas were divisionalized, with reps having exclusive consumer or medical territories.

During the 1960s and 1970s in both consumer first aid and in hospital products the principal competitor was Johnson & Johnson. Noxzema (Noxel Corp., now owned by Procter & Gamble) and Ponds (now owned by Lever Bros) were aggressive competitors to Nivea. As Hull-made OpSite became an important wound-care product in the 1980s, 3M and others joined the fray.

Like other advanced economies, the Canadian market environment changed considerably in the generation after 1950. Tender-bidding for hospital business was introduced along with government-sponsored medical care and required a transformation of selling techniques. Almost as radical, on the consumer side, self-service in drugstores and the rapid expansion of Smith & Nephew product distribution in non-pharmacy outlets, grocery and discount chains, required major packaging changes in Elastoplast and Nivea brands. How successful these alterations were may be judged by Elastoplast achieving a 50 per cent Canadian market share in the early 1980s.

With only Elastoplast, Gypsona and Nivea in its product mix during the 1960s, the Canadian company had one of the narrowest sales bases among Smith & Nephew's subsidiaries. Once local production and marketing were well established it was natural that remedying this weakness should become the subject of considerable effort. The Canadian company had been buying injection-moulded containers for Nivea and Atrixo since 1967. Acquisition of the supplier, St Lawrence Plastics, was therefore an obvious step.[26] Purchase of Toronto Plastics, a higher-technology injection moulder and extruder and its tool-making subsidiary, Star Tools Ltd, quickly followed in 1972. Propak Ltd, a thermoforming business, was the third acquisition in this group.

The oil crisis of 1974 created shortages of resins which provided unprecedented profit opportunities for the Canadian plastics conversion industry. Canadian GNP declined in 1974 and 1975 and customers soon reduced inventories. Plastics demand collapsed and the industry fell upon lean times. Smith & Nephew's enthusiasm for plastic conversion waned. St Lawrence Plastics was merged with Toronto Plastics and Propak was sold to its management.[27]

One other opportunity was taken by the Canadian company during the 1970s. In a marketing or business sense, Canada is one of the US contiguous states. US media, attitudes and people flow freely across the national border. Smith & Nephew's main competitors were all US companies, deriving great benefit from their US activities, as they operated in the awkward ribbon of the Canadian market 300 miles wide and 100 miles deep, holding a population the size of California's. Under the leadership of Don Seymour, the chairman of the Canadian company, in 1979 Anchor Continental Inc., based in South Carolina, was acquired as a first step towards expansion into the US. Anchor produced and marketed pressure-sensitive industrial tapes and plaster of Paris splinting bandages, activities in which Smith & Nephew had accumulated a wealth of experience.

THE UNITED STATES

For many years, the US was the main market in which Smith & Nephew would have liked a substantial presence but could not achieve one, though the priority attached to this aim varied over the years. Since 1936 L.O. Kojassar had been operating a subsidiary, Smith & Nephew Inc., in New York. The Smith & Nephew Board told H.N. to get rid of it during his visit in 1937/8 but he had not done so, despite the loss for the year ending 31 December 1937.[28] With the outbreak of war in Europe the American operation expanded. In 1940 activities grew to include San Fabrics Inc., also with Kojassar as president, which manufactured bandages for Smith & Nephew Inc.[30]

Smith & Nephew Inc. was charged almost 40 per cent more for cotton elastic bandages than they could be bought for from another supplier (Medical Fabrics Co., New Jersey) and more than twice as much in the case of plaster of Paris bandages. Excess profits tax was imposed retrospectively and Kojassar bowed out of Smith & Nephew Inc. in 1955 as Smith & Nephew bought the company. Wisby from Canada included the business in his sphere of management. The agency agreement for Gypsona with Institutional Products Corp., New York, begun in 1952, was wound up.[31]

The parent company felt that the agency business was not developing Smith & Nephew's interests in the American market as rapidly as the company wished. Purchase had been the only way to gain the necessary management freedom. The parent board rightly did not expect this company would produce any profits for several years. They knew successful investment in the US market was expensive and required long-term commitment.[31] But they were, with hindsight, unduly optimistic when they commented that Smith & Nephew Inc., New York 'should make an ever increasing contribution to the prosperity of the group'. Members of the Canadian company were enlisted to promote Gypsona sales and senior officers moved between Hull and New

York formulating promotional strategies.[32] Gypsona production began but quality problems arose and the company was wound up in 1957.[33] Thereafter the Bauer & Black division of the Kendall Company of Chicago manufactured Gypsona. Acquisition of the British hypodermic syringe maker Everett in 1954 brought into Smith & Nephew another US manufacturing subsidiary employing about 60 (1958) in Providence, Rhode Island. On behalf of Smith & Nephew, Wisby became president of this company as well in 1956 but not in any executive capacity. All correspondence on technical and management matters from the US subsidiary to Everett's in the UK was still channelled through Mr S.J. Everett personally.[34] Integration with Smith & Nephew operations as a whole was minimal.

Lacking the rights to manufacture Elastoplast and Nivea in the US, Smith & Nephew sales remained small until the product range could be extended. Exports to North America as a whole in the 1960s were also unspectacular because of Canadian production and very little market penetration in the US was achieved, as Table 10.3 shows. In 1968 a remedy was attempted when Smith & Nephew USA Inc., with offices on Madison Avenue, New York, was established to improve exports from Smith & Nephew.[35]

POORER COMMONWEALTH COUNTRIES AND BLACK AFRICA

In the late 1950s and early 1960s, the period of Prime Minister Harold Macmillan's 'Winds of Change' speech, Smith & Nephew were optimistic about the growth prospects of what were then called underdeveloped countries. Joint ventures and less than 100 per cent stakes in local companies were typically more acceptable politically to the host nation than fully owned susidiaries. In some cases early enthusiasm was excessive.

Smith & Nephew during 1958 acquired a small stake in India

> whose teeming millions and ever increasing population with its demand for improved standards of living will, in the not too distant future, be one of the largest consumers in the world.

Establishment of the plant near Bombay proceeded somewhat slowly, the first phase of manufacture of a small range of Smith & Nephew products by the Indian company being successfully accomplished in 1960. Like the Pakistan subsidiary, the Indian venture generated satisfactory but not outstanding expansion.

In conjunction with their local agents, Smith & Nephew acquired a controlling interest in Federal Industries Limited, Malaya, manufacturing surgical dressings and sanitary protection also in 1960. This company had only recently begun commercial production and did not become profitable until 1965.

Smith & Nephew (Nigeria) Limited was registered in 1960 as a means of exploring the possibilities for development in this newly independent country. A number of qualified technical executives were sent to study conditions and submit recommendations for expanding sales there. Africa was by far the largest regional market, as Table 10.3 shows, and therefore at first sight an obvious location for overseas subsidiaries.

Table 10.3   *Region and product distribution of Smith & Nephew export sales, 1962 (£'000)*

	W. Europe	N. America	Africa	S.E. Asia	Rest	Total
Elastoplast & medics	105.7	8.6	122	111.3	132.1	479.7
Tapes	133.9	0.2	1.7	1.8	16.7	154.3
Surgical dressings	39	–	201.5	44.3	92.4	377.2
Pharmaceut.	22.9	1.0	96	6.4	45.2	171.5
Hypodermics	62.2	8.9	9.7	11.2	25.3	117.3
Sanitary protection	16.8	–	37.2	16.1	3.7	73.8
Gypsona	39	–	122	30.3	25	216.3
Other products						521.7
Total non-group exports sales						1898.5

Source: *SANACO in the 1960s*, Smith & Nephew Board Report, File no. 13.

But extension of overseas investment to Africa proved problematic. Smith & Nephew reached a pioneering agreement in 1962 with the Ethiopian government to operate a small pharmaceutical unit in Addis Ababa. If successful, the plant was to be extended to meet more of Ethiopia's needs. Smith & Nephew's position in TB drugs and the prevalence of this illness in LDCs provided the industrial logic. Glaxo were originally also participating financially in the Ethiopian company but they withdrew early on and instead

Smith & Nephew developed the quality control system for Ethiopian production of penicillin and streptomycin.

Initially the Smith & Nephew board were almost euphoric:

> The happiest relations exist between us and the Ethiopian Government who share in the financial responsibility for the Company which is now in production and producing high-quality drugs.

The honeymoon was not to last. The chairman of the company, the Deputy Minister of Health in Ethiopia, proved uncooperative. So also did the Ethiopian government, which in 1964 demanded that the company produce antibiotics and Smith & Nephew traditional lines, as well as products for exports. The company was further expected to hold stocks of drugs to counter epidemics and could therefore expect violent fluctuations in activity. East European countries were tendering for tablet contracts in Ethiopia at prices which only covered the raw material contents of such tablets made in Ethiopia. By 1966 the lack of prospect for improving the Ethiopian company's poor profit performance forced Smith & Nephew's withdrawal from the project.[36] Smith & Nephew also abandoned drug synthesis the same year.

The second phase of Smith & Nephew investment in lower-income countries began in 1978 and centred on those with more dynamic growth records, Thailand, Indonesia and Mexico. These were all in regions where Smith & Nephew had not previously invested. The strategy was the culmination of the selling efforts of Stanley Clarke, who retired as deputy managing director of Smith & Nephew the following year. He had established Smith & Nephew in Japan, Taiwan, Indonesia and even made a start in communist China. The Australian company supervised a 50/50 venture with local partners in Indonesia, a new factory for dressings and Gypsona. Thailand had been a substantial market for many years and now high duties on imports justified a factory in Bangkok to manufacture and package first aid products, divided between 85 per cent Smith & Nephew ownership and a 15 per cent local stake. Both the Thai and Indonesian ventures quickly proved profitable.

In a break with established policy, acquisitions and joint ventures were also initiated in Central and South America in 1978. Although Wisby from Canada toured the areas in 1946 to consider sales and investment possibilities, Smith & Nephew then concluded that currency and political instability rendered commitments in the subcontinents too risky.[37] The Mexican acquisition, a 40 per cent share in Productos Higienicos Panamericanos S.A. de C.V. (Mexico), justified the policy switch by showing a 106 per cent increase in profitability in the first year (1979) and again in the second. Small joint ventures were also undertaken in Brazil and Venezuela.

CONTINENTAL EUROPE

Smith & Nephew acquired plants in Europe outside Britain almost entirely by purchase of less than 100 per cent of shares. They began buying only from the late 1950s, initially motivated by the desire to gain a foothold in the dynamic European Community in preparation for British entry, which Smith & Nephew enthusiastically supported. Smith & Nephew chose the joint venture route because they were then very conscious of their ignorance of the continental market, a problem compounded by the scarcity of European language competence in the company.[38]

An early and atypical European subsidiary was a fruit of the Southalls' merger. Smith & Nephew – Southalls (Ireland) Ltd – was fully integrated in 1959 and manufacturing facilities were expanded. Like the French subsidiary Fisch, in which a 50 per cent stake was bought in 1962, this was to prove a very successful geographical diversification.

Divisionalization of Smith & Nephew in 1960 facilitated the policy of gaining a European bridgehead. Division no. 5 was intended to develop interests on the continent, but Treasury restrictions on remittances of substantial sums to a foreign country inhibited the strategy. The board told shareholders in 1961:

> the entry of your Company into the European Common Market, without any previous manufacturing footholds having been obtained in the six countries, may well present problems of considerable magnitude which are difficult to assess at the present time. Politicians who support our entry have been at pains to point out the broadening of our present market of 50 million people to a total of 200 million people but do not emphasize the opening up of the British Market to Western European manufacturers, from which they have been to some extent excluded by duties, when free entry is established.

When General de Gaulle vetoed British membership of the Common Market in 1963, the company was disappointed but not dispirited. Smith & Nephew had begun preparing the ground for later entry by establishing either jointly or wholly owned companies with manufacturing facilities in Belgium, Denmark, France, Italy and Spain. Smith & Nephew Iberica S.A. was formed in partnership with Dr Pedro Junyent's company to manufacture plaster of Paris (the Gypsona process using solvents) and adhesive bandages. A Scandinavian subsidiary based near Copenhagen was formed the previous year, when the French investment was also made. Mr T.L. Whittaker, a director of the parent board with wide marketing experience, was appointed to give special attention to the development of the European market.[39] Judging by the profits achieved (Table 10.2), this attention was very necessary.

The second veto, on Prime Minister Harold Wilson's attempt at entry in 1967, was less traumatic. Effects of student riots, strikes and French economic difficulties carried severe consequences for French profits in 1968, but indirectly eased Britain's path by influencing the outcome of the referendum the following year. The Heath–Pompidou rapprochement of May 1971 opened the door to phased British membership of the European Community.

By the 1970s, when economic conditions in the UK were not helpful, the new European subsidiaries flourished. In 1976 companies in Scandinavia, France, Belgium, Spain and Italy were making consistently more important contributions to the company, generating sales of £21m and a satisfactory return on capital employed. Scandinavian operations were rationalized as Smith & Nephew A/S in Copenhagen, and cosmetics interests were eliminated in France and Italy.

Laboratoires Fisch S.A. became a wholly owned subsidiary at the beginning of the 1980s. As shown in Chapter 4, this company offers an important parallel to Smith & Nephew for they both acquired the Lohmann/Eichengrun licences at the beginning of the 1930s for their respective national and empire markets. The French company invented an alternative method to the German Cellona/Gypsona process. Fisch brought out Platrix 1 in 1952, followed by Platrix 2 five years later. Fisch introduced a third method of making plaster of Paris bandages, 'conversion', with Unitex in 1966. This method used the plaster of Paris converted to plaster on the dressing and not the plaster with solvent or the aqueous manufacturing process. Fisch terminated the contract with Lohmann in 1962, and developed European exports together with contacts with Smith & Nephew. Jean-Paul Fisch, son of the founder, employed P. Bouclier in 1969 to find a new technique of solvent recovery by condensation and not by charcoal. This technique raised productivity and in 1971 was embodied in a new machine FAS, and in 1975 FAT, at the Fisch plant, Vibraye. The following year a similar machine was sold to Smith & Nephew and later in 1979 a smaller one went to Saniteks.

CONCLUSION

Close cultural, economic and political links determined that Smith & Nephew's early overseas subsidiaries would be in larger English-speaking territories, the Commonwealth and to a much lesser extent, the US.[40] These were sales branches, extending into manufacturing plants from 1955. The second phase of expansion occurred at the beginning of the 1960s in continental Europe, and took the form of acquisitions of shares in established health care firms. The third phase was a move into South-East Asia and Latin America at the end of the 1970s. Since all these areas were on average growing faster than the British economy, presences in them ensured that they would account for a rising proportion of Smith & Nephew sales and provide a valuable cushion against periods of difficulty in the domestic economy, such as the 1970s. This pattern of expansion Smith & Nephew shared with other large UK companies. Smith & Nephew was distinguished however both by success, and by comparatively small company size at the time of the initial investments.[41]

NOTES

1. 'Meeting HN', *Sanaco News*, 1954 pp. 16–18; 'Our Companies Overseas – no. 2 Canada', *Sanaco News*, 1959, pp. 18–19.
2. 'Recollections of S Daly', *S & N Reporter*, 1967. H.N. Smith had appointed Thomas Reid of Montreal as his attorney in 1911. *S5 Copy Deeds 1911*, Smith & Nephew Archives, Hull.
3. *Agreement between H.N. Smith (161 Westbourne Avenue Hull) on behalf of Smith & Nephew and Downs Brothers of Wellington New Zealand*, giving sole agency to Downs of dressings etc. in New Zealand, 24 June 1909, S3, Smith & Nephew Archives, Hull.
4. *Chronology of Smith & Nephew Activities in Canada*, p. 1 S & N, Montreal.
5. Appointed sales manager in 1931 and later sales director, Medhurst organized the conversion of the company into a branded lines organization, both at home and abroad. From 1938 until 1945 he was chairman of the Surgical Dressings Manufacturers' Association. His services to the nation during this difficult time were recognized by the award of an MBE. He was the first chairman of Smith & Nephew Ltd, and both his sons, John and Patrick, worked for the firm. 'SANACO Board Changes', *Smith & Nephew Reporter*, January–February 1961.
6. 'Our Companies Overseas – no. 2 Canada', *Sanaco News*, 1959, pp. 18–19. Not until four years after he sailed was he 'forgiven' the $150 fare for which he had received an advance.
7. This lack of profitability of interwar overseas investment is widely observed for other British companies. See Jones (1986).
8. *Canadian Pharmaceutical Journal*, 15 June 1942, p. 76; *Minutes of Smith & Nephew Canada*, 22 February 1940.
9. *The History of Smith & Nephew in South Africa*, 1981? Natal.
10. *Chronology of Smith & Nephew South Africa*, 1991 p. 2.
11. 'Our Companies Overseas – no. 1 New Zealand', *Sanaco News*, 1959 pp. 17–18.
12. *Smith & Nephew Source* (Canada), Spring 1989, p. 8.
13. F.M. Medhurst, *Australia*, SANACO Board Memo., 22 December 1955, Smith & Nephew, London.
14. Formerly a member of the London Philharmonic Orchestra and professor of cello at the New South Wales State Conservatorium of Music in Australia, Fyfe joined Smith & Nephew as a trainee in 1946, returning to his home country in 1947 as Australian representative, and taking charge of the Australian company when it was formed in June 1950. See J.A. Thompson, 'Our Companies Overseas – no. 4 Australia', *Sanaco News*, Christmas 1959, pp. 19–20.
15. *Minutes of Board of Directors Smith & Nephew Canada*, 27 September 1951, p. 142, Montreal.
16. Tapes, textiles and syringes were still sold through agencies.
17. G. Whittaker, *A Handful of Shale*, 1979, unpublished ms, p. 198.
18. B.G. Hayes, *History of Smith & Nephew Australian Group*, typescript, 1991, pp. 3–4.
19. *Australia: Acquisition Vinyl Clad Pty Ltd*, Memo from S.J. Clarke and K.R. Kemp to Sanaco Management Committee, 1 October 1970, Smith & Nephew Archives, London.

20. *Smith & Nephew Annual Report 1977.*
21. Hayes, op cit., note 18, pp. 12–14.
22. Statement to Shareholders, Smith & Nephew Associated Companies Ltd, 21 February 1962.
23. *South Africa–Management*, SMC Agenda Item 5c, Meeting 7, October 1969, Smith & Nephew Archives, London
24. Nivea had been produced in Toronto before the acquisition of Herts Pharmaceuticals by Smith & Nephew. But until the transfer to the new factory at Lachine, Nivea manufacture remained a distant activity for Smith & Nephew personnel.
25. Martin Burke, *Notes on Smith & Nephew Inc* (Canada), 1991. Terry Winter letter to author, 20 October 1991.
26. *St Lawrence Plastics–Canada*, Smith & Nephew (Overseas), Minute no. 576/2 SANACO Board Meeting, 5 June 1970, Smith & Nephew Archives, London.
27. *Minutes of Shareholders' AGM Smith & Nephew Plastics Canada* 10 April 1976, p. 104, Montreal; Terry Winter letter to author, 20 October 1991.
28. Kojassar audit 18 January 1938, Smith & Nephew, Montreal; Smith & Nephew Minute Book 1937/8, London.
29. L.O. Kojassar sworn statement 20 September 1956, Smith & Nephew Archives, Montreal.
30. Agreement with Institutional Products Corp., 11 June 1952; Smith & Nephew Inc. to John W. Jackson, 27 April 1955, Smith & Nephew Archives, Montreal.
31. *Smith & Nephew Annual Report 1956.*
32. 'Welcome to Smith & Nephew Inc.', *Sanaco News*, Autumn 1955, p. 23.
33. *Chronology of Smith & Nephew activities in Canada* p. 2, Smith & Nephew Archives, Montreal.
34. Meeting of Directors of Everett's Products Inc., 25 October 1956; Wisby to Christine Johnson, *Sanaco News* Editor, 9 January 1958, Smith & Nephew, Montreal.
35. Smith & Nephew Canada Minute Book, p. 246.
36. *Ethiopia* minute no. 10 SANACO Board Meeting, 9 October 1963; Sanaco Executive Committee report to SANACO Board, 10 November 1964, Smith & Nephew Archives, London.
37. Kenneth Kemp interview, 1990; Smith & Nephew Canada Minute Book, 29 March 1946, p. 120.
38. Kenneth Kemp interview, 1990.
39. T.L. Whittaker came to Smith & Nephew in 1947 as general sales manager from Griffith Hughes and, before that, from Triumph Engineering.
40. Stephen Nicholas shows that a common language was a significant predictor of the destination of all UK direct investment overseas from 1870–1939. He also identifies the 'bunching' of the timing of foreign direct investment which is a clear feature of Smith & Nephew's history. See Nicholas (1991).
41. Smith & Nephew ranked 164th by capital employed among the *Times 300 Largest Industrial Companies* in 1964/5. Geoffrey Jones's summary of the historical pattern of British multinational corporate development shows Smith & Nephew to have been entirely typical of other much larger British companies. See Jones (1986).

11.   Finance, management and philanthropy

As Smith & Nephew expanded overseas and at home, management were obliged to grapple with problems of information, control and policy formation that were a side-effect of greater corporate size. New management structures and procedures were adopted and modified as experience accumulated and the business environment changed. Financial policy was a key concern, for it governed the ability to grow by acquiring other businesses or by expansion of existing products, and also the stock market value of the firm. Management continually monitored the share price, especially after the 1968 Unilever takeover attempt. Though occupied with cost control and incentive schemes, management did not forget the wider interests of the company's founders, donating increasing sums to the Smith & Nephew Foundation.

MANAGEMENT AND MANAGEMENT STRUCTURE IN THE 1950s AND 1960s

Growth after the Second World War was achieved more by new capital and by greater employee skills than by higher numbers of workers. Employment trends were rather similar to those of British manufacturing as a whole, peaking in 1974 (the year of the world oil crisis) at over 16 000, before declining to a trough in the recession year of 1982 (Figure 11.1).[1] Smith & Nephew employed more people 18 years earlier than in 1982. Even after the upward march was resumed, there were fewer jobs in 1990 than in 1970. Productivity growth driven by investment and embodying new technologies ensured that fewer and fewer people could manufacture more and more. Sales per employee in 1990 were more than 25 times higher than in 1961, whereas the retail price index had risen only 10 times between these years.[2]

Despite the legal name, SANACO (Smith & Nephew Associated Companies), in the 1950s and 1960s the management structure was not that of a true holding company.[3] The SANACO board allocated capital by giving or withholding approval for constituent company projects, although subsidiaries maintained a good deal of investment autonomy if they could generate their own cash. Each was visited annually by the chief executive, who checked

Figure 11.1   Employment, 1961–90

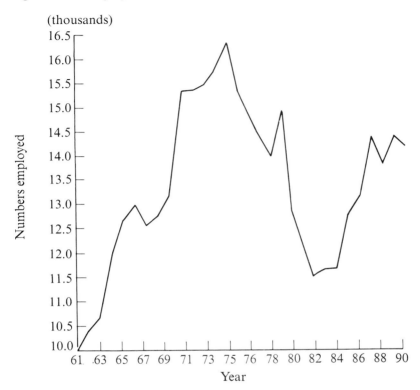

and approved their budget. As the scale of operations increased, the travelling became impossibly time-consuming and the post of deputy chief executive was created to share the burden.[4]

On the other hand, like a holding company, Smith & Nephew employed few headquarters staff, except for accountants, in marked contrast to Johnson & Johnson, an otherwise comparable (but larger) US corporation. Temple Place, the head office to which Smith & Nephew moved in 1962, could only accommodate 32 officers in total.[5] The choice of location was deliberate, intended to foster corporate decentralization. At the time of the search for a new head office, Smith & Nephew was arguably anyway too small to justify employment of many specialized headquarters staff. There was then no finance director, only a chief accountant. Some support services could be and were bought in when required, rather than constituting a permanent presence at head office. Even at the time of writing this is true of legal services. Research by contrast was institutionalized in Smith & Nephew with the acquisition of Herts in 1951 (Chapter 9) and a computer services bureau was operated early in the development of commercial mainframes (Chapter 8).

The board primarily monitored the financial consequences of divisional strategies, although Chairman George Leavey was concerned to take a view on more general policy.[6] Dominated by heads of operational divisions, the composition of the executive committee and of the board meant that policy formation might take second place to a contest for resources between different branches of the company during the late 1950s and early 1960s. In these years board members met at a London hotel on the Monday evening before the board meeting the next morning, discussing tomorrow's issues in an informal fashion, often until midnight.[7] Not surprisingly the official board minutes are rather uninformative about the formation of policy and the background to decisions. The SANACO executive committee (SEC) was established in 1954, and a special sales and marketing company was created at the same time. Research and Engineering were now also separate companies (Figure 11.2). Competition became more intense as import controls were abolished, overseas competitors recovered from the war and legislation, such as the 1956 Restrictive Trade Practices Act, became unfavourable to agreements limiting competition.[8]

By the beginning of the 1960s the board was larger than anybody thought ideal because inevitably the merger with Southalls and Arthur Berton's had raised the number of directors. Some senior long-serving Smith & Nephew directors left the board, having reached retirement age.[9] Five of the six new directors were managing directors of major subsidiaries. The sixth was H.N.'s daughter, Mrs Margaret Charlton, the first, and until December 1991 the only, lady ever on the Smith & Nephew board (although Southalls could boast a female director a generation earlier – see Chapter 5).[10]

Smith & Nephew in 1960 was divided into five divisions: medical products; personal hygiene and toiletries; plastics and tapes; textiles and clothing; and overseas. A change in management style is apparent, with a stronger emphasis on reports, documentation, and five-year plans and projections. The first corporate plan emerged in 1961, running to 109 pages. This document identified the need for growth overseas, for research and for new products, such as disposables. In the concern to restructure management organization Smith & Nephew was in advance of some other larger British companies in related fields.[11]

Three more new appointees, including Kenneth Kemp, joined the board in 1962. Under George Leavey's chairmanship a triumvirate of George Whittaker (a textile aficionado who entered from Glen Mills), Stephen Steen (a marketing-oriented consumer products man who joined Smith & Nephew with the acquisition of Arthur Berton) and Leslie Long (whose roots were in Hull's medical products) formed policy, not always harmoniously.[12] Alex Hastilow

Figure 11.2   Operating company relations and principal products, 1954

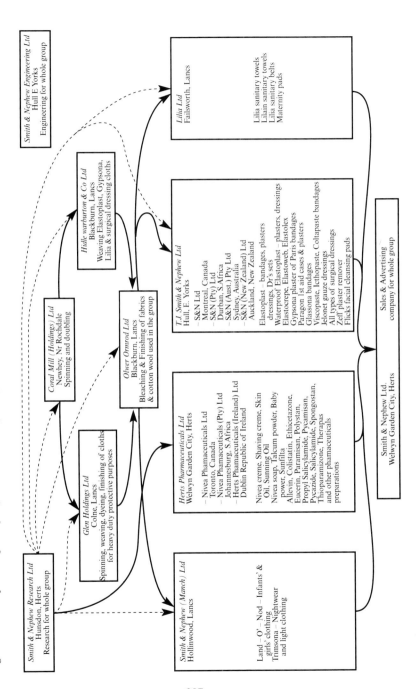

Smith & Nephew Engineering Ltd
Hull E Yorks
Engineering for whole group

Smith & Nephew Research Ltd
Hunsdon, Herts
Research for whole group

Coral Mill (Holdings) Ltd
Newhey, Nr Rochdale
Spinning and doubling

Hidle warburton & Co Ltd
Blackburn, Lancs
Weaving Elastoplast, Gypsona,
Lilia & surgical dressing cloths

Lilia Ltd
Failsworth, Lancs

Lilia sanitary towels
Lilain sanitary towels
Lilia sanitary belts
Maternity pads

Glen Holdings Ltd
Colne, Lancs
Spinning, weaving, dyeing, finishing of cloths
for heavy duty protective purposes

Olwer Ormrod Ltd
Blackburn, Lancs
Bleaching & Finishing of fabrics
& cotton wool used in the group

T.J. Smith & Nephew Ltd
Hull, E. Yorks

– S&N Ltd
  Montreal, Canada
– S&N (Pty) Ltd
  Durban, S. Africa
– S&N (Aust.) Pty Ltd
  Sydney, Australia
– S&N (New Zealand) Ltd
  Auckland, New Zealand

Elastoplast – bandages, plasters
  dressings, Dr's sets
Waterproof Elastoplast – plasters, dressings
Elastocrepe, Elastoweb, Elastolex
Gypsona plaster of Paris bandages
Paragon 1st aid cases & plasters
Giassona bandages
Viscopaste, Icthopaste, Coltapaste bandages
Jelonet gauze dressings
All types of surgical dressings
Zeff plaster remover
Flicks facial cleansing pads

Herts Pharmaceuticals Ltd
Welwyn Garden City, Herts

– Nivea Pharmaceuticals Ltd
  Toronto, Canada
– Nivea Pharmaceuticals (Pty) Ltd
  Johannesburg, S. Africa
– Herts Pharmaceuticals (Ireland) Ltd
  Dublin Republic of Ireland

Nivea creme, Shaving creme, Skin
Oil, Sunning Oil
Nivea soap, Talcum powder, Baby
  power, Sunfilta
Allevin, Colistatin, Ethicetazone,
Eucerin, Paramisan, Polystan,
Propyl Salicylamide, Pycamisan.
Pycazide, Salicylamide, Spongostan,
Thoparamizone, Therapas
and other pharmaceuticals
preparations

Smith & Nephew (Manch) Ltd
Hollinwood, Lancs

Land – O' – Nod – Infants' &
  girls' clothing
Trimsona – Nightwear
  and light clothing

Smith & Nephew Ltd.
Welwyn Garden City, Herts

Sales & Advertising
company for whole group

207

(from Southalls) took over as chairman when Mr Leavey retired in 1962.[13] Mr Hastilow was already past retirement age and was a stop-gap.[14] Under the executive triumvirate were three separate executive boards. George Whittaker, senior deputy chairman, chaired the board for UK operations, Steen chaired that for the rest of Europe and Long, that for Commonwealth and other overseas companies. The executive committee came to be a replica of the board except for the non-executive directors, so that board meetings continued to be formalities, the real decisions being taken elsewhere.

Each director was asked to write down how he thought the company should develop and Kenneth Kemp was given the task of synthesizing the contributions. The resulting 1964 corporate plan grouped UK product sales into three, sometimes surprising, categories by growth performance: group 1, expanding at the same rate as population, included Elastoplast, Gypsona and feminine hygiene; group 2, showing a moderate rate of growth, consisted of disposables, industrial tapes and pharmaceuticals; and group 3, products with a rapid expansion of demand, were plastics, textiles (denims, surgical dressings and cotton wool), toiletries and baby products.[15] Viewed from the perspective of developed market economies as a whole, pharmaceuticals were growing and textiles contracting. That Smith & Nephew deviated from this pattern reflects the relative managerial and investment effort that the executive committee allocated between the company's divisions. They did so because they regarded textiles as essential to their medical products. High-quality stretchable fabric for Elastoplast was difficult to make and to buy in but the material was essential and so the company was obliged to undertake the business itself.[16] Similar difficulties with the manufacture of substrate for Gypsona precluded purchase from other textile companies.

Research expenditure was set at 9 per cent of net profit. Although in comparison with large British companies, this was a low ratio of R & D to profit, the report indicated that Smith & Nephew might be unable to spend that sum.[17] Hence there was a need to enter new fields of activity. Unless the traumatic effect on the board of the Drazine incident is recalled (Chapter 9), the conclusion sounds odd against the background of corporate withdrawal from drug synthesis. It gave rise to one of the questions posed in the document: what direction should the research programme take? The other questions raised concerned the balance of effort between products and between geographical markets, and how much should be borrowed for diversification.[18]

Substantial sums were expected to be available for new investment over and above the requirements of the operating companies. Capital invested in textiles was now fully employed and boosting profits. Linear programming was improving resource allocation in denim, surgical dressings, cotton wool and blankets. Although the 1964 plan did not say so, improvements appeared to be much needed: the 8.4 per cent return on capital in textiles at the end of 1964 was one-third of that earned in the medical and toiletries division and less than one half of plastics (and half the group average). Four years later the net profit/turnover ratio in textiles was 9 per cent compared with a company average of 12.4 per cent.[19] Since the bulk of output was used within the company, textile profitability depended in part upon the transfer prices determined by company management. If these prices were unduly low then the true return in textiles would have been understated, as well as an insufficient incentive provided for medical dressings to economize on textile inputs.

Because division 2 (medical and plastics) was too large and diverse,[20] in 1967 it was split into four components: Hull (tapes, plastics, established branded goods), Mitcham (syringes, needles etc.) Scottish (Wallace Cameron), and Pharmaceuticals. Research and development was linked to Pharmaceuticals under D.E. Seymour.

After the 1964 corporate planning exercise, senior management structure and personnel were reviewed.[21] The upshot was a proposal to reduce SANACO board membership to between eight and 11, including president and chairman, by at the latest mid-1972. By that year the board was expected to consist of six executive directors and two non-executives plus the chairman; actually the goal was achieved in 1974. Heads of divisions were not necessarily to be board members.[22] A management committee of all SANACO executive directors was to meet at least once a quarter under Kenneth Kemp's chairmanship to review the company's activities, especially long term policy plans.

Stephen Steen replaced Hastilow as chairman in 1968 and Kemp became chief executive. Four years later Kenneth Bradshaw stepped into the chief executive's shoes and Kemp became executive deputy chairman. Stanley Clarke and Don Seymour were appointed deputy chief executives, a team that worked together well, especially in comparison with the earlier triumvirate.

Professionalization of top management continued during the 1960s when Smith & Nephew began sending executives to business schools. A second element was annual seminars from 1969 for board directors and 20 or so other senior divisional directors. These were run in a hotel at Chester by Professor Roland Smith of University of Manchester Institute of Science and Technology.

METHODS OF FINANCE

Top management's principal means of control was exercised through the flow of funds. These originated with sales revenue, from which production costs,

costs of borrowing, taxation and depreciation were subtracted, to leave net profits. A key Smith & Nephew management target became the ratio of profit to assets employed. Often known as 'Mr Kemp's 20 per cent', this figure referred only to a balanced project; on machinery the target was 33 per cent after depreciation. A simple objective, it was more easily understood than discounted cash flow returns, a technique used by the divisions in the 1960s but not then employed at board level. The board decided what proportion of profits to pay to shareholders as dividends and what to retain for new investment. Generally the 'dividend cover' was two or three (a payout ratio of one-half to one-third). The sum of retained profits and depreciation is generally called 'cash flow'. When insufficient cash was generated within the business for projected investment, external funds had to be raised, in the form of bank overdrafts, loans from consortia or from the stock market, or new shareholder capital, equity. Each source came at a different price and was most suitable for a different purpose.

Bank loans were the most flexible form of finance. Smith & Nephew's loans were originally overdrafts with the National Provincial Bank, later part of National Westminster. In 1962 loans were taken from the Royal Bank of Canada and later from Chase Manhattan. The profitable 1950s were marked by scrip issues and the less profitable 1960s by rights issues. The 200 per cent scrip issue in 1953 affected the 1954 accounts, the 50 per cent scrip issue in 1959, a one for two capitalization of reserves, showed up in the accounts for 1960. Scrip issues are expansions of the nominal capital of the company by proportionately distributing new shares to existing shareholders. The tactic may be employed to prevent share prices rising too high or it may be a means of popularizing a share, as Smith & Nephew management noted. When offered what looks like a free share, a considerable proportion of existing shareholders will give it to someone else. A larger number of shareholders means that at any time there are more likely to be buyers and sellers in the market, and that in turn makes Smith & Nephew shares more attractive (because more liquid) assets to hold. If they are more liquid, other things being equal, they will fetch higher prices. At the beginning of the 1980s, in three consecutive years, one for eight scrip issues were made with the annual results. By 1983 the greater marketability of the shares had attracted more than 24 000 investors. A decade later the number had more than doubled, if ownership through PEPs is included.

Unlike scrip, rights issues are means of raising fresh capital by giving existing shareholders the right to buy new shares at a pre-set price (also in a given proportion). Because there are markets in these rights, in effect any member of the public can subscribe the new capital. In 1961 Smith & Nephew made a one for five rights issue, in 1962 a one for three, in 1964 a one for four and in 1970 a one for six issue. The 1961 issue largely financed investment in Associated Tissues, a paper-making company, a joint venture with Wiggins Teape Ltd. It was to lead Smith & Nephew into a partnership in British Tissues, then the third largest soft tissue manufacturer in Britain.

More equity capital allows faster expansion but also dilutes the profit available for existing shareholders. Shareholders bear the risk of not receiving any income, although in fact Smith & Nephew's board ensured that the dividend stream was steady. Retained profits in principle were the buffer but in practice they grew steadily in the postwar period excepting only two years. Even had they proved inadequate, the company would not have been in terminal difficulties had it been forced to cut dividends.

In principle matters could be different with loan capital, where a company undertakes a contractual obligation to pay interest. The advantage is that such capital can be employed for faster expansion without extending the capital base on which dividends are payable. Moreover taxation was levied after the payment of interest and so the higher the rate of tax on profits, the greater the incentive to employ loans rather than equity finance. Smith & Nephew began to borrow from the market on a considerable scale for the first time in 1971. £7.368m (£7.5m less the cost of underwriting, now repaid) was received from Rothschild on 16 April, raised from loan stock. The £3m overdraft with the bankers National Westminster was eliminated and the balance temporarily invested at about 7 per cent.[23] Every shareholder had the right to subscribe £1 for every 19 shares, with interest payable at 8 per cent.

There is an upper limit beyond which it is unwise to raise the ratio of borrowing to equity (gearing); possible fluctuations in profits potentially render the firm unable to meet its debt service obligations. Precisely what that ratio is depends on the industry demand and the nature of the competition. Probably a more accurate gearing index is the ratio of profits to interest charges, which for Smith & Nephew since 1986 has indicated an ample cover of between eight and 17 times.

GROWTH STRATEGY

Finance is only a means of implementing a business strategy, which of course has financial implications. Smith & Nephew established some profitable market positions but they did not yield the growth rate to which the company aspired. Other products were needed that would achieve the necessary growth either through greater market penetration or by expanding sales along with a dynamic market. When the stock market looked on Smith & Nephew favourably, funds could be raised cheaply and the time was ripe for acquisitions, usually enterprises without access to the stock exchange, but with high earnings ratios. Integration of large acquisitions might then take some time, during which stock market favour would be lost, even though the process was necessary to long-term growth.

Cash flow from depreciation and retained profits in 1963 were quite sufficient to finance the normal growth of Smith & Nephew's business. But the rate of acquisition of small businesses was expected to create a £0.5m overdraft by the end of the year, increasing at an annual rate of £1m, with a considerably larger overdraft during the summer, when seasonal demands were at their height. Major acquisitions could be dealt with by cash raised specially for the purpose. Purchase of small companies presented difficulties. In general, acquisitions could not be financed by the issue of SANACO shares in place of cash because they gave a yield of 3 per cent whereas the acquired businesses had earnings yields of around 15 to 20 per cent.[24] Any exchange of shares would therefore cut the vendors' income. Many of Smith & Nephew's acquisitions bought at high earnings ratios were only available because the vendor was in a dangerous tax position or under threat of death duties and one of his main objectives was to liberate capital from his business by selling for cash.

Given unchanged policy on acquisitions and profitability, the board was obliged to decide between raising long-term finance immediately for future use or financing acquisitions on overdraft and raising the long-term money later. Choosing between these alternatives required a forecast of future interest rates and of government policy. A Labour government in 1964 was a possibility and therefore so was the introduction of capital controls within little more than a year. At the time of the last rights issue in 1961, Smith & Nephew had been able to borrow money at 4 per cent and lend it at 7 per cent while the funds were not being used for investment.[25] The likelihood was that long-term rates were going to rise and in 1963 short-term money could only be invested at around 4 per cent. Another rights issue so soon was likely to damage the company's reputation in the City, where it was already being criticized for being unable to generate growth from existing profits. The recommendation was that any capital raised immediately should be in the form of a loan, either from the public or from a consortium. This financial advice was ignored and fresh equity capital was raised. To the extent that the new issue lowered the share price relative to what it would have been, Smith & Nephew became more vulnerable to a hostile takeover bid.

After the failure of the Unilever bid, SANACO's 1969 price–earnings ratio was high at 19.5 relative to other shares. The timing therefore was right for using SANACO paper for acquisitions. Corporate eyes were directed to food/ household consumer products in the UK. Jeyes and Newton Chambers were identified as natural purchases, with synergy in the region of £0.75m expected.[26]

Acquisition policy, as well as the distribution of investment between established divisions and subsidiaries, raised a question to which Smith & Nephew gave different answers in the years after 1945 – which market was the company in? During the 1960s confidence in the ability of management to run conglomerates of unrelated products was greater than in the 1980s. Smith & Nephew never became a conglomerate but did accept a broader definition of its areas of expertise than the company does now. Growth could be sought either through products complementary with production technology and inputs, a direction that led to textile-related markets like carpets, or to plastics. Alternatively expansion could be pursued through new products in the market in which Smith & Nephew was established – health care.

Either way attention needed to be given to promising new developments that Smith & Nephew might utilize. In health care, up to a point, good marketing provided information about what was needed and what ideas practitioners had come up with. A complementary strategy was a 'travelling circus', like Allen & Hanbury's in the later 1950s, which specifically looked for products and ideas of potential commercial importance in universities and abroad.[27] H.N. Smith had performed this function before the Second World War and Seymour's identification of Hydron (Chapter 9) fits into this category. But the function was never formalized in Smith & Nephew and anyway firms capable of rapid 'organic' growth needed to generate innovations internally on a considerable scale. From time to time stockbrokers' assessments made disparaging references to Smith & Nephew's policy of growth by acquisition and licensing rather than by internal expansion.

Stockbrokers' judgements of the company were considered carefully because of their potential impact on share prices. In the early 1960s some brokers concluded that Smith & Nephew was no longer a growth company and that the shares should be sold. By 1964 shares were valued on a dividend yield of over 4 per cent compared with under 3 per cent a year or so earlier.[28] Lyster (originally Southalls' chief accountant) calculated annual indices of Smith & Nephew's dividends, earnings and earnings on capital for the period 1953–63. Since 1948, dividends had increased by five times but profits had not even doubled, his figures showed. Earnings on capital had declined from an average of 23 per cent in 1953–58 to an average of 19 per cent in 1959–63.[29] Although the numbers are slightly different, the trend is confirmed by the official accounts (Table 11.1 and Figure 11.3). Some temporary decline might be expected during the rationalization following the Southalls and Berton merger and during the concentration of textile production at Brierfield. But the persistence of the lower return during the early 1960s was the effect of textile investment. The informal method of communicating these rather fundamental facts (a letter to the chairman) indicates an idiosyncratic style of management that could allow such an investment strategy.

A stockbroker's circular calculated from published accounts Smith & Nephew's profits on sales (at the time the company did not publish sales figures

Table 11.1 Profitability and payouts in the 1950s

	1951 £'000s *($'000s)	1952** £'000s ($'000s)	1953 £'000s ($'000s)	1954 £'000s ($'000s)	1955 £'000s ($'000s)	1956 £'000s ($'000s)	1957 £'000s ($'000s)	1958 £'000s ($'000s)	1959 £'000s ($'000s)	1960 £'000s ($'000s)
Working capital (Total net assets)	4 554 (12 750)	4 240 (11 870)	5 095 (14 270)	6 025 (16 870)	6 576 (18 410)	7 231 (20 250)	7 592 (21 260)	11 316 (31 680)	12 159 (34 045)	13 120 (36 736)
Group profit % to working capital	30%	8%	21%	19%	20%	19%	20%	17%	18%	18%
Gross revenue (profit)	1 357 (3 800)	343 (960)	1 051 (2 943)	1 166 (3 265)	1 313 (3 676)	1 408 (3 942)	1 496 (4 189)	1 949 (5 457)	2 150 (6 020)	2 307 (6 460)
Net profit (after tax etc)	530 (1 484)	147 (412)	417 (1 168)	502 (1 406)	624 (1 747)	534 (1 495)	618 (1 730)	971 (2 719)	1 130 (3 164)	1 130 (3 164)
Ordinary shares*										
Earnings % (gross)	37.1%	11.6%	28.6%	27.6%	32.2%	31.6%	30.3%	28.2%	30.6%	30.8%
Earnings per share, in pence, gross	17.81	5.61	13.73	13.25	15.46	15.17	14.54	13.54	14.69	14.78
Dividend % (gross)	5.5	5.5	7.4	8.0	8.3†	8.3	9.0	10.4	11.8	12.5
Dividend per share, in pence, gross	2.64	2.64	3.55	3.84	3.98‡	3.98	4.32	4.99	5.66	6.00
Retention ratio	0.43	0.43	0.71	0.70	0.74	0.68	0.48	0.62	0.61	0.58

* Earnings and dividend calculations adjusted to end 1960 issued capital following 200% scrip issue in 1953 and 50% scrip issue in 1959.
** In this year – when for the first time the steady growth of profits was halted – it was entirely due to the sudden and serious drop in the international value of cotton. The management decided to face the position in a complete way by writing down the value of stocks of everything they made which contained cotton, by writing off all forward positions then open. The total cost of facing this issue was over £500 000 which was met out of current profits and without any reduction in the ordinary dividend. Its benefits assisted the group in subsequent years.
† Plus 1.7% centenary bonus, tax-free.
‡ Plus 0.82d. per share, centenary bonus, tax-free.

Source: Smith & Nephew Archives, London.

Figure 11.3   Rate of return on equity capital, 1961–90 (%)

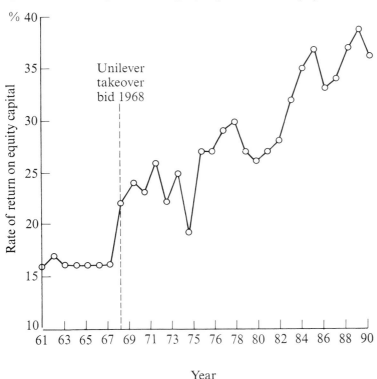

Year

but did give percentage variations). The index showed a steady decline from 1960 to the last available figure in the first half of 1964. In response to the broker's analysis, Kemp showed that the total investment funds spent by Smith & Nephew in the previous five years (£8.842m) increased profits by £1.618m, yielding a return of 18.3 per cent before depreciation.

Lyster maintained that much of this success came from good finance (for which Kenneth Kemp deserved credit). Smith & Nephew raised money on the stock exchange and the company gained from the difference between say the 5 per cent which the money cost and the 18.3 per cent earned on it. Kemp's figures showed that the new money earned a similar return to existing capital. But this return was still lower than previously and that was why Smith & Nephew's shares were trading at lower prices. Lyster added that the decline in share prices might have been greater had prices not been supported by a public unable to analyse the figures, looking merely at the record of dividend increase. He might have noted as well that there was no tax plan-

ning in Smith & Nephew before Kemp, and that Kemp's work raised after-
tax returns.

Ironically Lyster retired the year the tendency he identified, a low rate of
return on capital, was reversed; the year of the Unilever bid. But this indicator was not necessarily the right one, for the stock market took an increasingly favourable view of Smith & Nephew's prospects from 1964. The price–
earnings ratio showed a rising trend, peaking with the Unilever bid but
remaining well above 1964 levels until the oil crisis of 1973/4 (Figure 11.4).

Figure 11.4   Price–earnings ratio and dividend yield, 1964–91

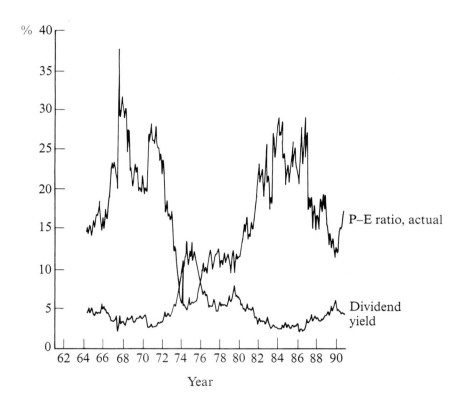

Source: Datastream

THE UNILEVER TAKEOVER BID

Share prices mattered to management for they determined whether another company might try to buy the business and, by running it more efficiently, raise the stock market value so as to reap a capital gain. After stock exchange hours on 16 April 1968, Lazard Bros announced to the press that, on behalf of Unilever, offers were to be made to acquire the whole of the issued capital of Smith & Nephew for cash and Unilever shares. Unilever dwarfed Smith & Nephew.[30] Unilever Group turnover was £2021.8m in 1967 and operating profit £145m. Smith & Nephew's sales to third parties in the same year were £32.8m and operating profit £3.8m. Moreover Unilever pointed out that their profits and dividends had increased faster between 1962 and 1967 than had those of their target. The timing of the bid seemed to be dictated by the apparent vulnerability of Smith & Nephew during a management interregnum; formally the chairman and chief executive had retired but Steen and Kemp were not to assume those positions until the beginning of May.

Smith & Nephew tried to dissuade their shareholders from accepting Unilever's offer by pointing out that Unilever lacked a medical background and therefore could not adequately handle a substantial portion of Smith & Nephew's sales; much of Smith & Nephew's selling was not like the marketing of detergents, margarine and other foodstuffs.[31] Nor did Smith & Nephew's overseas sales organization in over 100 territories require support from Unilever's international marketing. The truth was that Unilever wanted to cash in on Smith & Nephew's growth. Smith & Nephew forecasted a substantial jump in profits in 1968.[32] Their three-pronged financial defence was:

- Unilever's offer price for shares compared unfavourably with the potential market price;
- the offer of part payment in cash or fixed interest security would render the shareholder generally liable to capital gains tax and the cost of reinvesting the money; and
- Unilever's dividends were not going to be as high as Smith & Nephew's.

Chairman Stephen Steen also responded with a letter to shareholders that is instructive of how he saw his company:

> The main divisions of our Company emanated from three great family businesses, all of which have been in existence for over one hundred years... (Smith & Nephew, Southalls and Berton) ...who wanted to merge and did over ten years ago. They joined forces with enthusiasm and confidence and for convincing reasons; there was no takeover bid. The old family backgrounds and traditions are still with us. In fact they are peculiarly woven into the very fabric of our company.

Sympathy, sentiment, affection and even emotion, play quite a part. You have only to work for or with Smith & Nephew to realise their importance. We know that many of our shareholders appreciate this invisible and invaluable family bond. It is one of our driving forces.[33]

This stirring appeal to the virtues of 'personal capitalism', and against contested takeovers, prompted Unilever to place a revised offer on 17 May.[34] The new offer dealt with the capital gains tax issue by allowing payment entirely in Unilever shares. Unilever also substantially raised the offer price for Smith & Nephew ordinary shares. Smith & Nephew replied by pointing out that accepting Unilever shares would cut dividend income by 40 per cent and by illustrating graphically the stronger growth rate of Smith & Nephew profits since 1958 than Unilever's (Figure 11.5). They did not mention the increase

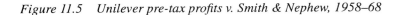

Figure 11.5   Unilever pre-tax profits v. Smith & Nephew, 1958–68

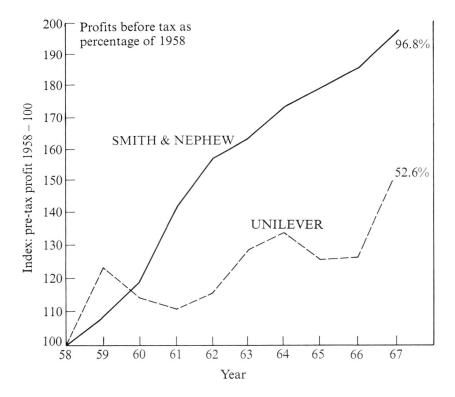

in equity capital (and therefore the greater claims on profit) during the 1960s that accompanied Smith & Nephew's expansion.

1968 marked a peak in Smith & Nephew's stock market rating but thereafter the rate of return on shareholders' capital rose (Figure 11.3).[35] The majority of shareholders were right with hindsight to reject the revised offer, a result which Unilever conceded on 31 May.

TIGHTENING UP

Tempted by the doubling of Smith & Nephew share prices during the Unilever bid,[36] professionals began dealing so that Smith & Nephew shares fluctuated in the same way as the *Financial Times* all share index. Previously turnover had been very small, probably between 8 and 10 per cent of the company's 60 million shares.[37] The company's profit and growth prospects were scrutinized more closely henceforth.

A new UK cash control system was introduced in 1971. Under this system each company in Britain paid 8.25 per cent (the cost of the newly raised loan stock) on all overdrawn balances at the NatWest Bank. The new rule encouraged divisions to maintain surpluses rather than deficits, saving Smith & Nephew as a whole considerable interest payments.[38] Even before this financial system was introduced, less than a year after the takeover bid, the board felt that diversification and/or improvement of existing product lines offered very little scope for spending all the profits the group was expected to generate.[39] Smith & Nephew therefore needed to break into new sectors. The problem was how to select these areas. Roland Smith's seminars addressed this issue and director J.A. Leavey suggested an arms-length investment company.

One possible new direction was suggested by Hydron. Share prices were given such a fillip in 1971 by rumours about Hydron's potential (Chapter 9)[40] that the chairman was obliged to tell the Society of Investment Analysts: 'it is too early to judge whether [Hydron] has the importance attached to it by various newspapers'.

Investor enthusiasm turned out to be right for the wrong reason. It was not merely, or mainly, Hydron that was responsible for *Management Today* in 1979 showing Smith & Nephew 14th in the UK corporate profit growth league.

Reorganization of the top management structure in 1972 was intended to complement the financial changes and clarify the direction in which the company should develop. Kenneth Kemp as executive deputy chairman and Kenneth Bradshaw as chief executive of operations worked as a team. But Kemp led on policy and special relationships, while Bradshaw led in opera-

Figure 11.6 Management structure, 1972

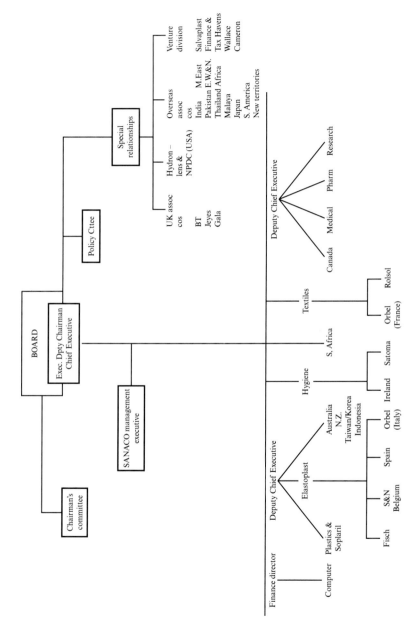

tional areas. The new SANACO management executive (replacing the SEC) was to be an advisory forum, meeting at Bradshaw's discretion. The executive deputy chairman and the chief executive were empowered to authorize capital expenditure up to £0.25m and acquisitions in cognate product areas of £100 000. The chief executive, with the executive deputy chairman, submitted annual budgets to the SANACO board and reported quarterly on the group's operations[41] (see Figure 11.6).

Management incentives were introduced in the early 1970s, as senior Smith & Nephew managers noted the financial rewards of owners of companies Smith & Nephew bought. Share option schemes allowed management to participate in the rising stock market value of the company to which they contributed. If they exercised their right to buy a number of Smith & Nephew shares, at a price fixed at an earlier date, after greater expected profitability had raised Smith & Nephew share prices, they would be rewarded for achieving these greater profits by the ability to realize a capital sum. These incentives were extended to all employees of Smith & Nephew through trustee share options. Share options were given to the trustees of the company pension fund who would use the option on behalf of the employee to whom it had been granted and enhance that employee's pension accordingly.

Smith & Nephew's growth by acquisition was not an unbroken upward trend. Diversification into cosmetics, at first very profitable, proved hard to manage in the turbulent world economy of the 1970s. Retrenchment in 1980 by selling Mary Quant, Outdoor Girl and Miners to Max Factor, a subsidiary of Norton Simon Inc. of the US, was expected to improve Smith & Nephew's cash position by around £7m in 1981. Around £3m was written off. Stock market confidence that this was the right decision was shown by the share price at the announcement remaining barely changed at around the 1980 peak.[42]

Corporate growth required by 1981 that non-board members be brought on to the executive committee. The name of SME was therefore altered to group management executive. Meeting each month, every member was assigned specific responsibilities on which they reported to the committee and for which they took instructions. For much of the 1980s constituent companies were encouraged to compete against each other; transfer prices for the same product could differ within the group according to relative bargaining power, as well as according to costs of supply. Towards the end of the decade, other approaches were adopted to ensure profit centres had incentives to minimize costs. One of Smith & Nephew's main costs was labour. Employment between 1984 and 1988 grew at 4 per cent a year, with the slowest expansion in direct production which accounted for almost 50 per cent of the labour force. Employment in R & D rose significantly faster than in other categories, showing the company's commitment to in-house innovation and organic growth.

When demand growth slowed, stock levels rose during 1988 from 68 days to 90 days. 'Just in time' investment was intended to address this problem. In response to worldwide cost-containment and competitive pressure, the health care division invested £2.5m in manufacturing techniques to reduce product costs, including a major 'just in time' project – a specially developed process control technique for improving productivity and reducing inventories. All departments used the same data base either to plan, manufacture or tabulate cost information.[43] The computer allowed the matching of raw material stocks against orders and the timing of deliveries of additional materials, if needed.

With the upswing from the recession of 1980–81, the stock market became more and more enthusiastic about Smith & Nephew.[44] The price–earnings ratio surged upwards (Figure 11.4). Commentators referred to the traditional 'dull but dependable' image of a company by contrast with pharmaceuticals but noted the success of OpSite, sales of which reached £20m worldwide in 1983, and Smith & Nephew's increasing focus on the US market. Between 1980 and 1984 share price quadrupled.

In the later 1980s shares lost their former rating because of the risk that the stock market associated with US acquisitions and because the pace of earnings growth slackened.[45] Between 1984 and 1988 annual turnover growth averaged 13 per cent a year. Underlying organic growth was 6 per cent per annum. Currency movements adversely affected turnover growth in 1988; the actual increase in gross revenue of 9 per cent would have been 14 per cent without currency changes. Gross profit margins grew faster than turnover because of the change in business mix with the acquisitions. Convertible debentures accounted for one-third of Smith & Nephew debt in 1988. If the option to convert debt to equity was assumed to be exercised then gearing was markedly reduced. Perhaps the return on equity was flattered by the write-off of goodwill on acquisitions but, even adjusted for that effect, returns remained above 21 per cent.[46]

THE SMITH & NEPHEW FOUNDATION

With continuous pressure from competition and monitoring by the stock market, top management in the postwar era was an occupation that demanded every available minute. No longer was it possible, as in the nineteenth century, for executive directors to devote a considerable proportion of their time to charitable and other public work. Instead Smith & Nephew contributed to a special charitable trust.

The original trust was created in 1938, the year after Smith & Nephew became a public company, quoted on the stock exchange. H.N. Smith had freed some of his capital from Smith & Nephew and was able to channel it into charitable activities through this trust, a company limited by guarantee. Smith & Nephew later also used the same vehicle for the Smith & Nephew Commonwealth fellowships, with a grant in 1961 and a covenant from 1964. The fellowship scheme supported physicians or surgeons, primarily but not exclusively from Commonwealth countries, to study in the UK for a year.

In 1974 the new Smith & Nephew Foundation, financed by an annual covenanted £50 000 from the firm, took over from the trust. A measure of the importance attached to the foundation was that the then chairman of Smith & Nephew, Stephen Steen, became the first chairman of the trustees. In his first annual report Steen set out the foundation's objective: to assist and encourage the advancement of knowledge, learning and experience in the medical, surgical and hospital fields of endeavour. A second vital trustee, who served the foundation and the predecessor H.N. Smith Trust for 18 years, was W.F. Davis, the general administrator of the Royal College of Surgeons.

Six Smith & Nephew fellowships and six Florence Nightingale nursing scholarships were awarded in the first year of the foundation. The contribution to the H.N. Smith Unit at the Royal College of Surgeons was also increased.[47] Research at this unit was primarily the study of changes occurring during the rejection of transplanted skin and the pharmacological mechanism involved in hypersensitive reactions.

As inflation reached an annual rate of 25 per cent in 1975, the purchasing power of the foundation's income was whittled away. It was decided to limit fellowship awards to alternate years. By 1977 Steen was announcing 'We now require another grant even to stand still'. Help came at last with SANACO's extra £25 000 annual grant in 1979. This additional support allowed the Nightingale nursing study scholarships to be extended to encourage visits to the rest of the European Community.

Don Seymour took over as chairman from Steen in 1979, when a new commitment was made to a five year Royal Society research fellowship in chemistry. A novel course in chemistry with toxicology and analytical chemistry at Hull University was supported from 1981, as was a seminar on wound dressing. By 1982, when Kenneth Kemp became chairman, the fellowship scheme was completely international, including in that year physicians from Hungary and Japan. During the 1980s a rising income from Smith & Nephew permitted the foundation to increase the number and variety of awards, reflecting the company's wider interests within the spheres of medicine and nursing. Quite independent proposals were also supported. The first Smith & Nephew fellowship in sports medicine, to allow a British medical practitioner to study for a diploma in the subject, was awarded in 1984. The following year a scholarship was established to enable a nurse to undertake a study of theatre management. Fellowships for Chinese surgeons to research and train in the UK were granted in 1986 and 1987.

In recent years, a fellowship in ophthalmology for a research project at Moorfields Eye Hospital, service doctor awards, Smith & Nephew/Richards fellowships in trauma for orthopaedic research, a midwife scholarship, and a cancer nursing care grant have been added to the foundation's health care benefactions. Longer-term projects have included support for research in the Department of Biochemistry at the Hunterian Institute, the Royal College of Surgeons of England which replaced funding for the H.N. Smith Unit in the Department of Pharmacology there. The University of Liverpool gained a three-year lectureship in pharmacology in the Department of Nursing.

In 1991 the foundation redirected long-term support for clinical research-based units to the newly created centre of excellence in wound healing at the University of Wales College of Medicine in Cardiff. Within the nursing profession the foundation continued its support for nurses working in the community, as well as for senior nurses. The foundation helped with bursaries for medical students undertaking intercalated B.Sc. degrees and students in science allied to medicine and nursing. It also aided medical and nursing students with the costs of their elective study periods abroad. From 1992 onwards the foundation decided to offer equal amounts of money to support education and research in the medical and nursing professions. The decision placed the foundation in the forefront of charities offering bursaries to the nursing profession. All this was possible because of a rising foundation income, exceeding £400 000 in 1990, directly or indirectly through annual donations from Smith & Nephew's profits.[48]

CONCLUSION

Profits were necessarily a key concern of management, for without them the company would not survive, but they were more an indicator of conformity of company policy with market pressures than an end in themselves. The falling rate of return on capital of the late 1950s and the weakness of the early 1960s reflected increasing size of operations and more intense competition. A strong commitment to textiles, where the rate of return was persistently below the group average, did not help either. Annual accounting rates of return were not an ideal guide to the efficiency of resource use; project appraisal is more accurately undertaken with discounted cash flow. But Smith & Nephew's textiles investment strategy was not short-termist, as the implicit one-year gestation period allowed for investment by the accounting rate of return might suggest.

Shortcomings were recognized in the 1960s and organizational reform initiated as well as new top managerial talent injected. The association of the turn-around in rates of return with the abortive 1968 Unilever takeover bid is striking, but stock market indices show a much earlier improvement. In the short run higher profits may be achieved by relatively minor changes. They were also boosted by higher borrowing from 1971. The real achievement was sustaining and enhancing these improved results over the following years. Closer cost control and higher gearing made their contribution on the side of finance; a successful international growth strategy and stronger focus on health care boosted the sources of corporate funds. High growth rates depended on judicious acquisitions and on new products developed within the company, because organic growth was necessarily low, given Smith & Nephew's established markets. Financing large acquisitions required paying close attention to stock market conditions and assessments. That imposed a tighter discipline on the company with the passage of the decades. A comparison of the appreciation of Smith & Nephew's share price with the market as a whole reveals how successfully the challenge was met. Between January 1965 and March 1987 the total industrial index rose 961.27 per cent while Smith & Nephew appreciated 3 416.73 per cent, an improvement of 231.37 per cent on the industrials index.

NOTES

1. For a comparison, Johnson & Johnson employed over 67 000 at the end of the 1970s. See Johnson & Johnson (1979), p. 13. Employment in British manufacturing as a whole began falling earlier, from 1966.
2. *Economic Trends*, Annual Supplement, 1990, and October 1991, HMSO.
3. Two types of British holding company have been classified in this period. In the first, senior executive management was composed of functional specialists (marketing, finance, production and so on) generally drawn from the original parent concern, together with general managers of senior subsidiaries, virtually completely independent of the parent. The second was primarily a form of ownership and a means of excluding competition, without integrating former or potential rivals. The first 'ideal type' resembled a functional structure in that parent board specialists were members of the senior executive group but there were no central policy-making, coordinating or strategic functions covering subsidiary operations. See Channon (1973), p. 15.
4. Kenneth Kemp interview. A Smith & Nephew chief executive is the managing director but the title was borrowed from American usage because under the 1937 constitution, the managing director was never required to resign at retirement age. Rather than change the constitution, the post was renamed.
5. Visitors to the rather larger Hever Castle, Kent, once the home of Ann Boleyn, will note the similarity of the wooden panelling to that in Temple Place. They were both refurbished for Lord Astor to his design.
6. George Leavey originally was a City financier who played a major role in the flotation of Smith & Nephew in 1937.
7. G. Whittaker, 'A Handful of Shale', 1979, unpublished ms.
8. The 1956 Act set up the Restrictive Practices Court which decided whether agreements among manufacturers were against the public interest or not. By June 1963 2 450 agreements had been registered and most were abandoned or reformulated. The Resale Prices Act of 1964 prohibited manufacturers enforcing recommended prices by withholding supplies from recalcitrant retailers. Pharmaceuticals were the only exemption allowed.

The Monopolies and Mergers Act of 1965 strengthened the earlier 1948 anti-monopoly legislation.

9. Fred Medhurst (see Chapter 10), Edwin Robinson (Chapter 4), J.W. Hamilton Jones and Colonel Jack Lockhart-Jervis all retired. Hamilton Jones edited and produced the first company history in 1956 and wrote three books on hermetic philosophy and alchemy. He began his career working for the merchant bankers Duncan, Fox & Co who had interest in Latin America and the US. In 1920 he contracted double pneumonia in Southern Chile and was advised to return to England. There he joined Buckley as a director of the Eversharp British Co. Lockhart-Jervis served in the Royal Engineers. Seconded to the Russian Army between 1913 and 1915, he returned to France, took part in sapper operations at Vimy Ridge and was awarded the MC and DSO. Joining the family consulting engineering firm of Hitchens Jervis & Partners in 1921, he participated in major hydroelectric, railway and paper-mill construction projects thoughout the world before joining Smith & Nephew as technical director in 1944.

10. Dr Nancy J. Lane, a Canadian-born cell biologist of Girton College, Cambridge, was appointed to the Smith & Nephew board as a non-executive director.

11. Only in 1962 did chairmen of ICI divisions become responsible for divisional performance, instead of divisional boards. Albright & Wilson maintained a holding company structure until 1967 when it reorganized into product and geographical divisions. Glaxo remained a holding company (but that did not prevent the company achieving sales second only to Merck in the world pharmaceutical industry during the 1980s). Precocious Beecham's established product divisions in the 1950s and Fisons also had five operating divisions from 1957 (Channon 1973, Chap. 5). Channon concluded that gains from the acquisitions by which most companies grew were frequently difficult to achieve because of a failure to bring about structural reform. When such reform did come it was generally introduced by outside consultants after changes in leadership. His sample excluded Smith & Nephew. The connection between management structure and performance is more often assumed than demonstrated.

12. Whittaker attributed his heart attack to their struggles. He retired in 1967. Long died three months after retiring in January 1969 but Steen survived to a ripe old age. ICI still has three deputy chairmen. Two are expected to leave the company when the third becomes chairman.

13. After gaining his B.Com. and M.Sc. degrees from Birmingham University, C.A.F. Hastilow CBE, FRIC joined Dockers, the paint manufacturers, as chief chemist, rising to chairman between 1946 and 1960. During the Second World War he worked for chemicals control in the Ministry of Supply and became director of paint materials 1944/5.

14. Leavey had groomed Roland Outen, a lawyer, board member and partner in Ashfield Morris, as his successor. Outen had died prematurely of a heart attack.

15. *SANACO in the 60's*, Smith & Nephew, London 1964.

16. During the 1950s fabric Elastoplast was expected to be replaced by plastic, but it remained popular because of the greater protection afforded by fabric. Johnson & Johnson eventually reintroduced a fabric elastic bandage, having earlier abandoned this type in favour of plastic.

17. In Channon's sample of 25 British- or European-owned companies, 'low' research and development expenditure was less than 2 per cent of sales, 'medium' was 2–4 per cent and 'high' was over 4 per cent (Channon 1973, p. 197).

18. Gearing in fact only began to rise from the beginning of the 1970s.

19. The pharmaceuticals ratio was 16.5 per cent, and Medical, including Everetts and Grahams, were making a loss, thanks to intense competition from imports of disposables – see Chapter 7.

20. SANACO executive committee, *Organisation Division 2 (Medical & Plastics)*, 3 October 1967 Minute no. 381–(8) Board Meeting, 10 October 1967.

21. In 1965, director J.A. Leavey circulated to the board 'A study of SANACO's Senior Management Structure & Plans for Succession'. J.A. Leavey was son of former chairman George Leavey and author of the second updated edition of Smith & Nephew's history.

22. Chairman's committee, *Organisation*, 7 February 1968, Smith & Nephew Board.

23. *Report of the SANACO Management Committee to SANACO Board*, 11 May 1971; Letter to Shareholders, 25 March 1971.
24. G.F.M. Lyster and K.R. Kemp, *SANACO Finance*, Memo to SANACO Board, 28 August 1963, Smith & Nephew, London.
25. When taxation was taken into account the net revenue earned on the borrowing was considerably higher than these percentages suggested. Interest charges were set against tax, lowering the effective cost of borrowing, while the loan was invested tax-free in Bermuda.
26. K.R. Kemp, *Strategy-Acquisitions*, 31 July 1969. Smith & Nephew already owned 33 per cent of Jeyes (manufacturers of Domestos bleach) which they had acquired in exchange for Parazone bleach. At the same time that Unilever put in a bid for Smith & Nephew, Newton Chambers attempted to take over Jeyes, of whom Steen was also chairman and Kemp a board member. The hostile bid for Jeyes was unsuccessful.
27. G. Tweedale (1990), p. 205. Channon notes that this corporate 'scanning function' as part of a strategy of diversification was quite widespread among large British firms and of vital importance to the growth of the economy. See Channon (1973), p. 238.
28. A higher yield meant a lower share price for a given pay-out. The market accepts low yields if it expects an appreciation of share price as a result of company growth; a low current return is expected to be compensated by future capital gains.
29. *Extract from a letter from Mr GFM Lyster to the Chairman 22nd Oct 1964*, Smith & Nephew, London.
30. *Offers by Lazard Brothers & Co Ltd* ... Minute no. 425, Smith & Nephew Board Meeting, 18 April 1968.
31. Smith & Nephew Associated Cos Ltd, *Offer From Unilever Limited*, 3 May 1968.
32. Profit forecasts had to be audited by the merchant banks during the bid. In order to improve the forecast Smith & Nephew was obliged to run faster, advertising expenditure was not raised and some money was taken from central provisions.
33. S. Steen, *A Personal Message to You – Our Shareholders*, May 1968.
34. *Lazard Bros to Members of S&N Ass. Co.*, 17 May 1968.
35. Defined as the ratio of operating profit to average net assets. Average net assets are fixed assets including investments and working capital. As such the value of the ratio is sensitive to the effects of writing-off of goodwill on the denominator.
36. *Investors' Guardian*, 21 May 1969.
37. *Economist* 1969.
38. *Management of Group Funds*, 1972, S & N, London.
39. J.A. Leavey, *Temple Holdings* 6 February 1969 Board Minute 483 (2), meeting 11 February 1969.
40. *Daily Telegraph*, 26 April 1971, Questor Column; *Investors' Guardian*, 14 May 1971; *Report of SANACO Management Committee*, 11 May 1971, item 221.
41. K.R. Kemp and K.W. Bradshaw, *Organisation*, 5 April 1972, Smith & Nephew, London.
42. *Glasgow Herald*, 10 December 1980.
43. *Smith & Nephew Source*, Spring 1989, p. 7.
44. *Financial Times*, 12 August 1982; *Money Observer*, October 1983; *Investors' Chronicle*, 23 March 1984; *Guardian*, 21 March 1984.
45. However necessary to long-term growth they are, the stock market rarely likes large takeovers because of the 'digestion' problem the parent is likely to suffer in the short term.
46. This was a common practice in the UK in the 1980s to impress investment analysts with the benefits of acquisitions. When a takeover was made, assets were written down as much as possible, large provisions were set up for estimated expenses in the future and the pension liability inflated. In effect this increased the goodwill, which was written back to the profit and loss account in the years immediately following the takeover. See 'Massaging Standards to Suit', *World Accounting Report*, 29 March 1985.
47. *The First Smith & Nephew Foundation Report*, 1974.
48. *Annual Reports of the Trustees of the Smith & Nephew Foundation 1974–1990*.

12. Globalization in the 1980s

By the 1980s, the health care industry was one of the few sectors of British manufacturing which were internationally competitive (Porter 1990, pp. 494–5). Detailed investigation of any major British firm in that sector might therefore unlock the secrets of competitive success. But Smith & Nephew is of particular interest because, although comparatively small, with a market capitalization of around £1.2bn, it was the most profitable British company of 1990.[1] The key to these profits includes at least four components: concentration on a limited range of health care activities which the business clearly did well; a strong presence in the largest world market, the US; a well established R & D programme; and high employee commitment reinforced by company institutions and culture.

MARKET POSITIONING

Health care expenditures can be counted on to grow faster than national incomes: any company attracting even a constant share of these outlays may expect profitable and rapid expansion. Ageing and longer-lived populations in the affluent West, together with advances in surgery and biologically compatible materials, ensure that synthetic 'spare parts' will be much in demand in the future. This is especially true of the US market, with half of the world's health care business, where new products and techniques spin off from universities at a great pace and where the American medical profession enthusiastically embraces innovation. Recognition of these facts was embodied in corporate policy from 1982 under Eric Kinder. Until then Smith & Nephew remained essentially a British company with subsidiaries in Commonwealth countries and part ownership of some continental European health care firms. Thereafter the company acquired health care businesses in the US so that by the end of the decade Britain was no longer the principal market and source of profit. Approximately two-fifths of sales and profits originated from North America, and two-fifths from Europe, including Britain (Table 12.1). Smith & Nephew had become a member of the very select club of world class British manufacturing companies.

Table 12.1   Geographical distribution of sales, 1980 and 1990

	1980	1990
UK	128.5 (54.1%)	190.5 (23.6%)
Europe	25.1 (10.6%)	168.1 (20.9%)
America	30.5 (12.8%)	300.6 (37.3%)
Rest of world	53.5 (22.5%)	145.8 (18.1%)
Total	237.6	805.0

Note: includes intergroup sales.

Simultaneously with geographical relocation of markets in the 1980s, sales of medical health care products grew rapidly to a dominant position within the company (75 per cent of sales at the end of the decade) and consumer products took second place (20 per cent). This shift of emphasis reflected a clear management strategy, influenced by rising R & D costs in the industry and intense international competition, coupled with rapid expansion. Very considerable fixed costs of new product development required larger sales of each product to recoup expenditures. In-house research, and licensing other companies, largely replaced buying in technology. Tighter environmental and safety standards in response to consumer lobbies also pushed up costs. Only by concentrating corporate efforts in a narrower product range and into the more rapidly expanding markets could Smith & Nephew maintain its high growth and profitability.

A good deal of growth had previously been achieved by acquisition rather than by rising sales of established products. Markets for this second group were not expanding as fast as required by the company's target rate of growth. Market shares were already typically high, so that the pace could not be maintained merely by increasing them. During the 1980s diversification into orthopaedics ensured that organic growth, rather than growth by acquisition, could be the pattern of the future.[2]

Established market positions are regularly challenged by technical developments. Keyhole surgery (endoscopy) reduced one component of demand for Smith & Nephew's products, that for surgical swabs. But with capacity in arthroscopy Smith & Nephew could far more than compensate for this loss by supplying equipment for keyhole surgery, the cameras and blades, through Dyonics, at the beginning of the 1990s experiencing 40–50 per cent growth a year. Arthroscopy is the treatment of injury by small portal incisions through which the surgeons repair damaged tissue in the joint. Fibre-optic viewing and motor-driven instruments allow these remarkable operations to be performed. Similar scientific and engineering advances in other fields as well have enormously extended the capacity of medical science, but the new techniques are expensive to implement. Consequently health administrations place a premium on reducing any avoidable costs to make room for these advances. Even US buying has become much more corporate in an attempt to gain better value for money. That creates an opportunity for the supplier of more cost-effective products to grow faster than the market by displacing competitors.

As in pharmaceuticals, only a few companies were large enough to support the development and marketing costs of these new products, and, to recover their investment, they needed to compete in all major markets. On the medical side of Smith & Nephew's business Johnson & Johnson, 3M and perhaps Beiersdorf were competitors. On the consumer side Johnson & Johnson again competed, together with Procter & Gamble and Unilever. Special soap manufacturers illustrate the process of concentration of the industry in response to pressures to market around the world. During the 1980s Procter & Gamble absorbed Ulay and Smith & Nephew bought Albion.

ESTABLISHED PRODUCT MARKETS IN THE 1980s

Tight monetary policies in America and Britain, together with oil price rises in 1979, squeezed demand at the beginning of the 1980s. From 1982 or 1983 recovery began, the upswing lasting until the stock market crashes of 1987.

Although the collapses did not precipitate the world depression that was feared, confused or inappropriate government policy reactions retarded recovery. Through much of the 1980s the US dollar exchange rate behaved unexpectedly, failing to decline despite a massive US budget deficit in the first half of the 1980s. Erratic exchange rate behaviour was both a challenge to corporate treasurers and an opportunity for well-timed acquisitions, as Smith & Nephew demonstrated. Established consumer products with high market penetration could count on steady but undramatic growth almost independently of market prosperity. A second group, including Gypsona and other medical supplies, were very dependent on stockholding and purchasing policies of health administrations, which could prove unpredictable. Plastics and textiles, partly providing specialized inputs to Smith & Nephew's health care products, experienced volatile sales outside the company, and certain peripheral businesses, though profitable, were abandoned.

Smith & Nephew's Flamazine burns cream was relatively new at the beginning of the 1980s. The bulk of the need in the UK comes from the 10 000 victims of mainly domestic accidents who are admitted to hospital burns units each year. But the large-scale tragedies in which Flamazine is used are more newsworthy: the St Valentine's day fire of 1981 in a Dublin nightclub (claiming 47 lives), phosphorous bombs in Beirut, Falklands' campaign casualties, all provided opportunities for Flamazine to prevent the spread of infection.[3] Special polythene gloves or bags allowed Falklands' casualties use of their hands and arms after the Flamazine had been applied. At the time of the fire at the Bradford football ground that killed 53 and injured 250, Smith & Nephew were asked to supply 620 50-gramme tubes of Flamazine to hospitals in Bradford and Leeds.[4] The Gulf War of 1991 boosted demand for Flamazine (fortunately most of the stocks did not need to be used) and staff worked overtime during the crisis, commemorated by sand-coloured 'singed desert rat' T-shirts. Other products were strongly demanded during crises as well. Hull's Gypsona department raised their normal splint production rate from 200 to 1 500 per week during the Falklands' emergency. Iraq's war with Iran brought about £780 000 of business each for Healthcare and Medical Textiles, including 2 million packets of gauze.[5] More Middle Eastern orders followed but then the market collapsed in 1984 with declining oil prices. The primary health care market showed increased sales in that year, reflecting the trend towards treating patients in their own homes rather than in hospital.

Smith & Nephew were one of the first manufacturers to recognize this opportunity. Financial stringency in national health care organizations held down health care sales from time to time. American hospital equipment sales stagnated in 1986 because of changes in the payment system to private hospitals by the US government for Medicare patients. This slowed the construction of new hospitals and the renovation of existing ones.

Health care took about 3–4 per cent of Net 909 output in the UK for use on adhesive dressings, where it lifted from a wound much more easily than the cotton equivalent.[6] A much higher proportion passed to the hygiene division. The special soft-net Dristock accounted for up to 23 per cent of output. Dristock does not retain moisture but maintains strength when wet and continues to feel soft and silky. It is therefore ideal for incontinence pads and disposable nappies. Around 17 per cent of Net 909 was exported in 1982, much in the form of D218 (a disposable cheesecloth) which also accounted for 30 per cent of sales to the British market. Industrial tape sales burgeoned in the early 1980s thanks partly to the electronics industry.[7]

Three-quarters of Smith & Nephew's specialist textiles were sold within the company, and were produced in seven Lancashire factories with a workforce of around 2 000 people. In 1991 Smith & Nephew Textiles was organized into five profit centres: medical textiles, surgical dressings, denim, polyfabrik and knitting. Medical textiles were centred on Brierfield, the largest site. Total weekly production averaged 1.2 million metres of medical textile fabric and 85 tons of yarn.[8] Also at Brierfield, Hollin Bank Mill concentrated on cotton wool and non-adhesive surgical dressings. Glen Mills and North Valley Mill manufactured denim. Coral Mill, Rochdale, was the centre of polypropylene extrusion and weaving operations and Adlington, Chorley, knitted and wove medical substrates.

Such sales were inevitably hit by NHS destocking and ward closures during the 1980s. Cotton price volatility continued to affect profits, falling between 1985 and 1986, rising to mid-1987 and declining thereafter to 1989. Denim demand pursued an equally erratic, but at times highly profitable, course through the 1980s, becoming profitable in 1983, helped by the addition of higher-margin products to the range (1984). Fashion trends on the European continent favoured denim in 1986 and peaked the following year. Cheap imports and strong domestic currencies squeezed textiles in 1988. Smith & Nephew's tactic in response was to move up-market, expanding specialized fabrics and reducing commodity cloth for hospital production. Two-thirds of denim output was exported but in 1990 production was only about breaking even.

Due to a continuing increase in competition from lower-cost sources in developing countries, Smith & Nephew carried out a strategic review of the whole of the textile division's operations. The conclusion was that the division could no longer compete effectively in its cotton-spinning and denim-weaving activities. As a result, at the beginning of 1993, the group decided to withdraw completely from these areas of business. Thereafter Smith & Nephew concentrated solely on the manufacture of technically advanced medical fabrics and health care products, of strategic importance to the group. A new medical fabrics division at the Brierfield site was created to handle this more focused business.

Smith & Nephew's mature consumer product lines continued to maintain high market shares through the decade: Elastoplast achieved more than 50 per cent in 1988. These levels of penetration carried with them the hazard of intervention by the Monopolies Commission, as shown in Chapter 8. Lil-lets share of the non-applicator tampon market in 1982 fell to a mere 92 per cent[9] and discounts were introduced for larger economy packs. The Monopolies Commission pronounced themselves satisfied in 1986 (Monopolies and Mergers Commission, 1986). At the end of the decade Lil-lets accounted for 32 per cent of internal feminine hygiene market and Dr White's for 23 per cent of the British sanitary towel sales. In toiletries, cooperation with Beiersdorf continued. The Limara range, launched in 1981, was another Beiersdorf product which Smith & Nephew was licensed to sell in specified territories, along with Atrixo and Labello. At the end of the 1980s, Nivea maintained 44 per cent of the UK skin care market.

Retailing of the health and beauty sector became more concentrated. By contrast with the large number of names in the 1960s (Chapter 7), Tesco and J. Sainsbury dominated the grocery trade in Britain, and Boots, Lloyds and

Superdrug retailed the bulk of the chemist trade. Large grocers continue to gain at the expense of smaller chemists.[10] At the beginning of the 1980s there were perhaps 30 large grocers; a decade later only five or six groups of significance were left. On the other hand in the early 1990s continental retailers, such as Aldi, entered the British market, intensifying competition.

Greater concentration in retailing conferred more bargaining power on the buyers' side of Smith & Nephew's market. J. Sainsbury would deal Smith & Nephew a heavy blow if they chose not to stock the company's products. Equally there would be an adverse effect on Sainsbury's sales. Marketing policy therefore needed to adjust to the far higher stakes of a smaller number of large individual contracts.

NEW PRODUCTS AND THE NORTH AMERICAN MARKET

With earnings growing at 20 per cent a year from 1982 to 1986, a favourable stock market rating placed Smith & Nephew in a strong position to finance acquisitions (shown in Table 12.2).

Growth by acquisition is constrained by what is for sale.[11] The company was lucky to find the three principal businesses, Affiliated Hospital Products Inc. (1985) Richards (1986) and Ioptex (1989), respectively for surgical gloves, for operating tables, trauma products, orthopaedic implants and for intraocular lenses, that were able to shift the company from health care products with only moderate growth possibilities into much more dynamic health care markets. But earlier operations in North America were based on a different strategy. As shown in Chapter 10, competitive advantage in the Canadian market was bound to be enhanced by more extensive operations in the US. Anchor, the newly acquired US industrial tapes business, was to be the spring-board. Under pressure in the early 1980s, Anchor hoped to strengthen its position with a new investment programme, begun in 1979, that came on stream in 1983. Relief was only temporary, for sales were dependent on the health of US manufacturing and the level of competitive imports, neither of which were favourable in these years, thanks to the strong dollar. In 1987 the subsidiary was sold to two Anchor executives. With the stronger focus on health care Anchor was no longer a core business. Toronto Plastics obtained high-technology orders from the US in 1983 and profits almost quadrupled. But it too was sold at the end of 1988 when operating at a small loss.

Unlike plastics, health care was the central concern of Smith & Nephew in the 1980s and this base was strengthened by the purchase in 1984 of H.M. Cote, a Quebec-based company making surgical dressings and cotton wool consumer products. A US bank undertook a search for suitable American

Table 12.2 Acquisitions, 1980–89

Year	Acquisition	Comment
1980	Stake in British Tissues (UK) increased from 25% to 50%.	In line with policy of extending interests in UK consumer hygiene products.
	Remaining 50% of Laboratories Fisch (France)	Strengthening of position in plaster of Paris and related products in Europe and French-speaking territories
1981	Avon Medicals Ltd (UK)	Manufacturer and distributor of disposable medical devices principally for use in life support
1982	Joubert and Joubert (Australia)	Cotton wool and surgical dressing supplier
1983	50% holding in small denim making-up business in Malta.	–
	Rolyan Manufacturing Co. (US)	Manufacturer and marketer of products for orthopaedic, occupational therapy and physiotherapy markets
1984	Outstanding 50% of Smith & Nephew Iberia (Spain)	Provides stronger base for development of hospital products in Spain and ultimately the EEC
	H.M. Côté Inc. (Canada)	Manufacturer of surgical dressings and cotton wool consumer products
1985	Affiliated Hospital Products Inc. (US)	Entry into manufacture and sale of latex gloves in North America. Other activities medical operating table, dental needles and generic drugs.
	3 Sigma Inc. (US)	Small adhesive tape operation, aimed at enhancing Anchor Continental business.
	Vulco Latex Industries (S. Africa)	Adds to range of latex medical products and technical expertise

Year	Company	Description
1986	Cold water orthopaedic cast business of the Hexcel Corporation (US)	Strengthens position in lightweight splinting materials.
	Richards Medical Company (US)	Entry into US orthopaedic market. Significantly increases penetration of US health care market
1987	Alberto Fernandez (Spain)	Leading Spanish manufacturer of latex surgeon's gloves, examination gloves and condoms.
	Lancashire Knitting Co (UK)	Extends existing Smith & Nephew interests in Spain
	Donjoy Inc (US)	Manufacturer of specialized knitted fabrics
	Sigma Inc (US)	Manufacturer of orthopaedic bracing products
	Balance of equity (50%) in Sanortho (France): S.F.F.C. (France); and MMS Quirurgica (Spain)	Manufacturer of medical peristaltic infusion pumps
		Orthopaedic manufacturing and distribution companies acquired with Richards Medical
1988	The Albion Group (UK)	Manufacturer of the Simple range of toiletries
	United Division of Pfizer Hospital Products (US)	Achieves effective critical mass of manufacturing and selling resources in wound care products
	Field Group Chemicals (Australia)	Manufacturer of X ray contrast media
	CeCorp Inc. (US)	Designer and manufacturer of Dyonics video systems
	Remaining 50% of Smith & Nephew-Orbel Spa (Italy)	Strengthens position in Italian market
1989	Ioptex Research (US)	Entry into replacement human eye lens field
	Purchase of Richards Italian distributor	Further strengthening of position in Italy
	Increase in equity stake in Cederroth Nordic (Sweden)	Strengthens position in European market for industrial first aid supplies

235

health care companies on Smith & Nephew's behalf. Attracted by Perry Gloves, Smith & Nephew first bought Affiliated Hospital Products (AHP) primarily as a means of building up critical mass in US. Wound Healing, previously at Columbia, South Carolina, was merged with the Perry division of AHP to become Smith & Nephew Medical Inc. in 1985. AIDS fears boosted sales of disposable examination gloves, not only for physicians but also for dental personnel, policemen and firefighters. US examination glove pieces sales soared to $3.8bn in 1987 and $10bn in 1988, when Perry held an estimated 13–15 per cent of this market. As the price of rubber rocketed during the first half of 1988, Perry was unable to obtain adequate supplies and was obliged to ration glove customers. Only a year before this boom collapsed, an extension to the Columbus, Georgia factory was completed; in the second half of 1988 selling prices of latex examination gloves were cut by almost 50 per cent. Canadian manufacturing capacity, which had only been expanded in the Spring with the opening of a $6m plant at Whitby, Ontario,[12] was closed and lines in the US were shut down in Georgia and Ohio in 1990. Glove profits fell from around $20m in 1989 to a first half loss in 1990 of $1–2m. The story was similar to that of the earlier hypodermic syringes and needles (Chapter 6), but the strategy of remaining a quality leader in a market where lower-range products were increasingly supplied from the Far East (helped by tax breaks and low wages), was more successful.[13]

The long-term growth potential of their products made Richards Medical of Memphis, Tennessee the ideal acquisition for Smith & Nephew. The £192.7m paid for Richards Medical was the group's most expensive purchase. Richards brought into Smith & Nephew six plants in the US and three in Europe, together with a workforce of 1 500,[14] organized into four divisions: orthopaedic, microsurgery, general surgery and international. The product range included hip replacement systems, fracture management devices, surgical instruments for joint repairs, ear implants and the necessary surgical instruments, post-operative and therapy equipment, cast-room and fracture-bracing products and electro-surgical equipment. Considerable thanks to Richards were due for the fact that by 1989 one-fifth of Smith & Nephew's profit and turnover derived from orthopaedics and trauma.

Richards was estimated to hold one-fifth of the trauma market, worth $200m in the US and $500m worldwide. Sports medicine was as dynamic a market for Richards products as was the ageing population, suffering from arthritis and rheumatism. Even arthritic dogs, used by the blind or the police, were candidates for hip replacement by the beginning of the 1980s. In 1988 Smith & Nephew Richards licensed the Ilizarov device, an external orthopaedic frame which allows bone regeneration to take place after certain surgical procedures. It was developed in Siberia to deal with complex diseases and bone defects including dwarfism.[15] Neatly complementing the Richards range were Dyonics products, acquired in 1988. Dyonics disposable cutter blades proved highly successful. Dyonics were also well placed in the specialized cameras and videos sector of arthroscopy. Donjoy (bought in 1987) further enhanced Smith & Nephew's position in the sports market with their knee braces.

The third major acquisition was the youngest. Ioptex, formed in California 1981, was by 1989 the sixth or seventh largest player in the US intraocular lens market.[16] Ioptex, uniquely, was working on soft acrylic-based lenses which allowed the lens to open up after insertion more gently than the conventional silicone-based lenses. A 6mm lens could be implanted through an incision no larger than 4mm. Clinical trials were underway in 1991 as they were on the multifocal lens. These last simulated the natural lens more accurately by allowing the eye to focus well at more than one distance, minimizing the need for spectacle correction after cataract operations. Ioptex also made 'surface passivated' lenses (launched July 1988), designed to reduce lens surface irregularities through the elimination of molecular defect sites, without bonding or coating new materials to the lens surface. Surface-passivated lenses are more compatible with eye tissue and so command a price premium of 40 per cent.

Profitability of Ioptex's American operation was threatened by a number of measures affecting sales at the beginning of the 1990s. In March 1990 Medicare reimbursement rates for intraocular lenses (IOLs) inserted at ambulatory surgical centers (ASCs) were reduced from 80 per cent of costs per IOL to $200. The rule change stemmed from proposals first put forward by the Health Care Financing Administration in 1988. ASCs were only 15 per cent of Smith & Nephew's IOL business, but from the more important hospital sector there was also price pressure. The average price of Ioptex IOLs fell by about 15–20 per cent in 1990 compared with 1989. Europe and Japan held the growth opportunities for Ioptex in the 1990s, for in Europe only half cataract operations resulted in the insertion of IOLs at the beginning of the decade and the proportion in Japan was probably similar. By August 1994, Smith & Nephew concluded Ioptex did not fit; among other reasons, specialist sales staff were required that could not also market Smith & Nephew's other products. Ioptex was sold to Allergan of California

Despite the general success of the American investments, Smith & Nephew had no wish to shift the corporate centre of gravity further towards the US after these three purchases. The legal and ethical environment in the US posed cultural problems for the company. An obvious example was the substantial pressure placed on the Federal Drugs Administration, because of vast corporate investments, the profitability of which depend on the timing of approval, or even on approval itself.

The US courts too behaved in a distinctive manner.[17] In 1987 Smith & Nephew Richards signed a $140 000 agreement with the California-based company Polteco to research and develop a longer-lasting material (ultra-high molecular weight polyethelene) for use on the surfaces of its orthopaedic implants, such as hip and knee joint replacements (Krikler 1991). Included in the $140 000 payment was a $10 000 fee as payment for an agreement to license the technology. The following year Smith & Nephew claimed that Polteco had not met the standard required of the material and that a licence agreement had not been signed. Polteco maintained that Smith & Nephew secretly incorporated the technology into its Optifix and Genesis knee and hip products, which Smith & Nephew denied and contested. In 1990 the Superior Court of the State of California awarded $83m in damages against Smith & Nephew Richards to which the jury added $19m – 'a gross miscarriage of justice' according to Smith & Nephew.[18] At the beginning of 1992 an out-of-court settlement was reached with Polteco, to the approval of the stock market. Regardless of the rights and wrongs of the case, the ratio of damages awarded by the court to the value of the original contract was fantastic. Such awards add to the risks for any company of doing business in California.

OTHER WORLD MARKETS

The growth strategy of the 1980s required close attention to high-income markets outside North America as well: primarily Western Europe, Japan and Australasia. Other economies in Asia were growing so rapidly, or might well do so in the future, that a presence was justified to ensure a strong position when the right time arrived. Incomes in a third group of markets were sufficiently low that there was little prospect of large sales of Smith & Nephew's advanced products. New strategies were required if they were to be served.

Europe

In the UK rationalization of Smith & Nephew's activities was the inevitable consequence of a stronger focus on health care. Production was concentrated at Birmingham and Hull. Non-core business, like plastics, was sold off and existing strengths in health care were supported by acquisitions. Avon Medicals, suppliers of plastic tubing and other devices to convey fluids to and from a patient in hospital, such as in kidney dialysis, was bought in 1981. The Albion Simple soap and cosmetics range was acquired seven years later. The Birmingham site development (completed in 1984) raised factory efficiency and from 1985 all consumer products were sold through the consumer division in Birmingham, while Hull marketed medical and hospital products.

Smith & Nephew's 50 per cent holding in British Tissues was passed to Nokia for £50m in 1989.[19] In the same year Smith & Nephew disposed of Wallace Cameron industrial first aid and hygiene for an increased holding in the Swedish company Cederroth Nordic. After two decades in the company the plastics injection and moulding business was transferred to a group specializing in high-quality packaging. Smith & Nephew continued to buy much of their plastic containers from the organization. Watson Marlowe was sold in 1990 for the same reason as all these others: it was not health care business. A leading European supplier of peristaltic pumping and metering products, with a factory at Falmouth, exporting to Japan, North America and Germany, Watson Marlowe had been acquired in 1977. Subsequent development took the company further away from the medical field into manufacturing and service industry applications.[20]

Creation of the single European market in 1992 required further concentration into national specialist centres: France focused on plaster of Paris, the UK on wound care, and Spain on latex products. Marketing infrastructure was strengthened with recruitment of a special sales team for Dyonics in West Germany. Market unification was not completed by 1992 for not until the mid-1990s would common registration of health care products across Europe and good manufacturing practice standards be accepted throughout. Beiersdorf's control of continental licence rights blocked further development of the more obvious consumer products. This was the main factor in Smith & Nephew's decision to sell its Nivea trade mark to Beiersdorf at the end of 1992. The agreement provided that Smith & Nephew would continue to sell and distribute the Nivea range on commercial terms in its existing consumer markets into the twenty-first century.

Germany is the second largest health care market in the world and one from which Smith & Nephew traditionally bought rather than to which it sold. Smith & Nephew's entry began through a joint venture with the family-owned B. Braun Melsungen (BBM) in 1985 to form a new marketing company specializing in high-technology wound dressings and orthopaedic splinting products. BBM, one of the biggest and most respected German hospital health care companies, employed more than 10 000 in the Melsungen/Spangenberg area.[21] Germany remains a market where Smith & Nephew would like a stronger presence but one that presents unusual difficulties for growth by acquisition because of the persistence of family ownership and the attitude of German financial institutions.

Australasia and Asia

Australian operations in 1978 were restructured into two trading companies, Smith & Nephew (Australia) and Smith & Nephew Plastics (Australia), with all divisions operating within one or the other. Australia in the late 1980s was the only region where Smith & Nephew maintained an interest in plastics. Investment in modern injection moulding machinery improved productivity from 1985 and reversed previous unsatisfactory results. The optics division was sold in 1982 as being of peripheral interest but Field Group Chemicals Pty, a producer of barium meals and related items for use with X ray technology was bought in 1987. The Wonthaggi facilities were upgraded by the purchase of OpSite IV Dressing Conversion and OpSite WDC machines. Investment there and at Clayton allowed replacement of imports.

In South-East Asia, the Malaysian textile plant was disposed of and the business relocated in smaller premises dedicated to surgical dressings. The Thai subsidiary, required to divest down to 49 per cent, was joined by Jack Chia Industries. A new factory in Thailand was completed in 1987. Like the Thai company, that in Indonesia was growing rapidly through the 1980s. (The Venezuelan subsidiary was in a similar position, placed to take advantage of future developments.)

Distribution was strengthened in Japan – Smith & Nephew (Japan) was formed in 1987 – but product registration requirements slowed progress. By far the largest market in the Pacific basin, particularly for orthopaedic implants, Japan was an obvious target for greater sales in the 1990s. During the 1980s, regular visits were made to China in an attempt to develop that huge, but low-income, market. A 1988 symposium in Beijing was attended by 700 senior representatives of major Chinese hospitals. All these efforts in China were set back by the Tiananmen Square massacre in June 1989.

Africa

During the 1980s, the South African subsidiaries took over the distribution of Richards products. There continued to be no discrimination on the basis of race within the company and all non-whites were encouraged to train for positions of responsibility. In the community Smith & Nephew maintained their contribution to improvement of the black population with particular emphasis on education and housing.[22] During 1987 company activities in Mauritius increased with exported surgical dressings and latex gloves, assisted with advice and management services from Rogers & Co.

As apartheid began unravelling at the beginning of the 1990s, new opportunities emerged for Smith & Nephew's exports to the rest of Africa, and new international competitors appeared in the South African market. Sales to the rest of Africa were boosted by regular workshops arranged throughout the continent in partnership with the College of Medicine of South Africa. A working group in South Africa was established to examine the possibilities for offering a portfolio of Smith & Nephew products that were cheap but effective. Even plaster of Paris was too expensive for many poor countries. The challenge was to develop cheaper substitutes that would maintain Smith & Nephew's reputation for effective health care.

R & D AND IN-HOUSE NEW PRODUCTS

Organic growth needed the continual development and innovation of new products. So as to ensure these were what the health care market wanted, among Eric Kinder's first moves as chief executive was his attempt to bring research and business closer together. From 1982, a customer–contractor relationship between Research and the operating divisions was established. Either could initiate projects but the divisions contributed the bulk of Research's funds. This regime led to a number of important customer-centred products such as Allevyn, OpSite IV 3000 (fundamentally different from old OpSite, being used for catheters), and Dynacast casting bandages. (Major new products since 1980 are shown in Table 12.3).

Table 12.3   Principal new products

Product	Date launched	Application
OpSite	1978	Interactive wound dressing. Avoids formation of scab and promotes quicker healing
Crystona	1979	Synthetic casting material
Pryme	1985	Range of soft contact lens care
Allevyn	1987	Ulcer dressing product
Transite	1987	Wound contact layer
Dynacast XR	1986	Synthetic casting material
Glauline	1986	Glaucoma treatment
Intrasite	1988	Ulcer dressing product

A limitation of the new approach turned out to be the spreading of resources over too many projects (around 50 or 60 a year). A second phase was introduced to counteract short-termism and parochialism, which the first customer–contractor mode was suspected of encouraging. The Research Steering Group, formed in 1989, chaired by the present chief executive John Robinson, allocated research budgets by sector and project. Eighty per cent of the research company's income derived from divisional projects and 20 per cent from general research support. These resources were divided among a smaller number of projects, about 25 per annum, a figure which may in the future be reduced to 10 a year. Eight largely separate multidisciplinary project teams, irrespective of divisional funding support, covered each of the core product/technology areas judged to be central to the future of the supported businesses.[23] From 1992 research costs were charged to all divisions throughout the world according to sales in product sectors supported by the research.

Research up to clinical evaluations was centralized; development including manufacturing technology and marketing was a matter for the divisions. Both Richards and Ioptex, acquired in the second half of the 1980s, owned integrated R & D groups which were retained but the research components were coordinated through budgeting. Research and development in both companies was complementary with Smith & Nephew's established interests. Ioptex's technology, particularly optical technology, was similar to the polymer chemistry of films and adhesive on which Smith & Nephew had worked for many years. Richards' orthopaedic implants were influenced by the biology and coatings of metals, a strength of Gilston Park.[24] Bones need weight on them to prevent wastage. Metal replacements remove that weight and so resorb away bone; the cells do not replace. Materials are needed that do not produce that effect.

As Chapter 9 showed, long before the 1980s Smith & Nephew were moving away from licensing technology, as a general policy, to in-house development exemplified by polymer science applied to wound healing in OpSite. Polymer science also was central to synthetic lightweight splint casting, Crystona. The clinical research group continued to develop links with key centres of international repute. Studies were undertaken in four during 1989: Cardiff (Hughes, Intrasite Cavity Dressing), Edinburgh (Ruckley, Allevyn), Aberdeen (Wardlaw, orthopaedics) and Wisconsin (Maki, OpSite IV 3000).

From 1975 onwards, research funding increasingly came from health care at Hull. The success of OpSite, and the considerable revenues produced, together with the development of the Hull Technical Centre which collaborated closely with Smith & Nephew Research, were responsible. Hence the chief projects of this later period were all in the health care area. The £600 000 Technical Centre, opened in 1981, was intended to build a bridge between the research division at Gilston Park and the production facilities at Hull. New products and processes were developed up to the semi-production stage. In 1986 the Technical Centre staff in engineering, electronics, new product development, analytical chemistry and bacteriology came together under the same roof for the first time.[25]

In the shift towards successful health care research the Hydron project was seminal in two ways. To cope with the new work, polymer chemists were employed for the first time, associating with and being influenced by synthetic organic chemists, to their mutual advantage. The other effect was to direct attention to the construction of special polymers with the correct properties for the desired medical end-use. OpSite, Haemocol and later, polymethanes, demonstrated the pay-offs from this approach. Departments which previously had relied on standard bought-in polymers and their own ingenuity in design to develop medical devices now could employ in-house polymers, a combination that proved very fertile[26] (Table 12.4).

Table 12.4   Polymer technology at SNR, 1980–87

Date	Event	Significance
1980	Polymer blends patent	Extension of melt technology to films
1980	No 8 adhesive patent	First acrylate *medical* adhesive
1981	Allevyn patent	First foam composite dressing
1981	Curable adhesive patent	Entry into radiation curing technology
1981	NODS patent	Significant polymer drug delivery system
1982	OpSite 3000 patent	First hydrophilic polyurethane product
1985	3D coverstock patent	Further extension of polymer melt technology
1986	Transdermal delivery patent	Further extension of drug delivery from polymers
1987	Powder-free glove patent	First patent on polymer coated latex

Note: Not an exhaustive list – only significant jumps in polymer technology shown.

Source: J Fennimore, Smith & Nephew Research.

New Splinting Products

Splints were an early beneficiary of this approach. Smith & Nephew added substrate, the gauze or knitted bandage on to which polymer resin was impregnated, and fibreglass, to create Crystona. The resulting product was lighter, more robust than plaster of Paris and also waterproof; this was useful when the patient had to walk home long distances as in South Africa, but was two to three times more expensive than plaster.

Polyurethane quickly emerged as the basis for splints with greatest future potential. As a first step towards their development, an existing product, 'Dynacast', was obtained by licence from an American aerospace company, Hexcel Corporation, from whom Smith & Nephew also acquired urethane technology. The research company improved Dynacast in the mid-1980s, as a result of experience with hydrophilic polyurethenes (existing products were based on hydrophobic or conventional polyurethanes, see Chapter 9). Ultimately, an advanced form of the splint was produced and marketed under the name of Dynacast Extra in 1988, as a collaborative venture between Research and the Hull Technical Centre, which was followed by an additional development called Dynacast Pro. This used a material which generated less dust than fibre glass and offered excellent X-ray translucency, among other improved properties. About one-seventh of turnover and operating profits in 1989 came from orthopaedic casting and support, mainly in-house developments or long-established products.

New Wound Healing Products

A similar proportion was accounted for by wound management. Wound healing was the area of most recent in-house innovation. The success of OpSite demonstrated the correctness of the moist-wound healing approach (see Chapter 6). An optimum wound healing system must be biocompatible, adhere well using a 'hypo-allergenic' adhesive (with a low tendency to produce allergic reactions to the skin), provide a bacterial barrier to prevent infection, maintain a moist environment, and permit the dispersion of large amounts of wound exudate. A series of advanced wound dressings were developed conforming with these criteria during the 1980s (again in close collaboration with Hull). Among products marketed or about to be marketed in this area at the beginning of the 1990s were Transite and Transigen, film dressings with the capacity to release bulk fluid but prevent drying out, and Allevyn, a composite non-adherent three-layer dressing involving films, foam and a polyurethane net surface. Layer 1 is OpSite, to let moisture through, layer 3 is polymer net (non-stick) next to the skin so that the newly formed tissue is not torn off when the dressing is removed. In the middle is polyurethene foam for absorbency. In addition there was OpSite IV 3000, a highly permeable film dressing designed to protect I.V. catheter sites over long periods. The skin allows water vapour to permeate at a rate of about 2000 gms per m^2 over 24 hours. Original OpSite achieved 1500. OpSite IV 3000 is more permeable than skin at 3000 gms per m^2. Allevyn cavity wound dressings, like tea bags in shape, remove the necessity for daily insertion and removal of cotton wool strips. They were developed from Net 909 technology. The Net 909 cover allows fluid to pass one way but not the other. Research on Allevyn in the early to mid-1980s culminated in a product launch in the UK at the end of the decade. All these products are highly innovative, combining ingenuity in device design with novel high water-uptake polyurethanes developed at Smith & Nephew Research.

Net 9000 lightweight coverstock was introduced in 1988 and sold well especially in Japan. The new Airstrip film with improved performance and viral barrier properties was added to Elastoplast first aid dressings.

Pharmaceuticals and eye care products including the intraocular lens business (and Flamazine) accounted for 8–9 per cent of 1989 turnover and sales. Glauline, a beta-blocking drug used for the treatment of Glaucoma, was introduced to UK ophthamologists in 1986,[27] but was subsequently withdrawn. NODS (new ophthalmic delivery system) allows the administration of drugs through the eye via a small soluble polymeric 'matchstick'. Pharmaceuticals were a small proportion of the UK market and new products were licensed from other companies. One of the most recent examples is the incontinence treatment, Ditropan. A 'Derma-alliance', with pharmaceutical companies in Scandinavia, Germany, France and Spain, to search for dermatology product licenses primarily outside Europe, promised expansion in this niche market during the 1990s. In late 1993 Smith & Nephew sold the ophthalmic side of the business to the French company, Chauvin. The remaining two products, Flamazine and Ditropan, were transferred to Smith & Nephew in Hull.

The Future

In April 1991 Smith & Nephew announced the move of its 200 research scientists from Gilston Park to a new science park next to the University of York campus. The aim was to encourage the cross-fertilization of ideas; Smith & Nephew researchers were to have the same senior common room rights as the University teaching staff. Not only had York achieved top university finance committee ratings in chemistry and biology but probably the largest health economics unit in the world was located there. An added advantage was that funds released from the sale of Gilston Park could be employed to provide the most modern equipment for the new leased laboratories.

Future development was based on five-year-ahead R & D planning. No fundamental innovations were projected in the implants sector, though improvements to reduce post-surgery complications were planned. However, the lack of innovation in this area may be addressed by the 1994 collaboration agreement with Advanced Tissue Sciences of California which could improve cartilage surgery through the use of cell-based therapies to repair and resurface damaged joints. Similarly in wound healing a satisfactory portfolio had been built up that would grow faster than the market over the next five years, so that development, rather than research, was needed in that range as well. Longer-term sustained growth required new products in areas where Smith & Nephew possessed expertise. Two areas in particular were under consideration in 1992, pain control and dermatology. Changing attitudes to pain, exemplified by the hospice movement and by the pro-active role increasingly taken by anaesthetists, could be summarized by a concern to enhance the quality of life. One such enhancement is the employment of adhesive technology to administer a local anaesthetic for children, with a patch before an incision.

In the field of dermatology, flaking and itchy skins are widespread yet palliative treatment is expensive and not very effective. An early example of Smith & Nephew's new concerns here is the result of a three-year research programme on surgeons' gloves. Surgeons' gloves must have absolute sensitivity, they must be puncture-proof to avoid any possible transmission of AIDS and, in some uses, such as orthopaedics, they must be extremely tough. Traditionally these gloves have powder inside them for, before operating, surgeons dip their hands in liquid to kill bacteria. Without powder, inserting wet hands into latex gloves is difficult. Should some of this powder find its way out of the glove into the patient's body, lesions can be caused. The problem then is to find a material that will slip easily without talc. Some surgeons anyway are allergic to latex (2–10 per cent of the population as a whole suffer in this way). An experimental product now has polyurethane coating on the inside, thereby avoiding the need for powder. This market is not growing significantly; gains are made by creating a new product that displaces the old.

ORGANIZATION, MANAGEMENT AND PERSONNEL

In addition to a strong product range based on detailed R & D and an international spread of markets, sustained company growth was rooted in the work of highly motivated employees. A health care business begins with an advantage, for employees find identification with the company goals far easier than in industries whose products are less central to well-being. During the late 1970s Joe King, a former member of the Trades Union Congress General Council, advised Smith & Nephew on industrial relations.[29] One consequence of his advice was the introduction of a more open style of management during the 1980s. In Hull John Robinson talked to the whole workforce at least four times a year about all and any matters of concern to them. The company shifted from traditional paternalism to a more participative style. Instead of gold watches, long-standing employees were awarded shares in the business. Fifty-five per cent of employees were members of savings-related share option schemes by the beginning of 1988. For every two shares applied for under this scheme the board allocated a third. In addition £250 000 of shares were handed to Smith & Nephew long-serving employees in 1985.[30]

Employees as shareholders expressed their views of company policy and performance based on their work experience. The improved flow of information to top management enhanced company operations. Videos and the company newspaper kept the workforce informed and regular contact was maintained with former employees.[31]

'Just in time management' mixed traditional management and workforce roles. Graded dining rooms were phased out in the 1980s. The, by British standards, egalitarian culture of Smith & Nephew was encouraged by the diffusion of Southalls' single-status pension scheme (Chapter 5) throughout the organization after the merger. An objective reminder of the rewards for merit in the 1980s was that the chief executive had begun working for the business as a mill shift foreman.

Personnel issues in the US contrasted with those in Britain. Lacking a class system, the effort required to reach a one-status workforce was much less. But America had evolved its own barrier of highly bureaucratic, legally regulated industrial relations. Positive discrimination could create resentment among non-beneficiary groups even though particular promotions or appointments were made solely on merit.

Top management had always gained 10 to 30 years of senior executive experience within the company, contributing to a coherent management culture. Eric Kinder took over as chief executive in 1982, succeeding Kenneth Bradshaw. Kinder joined the company in 1957 as a shift manager at the Victoria Works, Rawtenstall. He eventually followed Bradshaw as managing director of the Textile Division. His successor, John Robinson, trained as a chemical engineer, worked for ICI and came to Smith & Nephew from a spring company, after consultancy. A considerable proportion of top managers of Smith & Nephew originated outside the company but a strong training programme, taking 50 graduates in science or marketing each year in the UK, may reduce the number in the future.[32]

The board of Smith & Nephew was geographically structured for operating – one director for each area. A North American business development group was formed in 1987 in recognition of the new importance of that market to the company. This sub-group of the management executive met bi-monthly in North America with a view to monitoring progress, ensuring exploitation of intercompany synergies and developing regional strategy. Similar geographical groupings were established the following year covering the other regions of the company's activities.

An immovable corporate objective which all divisions and subsidiaries were obliged to achieve was to compound pre-tax profits at (Kemp's) 20 per cent per annum.[33] During the 1980s and later, cash was sufficiently tight that the budgets and operating plans for new developments had to be agreed for the whole group. Innovatory products were so expensive by the beginning of the 1990s that they could not be undertaken by semi-autonomous divisions as they were ten years earlier. Launches were synchronized in a number of geographical markets, as was the new hip implant (RMHS), marketed simultaneously in North America and Europe.

The annual budget embodying corporate strategy was monitored by monthly reports of sales and forecasts. In 1992 the future target rate of growth of core business was 10 per cent per annum real growth. Actual performance of about 9 per cent a year nominal growth was divided between 3 per cent price increases and 6 per cent volume expansion. Some considerable acceleration was yet to come, but in comparison with probable real core growth of perhaps zero with the product mix at the beginning of the decade, the most rapid acceleration had already occurred. The difference was in the switch from growth by acquisition to organic expansion that had been accomplished during the 1980s.

REGULATION AND THE ENVIRONMENT

Sales revenues are grounded in legal rights to dispose of products. Where innovatory ideas are embodied in devices, exclusive rights are not always well-defined. Establishing property rights in products developed by Smith & Nephew, both by patenting and by satisfying state regulatory requirements, absorbed a significant and increasing volume of corporate resources. Rising public concern with the right not to consume various chemicals as by-products of other activities towards the end of the 1980s encouraged Smith & Nephew to regulate its own activities to conform with these wishes.

Product registration added to fixed costs and European directives on product specification and testing occupied more management time. The trade mark portfolio of the group included 4 500 devices at the beginning of 1990. One hundred and thirty-six applications werè granted in 1989. Smith & Nephew's patent portfolio was enhanced by 56 applications by the research company in 1989 and 21 from other group companies. Defence of patents also was an interest, particularly to protect against the infringement of OpSite. Patents were exploited by licensing as well as by working; 3M and Johnson & Johnson were permitted to operate under the OpSite patent in the US and NODS was licensed to Alcon.[34] By 1989 these activities were sufficiently important for a central clinical research and regulatory affairs unit to be established.

Responding to environmental pressure groups, in early 1989 Smith & Nephew abandoned chlorine bleached pulp for any of its products (Krikler 1991, p. 20). Later the company launched the first environmentally friendly press-on sanitary towel, Ecosense. Ecosense was 97 per cent biodegradable (the remaining 3 per cent was due to an adhesive strip) and half of the constituent materials were recycled. To maintain company awareness of environmental issues, Smith & Nephew's Information Department publish for internal circulation a monthly bulletin 'Green Issues' with abstracts of publications which may be relevant to any of Smith & Nephew's products.

Publicity gained by the Women's Environmental Network and by one of their books,[35] together with an ITV *World in Action* programme, precipitated the 'greening' of Smith & Nephew. The book and the programme claimed that some tampons and sanitary towels contained a cancer-promoting toxic chemical, dioxin. Bleaching wood pulp with chlorine to make soft-tissue products resulted in the production of a variety of highly toxic chemicals including dioxin, they claimed. These chemicals eventually found their way into the seas and rivers, harming birds and fish. In the products themselves tiny concentrations of these chemicals remained. Disposable nappies had earlier been subjected to a similar attack and some sanitary products contained four times as much dioxin. An independent Rechem laboratory test found Smith & Nephew's Dr White's sanitary towel contained 400 parts of dioxin per trillion (sic). The *World in Action* programme suggested that use of such products could cause a harmful build-up of toxins, but the safety level was generally placed nearer 5 000 parts per trillion. Products absolutely free of dioxins are impossible because of the continuous cycle of pollution from factories and cars to the sea and soil. Lil-lets and Dr White's Contour tampons were anyway manufactured without chlorine gas and so did not acquire dioxin from the production process.[36]

In North America, Smith & Nephew undertook an environmental audit of all operations during 1991, and, in Europe as well, senior personnel were assigned responsibility for environmental issues. US legal regulation had unintended consequences in this as in other areas. While Smith & Nephew at the time of writing has an explicit European environmental policy, the possibility of legal action based on any written group policy deters a formal extension to the US.

CONCLUSION

At the beginning of the 1990s Smith & Nephew had established a strong position in the growing and competitive world health care industry. The strategy that had proved so successful was to maintain close links with medical practitioners and a strong marketing thrust, together with tight cost controls and highly innovative research in sectors where health care organizations were anxious to bring down their costs and improve their effectiveness.

Geographically the strategy required a marked presence in the American market, as the largest and most sophisticated health care market in the world. Product strategy entailed a closer focus than hitherto on health care. Within this field Smith & Nephew had already achieved high market shares in established lines. Rapid growth therefore needed a jump into new products, such as artificial hips, the demand for which burgeoned from an affluent and ageing population.

Having maintained an innovative research department over the preceding generation, Smith & Nephew found little difficulty in identifying and integrating the important advances made by acquired companies. Acquisition strategy was only to buy businesses with potential that Smith & Nephew could develop. With Richards this approach clearly paid off, for the subsidiary's 30 per cent per annum growth rate was attained only after joining Smith & Nephew. Thanks to the restructuring of the 1980s, rapid organic growth could be based on two product areas, wound care and orthopaedics. Consumer products remained in effect a separate business which could not be further developed because of rights possessed by Beiersdorf and Johnson & Johnson. But consumer products provided cash for development in the medical field.

Through its constituent businesses Smith & Nephew's history stretches back to the industrial revolution. Over many generations a great number of formerly independent enterprises have voluntarily been welded into an organization that has been enabled to accomplish far more than each could have achieved separately. This pattern links Lancashire textile mills of the eighteenth century, a Birmingham pharmacy of the early nineteenth and T.J. Smith's Hull shop of the mid-nineteenth century with Tennessee orthopaedics and Californian intraocular lens manufacturers. Smith & Nephew have shown that this distinctive corporate form, partly dictated by British economic history, clearly works well. It did so, however, only because the right decisons were made at crucial moments in company history. The first was H.N. Smith's move into surgical dressings and abandonment of cod liver oil at the beginning of the twentieth century. Acquisition and marketing of branded lines during the 1930s was the second. The development of corporate research marked the third big leap in Smith & Nephew's history. During the 1950s and 1960s this research potential, acquired with Herts, was not fully utilized while so much of the company's energies were absorbed by textiles. But ultimately research in materials, especially plastics, paid off with valuable new dressings: Net 909, OpSite, Alleyvn and many other contributions should be seen as the outcome of a common research programme. By the 1970s Smith & Nephew was beginning to consolidate its position as a business large enough to generate its own new technology. During the 1980s concentration of product activity in wound care and orthopaedics ensured that Smith

& Nephew flourished as one of the few world players in the health care business.

T.J. and H.N. Smith would not recognize all the science and technology employed by the company that now bears their name but we may imagine they would be delighted that Smith & Nephew is employing for the improvement of health so many of the subjects in which they took a purely intellectual interest. Equally we might expect they would be gratified to know that their concern for the well-being of the wider society in which their business operated, that prompted them to give so much of their time to improving health and education in Hull and elsewhere, was still maintained by the Smith & Nephew Foundation's charitable activities across the world.

NOTES

1. 'Winners and Losers: MT250', *Management Today*, June 1991, pp. 32–42. Profitability was measured by net profit as a percentage of investment among the 250 largest publicly quoted industrial and commercial companies measured by market capitalization of equity on 2 April 1991. Smith & Nephew has consistently been a high performer in intercompany comparisons. *Management Today* identified the company as one of Britain's eight best-managed firms in 1986. 'Britain's Best Eight', *Management Today*, April 1986, pp. 58–9.
2. Marris's model of the growth of the firm corresponds very closely with Smith & Nephew's growth pattern in the 1980s (Marris 1964).
3. 'Flamazine used in Beirut', *Smith & Nephew Reporter*, October 1982, July/August 1982.
4. 'Experts learn from Bradford Disaster', *Smith & Nephew Reporter*, January 1986. A one-day conference on accident and emergency burns – lessons of the Bradford disaster – was organized by the Royal Society of Medicine at Bradford Town Hall and sponsored by Smith & Nephew. *Bradford Star*, 3 October 1985.
5. *Smith & Nephew Reporter*, April 1981.
6. *Smith & Nephew Reporter*, May 1982.
7. *Smith & Nephew Reporter*, July/August 1982.
8. *Smith & Nephew Reporter*, April 1991, p. 5.
9. *Smith & Nephew Reporter*, September 1982.
10. 'Pharmacy Markets under Attack', *Chemist & Druggist*, 11 March 1989, p. 386.
11. Smith & Nephew has never considered making a hostile bid, on the grounds that in any company worth acquiring, management is an essential asset, with distinctive knowledge of markets and products.
12. 'New Plant Opens as Demand for Latex Gloves Burgeons', *Canadian Medical Association Journal*, vol. 138, June 1988.
13. *Smith & Nephew Source*, Spring 1989, p. 4.
14. 'Group gains Richards in biggest ever buy', *Smith & Nephew Reporter*, November/December 1986.
15. Smith & Nephew Press Release 18 May 1988, 'Smith & Nephew Subsidiary in Russian Joint Venture'; also C. Cookson, 'The Door Starts to Swing Open', *Financial Times*, 19 May 1988; J. Randall, 'US Physicians Adopt Soviet Bone Technique', *Washington Post Health*, 1 March 1988; 'Doctors Stretch Dwarf an Amazing 12 Inches', *The National Enquirer*, 12 June 1988; 'S and N in an Historic New Medical Venture', *Burnley Express*, 1 July 1988.
16. The three biggest players were Alcon (Nestlé), Iolab (Johnson & Johnson) and Allergan.

17. Although readers of Charles Dickens's *Pickwick Papers* might see in the fictional case of Bardell v. Pickwick some parallels with the British legal system of the 1820s and 1830s.
18. *Smith & Nephew Press Release*, 14 May 1990.
19. British Tissues held around 20 per cent of the UK market for disposable paper products and generated pre-tax profits of £12.8m on revenues of £109m in 1988. British Tissues turned out a profitable investment for Smith & Nephew for the 20 years when the group held some of its shares. It also proved so profitable for the joint owner, the Finnish conglomerate Nokia, that the then chairman Kenneth Kemp was appointed a Commander of the Order of the Lion of Finland by the President of the Republic of Finland in recognition of Smith & Nephew's support for the Finnish economy.
20. *Smith & Nephew Press Release*, 12 June 1990. Less than 10 per cent of Watson-Marlowe sales were for medical applications.
21. *Smith & Nephew Reporter*, June/July 1985.
22. Annual reports on employees' working conditions were deposited with the UK Department of Trade and Industry.
23. Smith & Nephew Research Ltd, *Budget Proposals 1990*, p. 1.
24. A chemical treatment for osteo-arthritis is not likely to be available over next 10–15 years.
25. *Smith & Nephew Reporter*, April 1981; September/October 1986.
26. J. Howes, 'Research and Development at Gilston Park', unpublished ms, 1991.
27. Beta-blockers, originally developed by James Black and colleagues at ICI Pharmaceuticals, antagonize the actions of adrenaline and sympathetic nerve stimulation at Ahlquist's beta-receptors which, among other things, control the rate and force of cardiac contraction.
28. The contribution of employee loyalty to Smith & Nephew's performance suggests that what according to one commmentator is the secret of Japan's postwar economic success is not unique to Japan, though it may be most abundant there. See Morishima (1982).
29. King represented the National Union of Textile and Allied Workers on the Council for 1972–73.
30. Over 20 years' service was rewarded by £400, over 30 by £600–700. *Smith & Nephew Reporter*, November/December 1985.
31. The Hull pensioners' club has proved a useful source of oral history of the company.
32. A full-time management trainer and recruiter was employed, and trainees were appraised every six months for the first three years.
33. 'Smith & Nephew's Speciality', *Management Today*, April 1986, p. 64.
34. Smith & Nephew Research op. cit., note 23.
35. *The Sanitary Protection Scandal*, by Alison Costello, Bernadette Vallely and Josa Young.
36. B. Coleman, 'The Right to Know', *Guardian*, 28 February 1989.

A chronology of Smith & Nephew

1820   Thomas Southall, chemist and druggist, opened his Birmingham shop.

1856   Thomas James Smith opened a pharmaceutical chemist shop in Hull, England.

1860   T.J. Smith visited Norway to buy refined cod liver oil.

1861   Thomas Barclay joined Southall's as a commercial traveller.

1880   Southalls patented the first disposable sanitary towel.

1896   Horatio Nelson Smith, the founder's nephew, entered into partnership with his uncle and the firm became known as T.J. Smith & Nephew.

1898   Southall Bros & Barclay went public with an issued capital of £150 000.

1906   First overseas contracts were secured with Canadian Hospital Authorities for Smith & Nephew.

1907   T.J. Smith & Nephew became a limited company with paid-up capital of £207.

1912   SASHENA Limited, manufacturers of sanitary towels, was purchased by Smith & Nephew.

1914/   Expansion during the war years increased Smith & Nephew staff
1918   numbers from 50 to over 1 200.

1921   The Canadian branch was established as a separate company of Smith & Nephew.

1928   The development of Elastoplast began.

        Lilia Limited was formed (the SASHENA name dropped).

1930   Plaster of Paris bandages were launched (Gypsona).

1935   Southalls sold their chemist and druggist business to Sangars Ltd.

1937   Smith & Nephew Associated Companies Limited launched as a public company.

1943   S.N. Steen joined Arthur Berton Ltd.

1950   Smith & Nephew formed a company in Australia to be followed three years later by a concern in New Zealand.

1951   Herts Pharmaceuticals Limited, who sold preparations under the Nivea brand, acquired by Smith & Nephew.

1952   Smith & Nephew Research Limited (formed out of Herts Pharmaceuticals Limited).

1953   Glen Mills at Colne and Rawtenstall acquired by Smith & Nephew.

1954   An agreement was made with Dr Carl Hahn to produce Lil-lets in Britain on his machines.

1955   A joint selling company was formed between Lilia Limited (a Smith & Nephew subsidiary) and Arthur Berton Limited, the manufacturers of Dr White's – now to be known as Lilia-White (Sales) Limited.

1956   Smith & Nephew Pharmaceuticals Limited formed.

1957   Smith & Nephew Plastics formed.

1958   Southalls (Birmingham) Limited and Arthur Berton Limited both acquired. These new acquisitions were merged with the existing Lilia business and Lilia-White (Sales) Limited became the largest supplier in the sanitary protection market in the UK.

1962   No. 2 Temple Place was purchased as the Group headquarters.

         Smith & Nephew Scandinavia founded with a base near Copenhagen, Denmark.

1963   In Spain, Smith & Nephew Iberica S.A. was formed in partnership with the company of Dr Pedro Junyent, to manufacture plaster of paris and adhesive bandages.

1966   The Airstrip variant of Elastoplast was launched.

1968   Smith & Nephew successfully fought off a hostile take-over bid from Unilever.

1970   Acquisition of control (55 per cent) of Gala Cosmetics Group and subsequent merger with Nivea business.

1971   Smith & Nephew subsidiary set up in Norway.

1973   Flamazine, a new treatment for burns, was successfully launched.

1974   The Smith & Nephew Foundation was established to become the central coordinator for all Smith & Nephew charitable work.

1977   International interests, including UK exports were responsible for over half of the group's profits.

Watson-Marlow Limited (UK), a manufacturer of medical pumps, joined the group.

1978   Smith & Nephew purchased a 40 per cent share in Productos Higienicos Panamericanos S.A. de C.V. (Mexico), a sanitary protection and diaper producer.

New factories were opened in Thailand and Malaysia.

1979   Smith & Nephew subsidiaries set up in Stockholm and Gothenburg, Sweden.

1980   Laboratoires Fisch S.A. of France became a wholly owned subsidiary.

Smith & Nephew doubled its interest in British Tissues to 50 per cent.

1981   Smith & Nephew establish companies in West Germany and Holland.

Gala Cosmetics sold.

Avon Medical Company Limited acquired.

1984   Smith & Nephew Iberica S.A. in Spain became a wholly owned subsidiary.

1985   A joint venture was set up in Germany with B. Braun GmbH to distribute medical health care products in Germany.

Smith & Nephew expanded within the US, with the purchase of Affiliated Hospital Products Inc. and 3 Sigma Inc.

1986   Purchased Hexcel Medical Corporations (US) cold water cast business.

Richards Medical Company is purchased, leaders in many orthopaedic fields. The largest single acquisition to date – £201m. With this acquisition Smith & Nephew became a major force in the US medical market.

1987   Alberto Fenandez S.A. joined the group. A leading Spanish manufacturer of condoms and surgeons' latex gloves.

Two more companies in the US are purchased. Donjoy Inc., specializing in the prevention and treatment of sports injuries, and Sigma Inc., an important manufacturer of peristaltic infusion pumps.

Field Group Chemicals Pty Ltd acquired in Australia, a company involved in soluble and insoluble x-ray contrast media.

Acquisitions in France of Cogemo S.A., maufacturers of continuous passive motion machines, and Sanortho S.A., a leading manufacturer of general orthopaedic implants.

Over £100m profit threshold passed (£109.6m).

1988   Purchased the Albion Group Limited, manufacturers of the Simple range of 'additive-free' toiletries.

A further joint venture with B. Braun Melsungen was begun, this time in Switzerland.

The remaining 50 per cent of Smith & Nephew Orbel S.p.A., Italy was purchased.

United Medical Division of Pfizer Hospital Products Inc. in Florida was acquired, manufacturers of special surgical dressings.

Dyonics Inc. acquired CeCorp Inc. Oklahoma, a company which designs and manufactures their video systems.

1989   In January Ioptex Research Inc., a leading US manufacturer of replacement human eye lenses for the treatment of cataracts, was acquired.

1990   Watson Marlowe, supplier of peristaltic pumping and metering products, sold.

Damages awarded by Superior Court of California to Polteco against Smith & Nephew Richards.

1992   Polteco out of court settlement reached.

Nivea trade mark sold to Beiersdorf. Smith & Nephew would continue to sell and distribute the Nivea range in existing markets.

1993   Smith & Nephew withdraws from cotton spinning and denim weaving.

Smith & Nephew sells the ophthalmic side of its UK-based pharmaceutical business to the French company, Chauvin.

1994   Loptex sold to Allergan.

Collaboration agreement with Advanced Tissue Sciences to improve cartilage surgery.

Bibliography

This bibliography covers sources other than company reports, local newspapers, archive material and unpublished data, references to which will be found in the notes following each individual chapter.

Andreopoulos, S. (1975), *National Health Insurance*, New York: J. Wiley.

Apple, D.J., M.C. Kincaid, N. Mamlis and R.J. Olson (1989), *Intraocular Lenses; Evolution, Designs, Complications and Pathology*, Baltimore: Williams & Wilkins.

Armstrong, J. (1987), 'The Role of Coastal Shipping in UK Transport: An Estimate of Comparative Traffic Movements in 1910', *Journal of Transport History*, 8.

Association of British Chemical Manufacturers (1949), *Report on the Chemical Industry*.

Baly, M.E. (1986), *Florence Nightingale and the Nursing Legacy*, London: Croom Helm.

Barnett, C. (1986), *The Audit of War*, London: Macmillan.

Bartrip, P.W.J. (1985), 'The Rise and Decline of Workmen's Compensation' in P. Weindling (ed.), *The Social History of Occupational Health*, London: Croom Helm.

Bartrip, P.W.J. (1990), *Mirror of Medicine: A History of the British Medical Journal*, Oxford: Oxford University Press.

Bavin, E.M. (1965), 'Smith & Nephew Research Ltd, Gilston Park', *Chemistry and Industry*, 15 May, pp. 820–25.

Bellamy, J. (1966), 'Some Aspects of the Economy in Hull in the Nineteenth Century with Special Reference to Business History', University of Hull PhD thesis.

Bellamy, J. (1968), *One Hundred Years of Pharmacy in Hull*, Hull: Hull Pharmaceutical Society.

Bellamy, J. (1971), *The Trade and Shipping of Nineteenth Century Hull*, East Yorkshire Local History Society.

Berridge, V. and G. Edwards (1987), *Opium and the People: Opiate Use in Nineteenth Century England*, New Haven and London: Yale University Press.

Bishop, W.J. (1959), *A History of Surgical Dressings*, Chesterfield: Robinson & Sons.

Bishop, W.J. (1960), *The Early History of Surgery*, London: Robert Hale.

Bliss, M. (1982), *The Discovery of Insulin*, Basingstoke: Macmillan.

Bowker, B. (1928), *Lancashire Under the Hammer*, London: Hogarth Press.

Braithwaite, W.J. (1957), *Lloyd George's Ambulance Wagon*, London: Methuen.

Brown, P.S. (1980), 'Providers of Medical Treatment in Mid-Nineteenth Century Bristol', *Medical History*, 24.

Bryder, L. (1990), *Tuberculosis and the State*, Oxford: Oxford University Press.

Bull, J.P., J.R. Squire and E. Topley (1948), 'Experiments with Occlusive Dressings of a New Plastic', *The Lancet*, 7 August, pp. 213–5.

Burroughs Wellcome (1980), *One Hundred Years Wellcome 1880–1980*, London.

Caldwell, M. (1988), *The Last Crusade: The War on Consumption 1862–1954*, New York: Athenum.

Carr, W.I. Sons & Co. (1962), *Smith & Nephew; An Analytical Report*, February.

Cartwright, F.F. (1972), *A Social History of Medicine*, London: Longman.

Chandler, A. (1990), *Scale and Scope: The Dynamics of Industrial Capitalism*, Cambridge, Mass.: Belknap.

Channon, F. (1973), *The Strategy and Structure of British Enterprise*, London: Macmillan.

Chapman, S. (1973), *Jesse Boot of Boots the Chemist*, London: Hodder & Stoughton.

Checkland, S.G. (1965), *The Rise of Industrial Society in England 1815–1885*, London: London.

Coleman, D.C. (1973), 'Gentlemen and Players', *Economic History Review*, 26.

Coleman, D.C. (1980), *Courtaulds: An Economic and Social History. Vol. III, Crisis and Change 1940–1965*, Oxford: The Clarendon Press.

Cook, E. (1913), *The Life of Florence Nightingale*, London: Macmillan.

Cooper, M.H. (1966), *Prices and Profits in the Pharmaceutical Industry*, London: Pergamon Press.

Corley, T.A.B. (1987), 'Interactions between the British and American patent medicine industries 1708–1914', *Business and Economic History*, 16.

Crafts, N.F.R. (1991), 'Economic Growth' in N.F.R. Crafts and N. Woodward (eds), *The British Economy Since 1945*, Oxford: Clarendon Press.

Cripps, E. (1927), *Plough Court: The Story of a Notable Pharmacy 1715–1927*, London: Allen & Hanbury.

Culyer, A.J. (1976), *Need and the National Health Service*, London: Martin Robertson.

Culyer, A.J., A. Maynard and J. Posnett (eds) (1990), *Competition in Health Care: Reforming the NHS*, London: Macmillan.

Dagger, Stanley H. (1971), 'News about Phyllis', *Smith & Nephew Reporter*, August.

Davenport-Hines, R.P.T. and J. Slinn (1992), *Glaxo: A History to 1962*, Cambridge: Cambridge University Press.

Davies, W. (1967), *The Pharmaceutical Industry*, London: Pergamon Press.

Davis, K. (1975), *National Health Insurance: Studies in Social Economics*, Washington: Brookings Institution.

Department of Prices and Consumer Protection (1978), *Southalls (Birmingham) Ltd. Sanitary Protection and other Hygiene Products*, London: HMSO.

Dickinson, R.L. (1945), 'Tampons as Menstrual Guards', *Journal of the American Medical Association*, 128, 16 June.

Dickson Wright, A. (1931), 'The Treatment of Indolent Ulcer of the Leg', *The Lancet*, pp. 457–60.

Dickson Wright, A. (1940), 'Treatment of Varicose Veins', *British Medical Journal*, 20 April.

Dubos, R. and J. Dubos (1953), *The White Plague: Tuberculosis, Man and Society*, London: Victor Gollancz.

Eder, R. (1982), *National Health and the Medical Profession in Britain 1913–1939*, New York: Garland.

Elliott, I.H.Z. (1964), *A Short History of Surgical Dressings*, London: The Pharmaceutical Press.

Floud, R., K.W. Wachter and A. Gregory (1990), *Height, Health and History: Nutritional Status in the United Kingdom 1750–1980*, Cambridge: Cambridge University Press.

Foreman-Peck, J. (1987), 'Death on the Roads: Changing National Responses to Motor Accidents' in T.C. Barker (ed.), *The Economic and Social Effects of the Spread of Motor Vehicles*, London: Macmillan.

Gillett, E. and K.A. MacMahon (1989), *A History of Hull*, Hull: Hull University Press, 2nd edition.

Godlee, R.J. (1917), *Lord Lister*, London: Macmillan.

Grabowski, H.G. (1976), *Drug Relation and Innovation*, Washington DC: American Enterprise Institute.

Griliches, Z. (1986), 'Productivity, R & D and Basic Research at the Firm Level in the 1970s', *American Economic Review*, 76, March.

Haber, L.F. (1971), *The Chemical Industry 1900–1930: International Growth and Technological Change*, Oxford: The Clarendon Press.

Harris, R.W. (1946), *National Health Insurance in Great Britain 1911–1948*, London: Allen and Unwin.

Holloway, S.W.F. (1987), 'The Orthodox Fringe: The Origins of the Pharmaceutical Society of Great Britain', in W.F. Bynum and R. Porter (eds), *Medical Fringe and Medical Orthodoxy, 1750–1850*, London: Croom Helm.

Holloway, S.W.F. (1991), *The Royal Pharmaceutical Society of Great Britain 1841–91: A Political and Social History*, London: Pharmaceutical Press.

Jephcott, H. (1969), *The First Fifty Years*, Glaxo Ltd.

Jeremy, D.J. (1993), 'Survival Strategies in Lancashire Textiles: Bleachers' Association Ltd to Whitecroft plc 1900–1980', *Textile History*, 24, pp. 163–209.

Jewkes, J. (1946), 'Is British Industry Inefficient?', *Manchester School*, 14.

Johnson & Johnson (1979), 'A Brief History of Johnson & Johnson', unpublished.

Jones, G. (1986), *British Multinationals: Origins, Management and Performance*, Aldershot: Gower.

Kleinwort Benson (1988), *Investors' Brief*, no. 101, December.

Krikler, P. (1991), *Investment Research: Smith & Nephew*, Goldman Sachs, February.

Last, J.M. (1963), 'The Iceberg: Completing the Clinical Picture in General Practice', *The Lancet*, July, pp. 28–31.

Lawrence, J.C. and M.J. Payne (1984), *Wound Healing: User's Guide, an Update Workshop sponsored by Smith & Nephew*, London.

Lazell, H.G. (1975), *From Pills to Penicillin*, London: Heinemann.

Lazonick, W. (1986), 'The Cotton Industry' in B. Elbaum and W. Lazonick (eds), *The Decline of the British Economy*, Oxford: The Clarendon Press.

Lehmann, J. (1946), 'Para-aminosalicylic Acid in the Treatment of Tuberculosis', *The Lancet*, 252.

Le Vay, D. (1990), *The History of Orthopaedics. An Account of the Study and Practice of Orthopaedics from the Earliest Times to the Modern Era*, Carnforth, Lancs and Park Ridge, NJ: Parthenon.

Liebenau, J. (1986), 'Marketing of High Technology: Educating Physicians to Use Innovative Medicines' in R.T.P. Davenport-Hines (ed.), *Markets and Bagmen*, Cambridge: Cambridge University Press.

Liebenau, J. (1987), *Medical Science and the Medical Industry*, Baltimore: Johns Hopkins University Press.

Macfarlane, G. (1979), *Howard Florey: the Making of a Great Scientist*, Oxford: Oxford University Press.

Mansfield, E. (1980), 'Basic Research and Productivity Increase in Manufacturing', *American Economic Review*, 70, December.

Martin, D.D., F.S. Spring, T.G. Dempsey, C.L. and D.E. Seymour (1948), 'p-Aminosalicylic Acid in the Treatment of Tuberculosis', *Nature*, 161, 20 March.

Marris, R. (1964), *The Economic Theory of 'Managerial' Capitalism*, London: Macmillan.

Mass, W. and W. Lazonick (1990), 'The British Cotton Industry and International Competitive Advantage: The State of the Debate', *Business History*, 32.

Matthews, L.G. (1962), *History of Pharmacy in Britain*, Edinburgh and London: E. & S. Livingstone.

Maxwell, R.J. (1981), *Health and Wealth*, Lexington, Mass.: Lexington Books.

McCulloch, J.R. (1837), *A Statistical Account of the British Empire*, London.

McKeown, Thomas (1988), *The Origins of Human Disease*, Oxford: Blackwell.

Miall, S. (1931), *A History of the British Chemical Industry*, London: Ernest Benn.

Monopolies and Mergers Commission (1986) *Tampons: A Report on the Supply in the United Kingdom of Tampons*, Cmd 9705, London: HMSO.

Morishima, M. (1982), *Why has Japan 'Succeeded'?* Cambridge, Cambridge University Press.

Nenadic, S. (1991), 'Businessmen, the Urban Middle Classes, and the "Dominance" of Manufacturers in Nineteenth Century Britain', *Economic History Review*, 44.

Nicholas, S. (1983), 'Agency Contracts, Institutional Modes and the Transition to Foreign Direct Investment by British Manufacturing Multinationals before 1939', *Journal of Economic History*, 43, pp. 675–86.

Nicholas, S. (1991), 'The Expansion of British Multinational Companies: Testing for Managerial Failure' in J. Foreman-Peck (ed.), *New Perspectives on the Late Victorian Economy: Essays in Quantitative Economic History 1860–1914*, Cambridge: Cambridge University Press.

Orr, D.W. and J.W. Orr (1938), *Health Insurance with Medical Care; the British Experience*, New York: Macmillan.

PEP (1937), *Report on the British Health Services*, London.

Peterson, M.J. (1978), *The Medical Profession in Mid-Victorian England*, Berkeley; University of California Press.

Pettigrew, A. (1985), *The Awakening Giant: Continuity and Change in ICI*, Oxford: Blackwell.

Pollard, S. (1989), *Britain's Prime and Britain's Decline: The British Economy 1870–1914*, London: Edward Arnold.

Porteous, C. (1965), *Pill Boxes and Bandages: A Documentary Biography of the First Two Generations of Robinsons of Chesterfield 1839–1916*, Chesterfield: Robinson & Sons.

Porter, M. (1990), *The Competitive Advantage of Nations*, London: Macmillan.

Prest, A.R. and A.A. Adams (1954), *Consumers' Expenditure in the United Kingdom 1900–1919*, Cambridge; Cambridge University Press.

Reader, W.J. (1975), *Imperial Chemical Industries: A History, vol. II*, Oxford: Oxford University Press.

Reed, P. (1992), 'The British Chemical Industry and the Indigo Trade', *British Journal for the History of Science*, 25.

Reed, S. (1988), '300 Years of the Cod Liver Oil Industry', paper presented to the 1988 Spring Conference of the British Society for the History of Pharmacy.

Reekie, W.D. (1973), 'Patent Data as a Guide to Industrial Activity', *Research Policy*, 2.

Reekie, W.D. (1975), *The Economics of the Pharmaceutical Industry*, London: Macmillan.

Reekie, W.D. and M.H. Weber (1979), *Profits, Politics and Drugs*, New York: Holmes and Meier.

Richardson, H.W. (1968), 'Chemicals' in D.H. Aldcroft (ed.), *The Development of British Industry and Foreign Competition 1875–1914*, London: Allen and Unwin.

Riley, J.C. (1989), *Sickness, Recovery and Death*, London: Macmillan.

Robson, Michael (1988), 'The British Pharmaceutical Industry and the First World War' in J. Liebenau (ed.), *The Challenge of New Technology: Innovation in British Business since 1850*, Aldershot: Gower.

Rolleston, Sir Humphrey (1933), 'Some Changes in Medicine During the Last Hundred Years', *The Medical Press*, 4 January.

Rosenberg, N. (1990), 'Why do Firms do Basic Research (with Their Own Money)?', *Research Policy*, 19, April.

Rostas, L. (1948), *Comparative Productivity in British and American Industry*, Cambridge: Cambridge University Press.

Schilling, R.S.F., M. Roberts and N. Goodman (1950), 'Clinical Trial of Occlusive Plastic Dressings', *The Lancet*, 18 February, pp. 293–6.

Shearson Lehman Bros (1991), *Orthopaedic Review and 1991 Outlook*, February.

Singleton, J. (1986), 'Lancashire's Last Stand: Declining Employment in the British Cotton Industry 1950–1970', *Economic History Review*, 32, pp. 92–107.

Slinn, J. (1984), *A History of May & Baker*, Cambridge: Hobsons.

Smith, F.B. (1988), *The Retreat of Tuberculosis 1850–1950*, London: Croom Helm.

Sneader, W. (1985), *Drug Discovery: The Evolution of Modern Medicines*, Chichester and New York: J. Wiley.

Social Services Committee (1989), *Public Expenditure on Health Matters, H.C. 1988–89*, June, London: HMSO.

Southall, H. and E. Garrett (1991), 'Morbidity and Mortality among Early Nineteenth Century Engineering Workers', *Social History of Medicine*, 4.

Southall, K.H. (1957), *Wilfred F. Southall*, FHSC, privately published.

Sournia, J.-C. (1990), *A History of Alcoholism*, Oxford: Blackwell.

Spriggs, H.J. (1948), 'The Story behind Paramisal: A Research Project that Nearly Got Scrapped', *Nivea News*, May.

Stone, J.R.N. and D. Rowe (1966), *The Measurement of Consumers' Expenditure in the United Kingdom 1920–1938*, Cambridge: Cambridge University Press.

Summers, A. (1987), 'Campaigns of a Victorian Lady', *Nursing Times*, 11 March.

Temin, P. (1980), *Taking Your Medicine: Drug Regulation in the United States*, New York: Harvard University Press.

Trease, G.E. (1964), *Pharmacy in History*, London: Ballière Tindall and Cox.

Turner, E.S. (1953), *Shocking History of Advertising*, New York: Dutton.

Turner, G. (1973), *The Leyland Papers*, London: Pan.

Turner, H. (1980), *Henry Wellcome: The Man, His Collection and His Legacy*, Wellcome Trust and Heinemann.

Tweedale, G. (1990), *At the Sign of the Plough: Allen & Hanbury and the British Pharmaceutical Industry 1715–1990*, London: John Murray.

van Abbe, N.J. (1974), 'Cosmetics Today and Tomorrow', *Chemist & Druggist*, 24 August.

Waksman, S.A. (1964), *The Conquest of Tuberculosis*, Berkeley: University of California Press.

Waugh, W. (1990), *Charnley: The Man and the Hip*, New York: Springer Verlag.

Webster, C. (1984), 'Health: Historical Issues', CEPR Discussion Paper, 5.

Whiteside, N. (1987), 'Counting the Cost: Sickness and Disability among workers in an era of industrial recession 1920–1939', *Economic History Review*, 40.

Wiener, M. (1981), *English Culture and the Decline of the Industrial Spirit 1850–1980*, Cambridge: Cambridge University Press.

Wilsher, P. (1963), 'Big Name in Bandages', *Sunday Times*, City Section, 16 June.

Wilson, C. (1954), *The History of Unilever: A Study in Economic Growth and Social Change*, London: Cassell.

Young, J.H. (1961), *The Toadstool Millionaires. A Social History of Patent Medicines in America Before Federal Registration*, Princeton, NJ: Princeton University Press.

Youngson, A.J. (1978), *The Scientific Revolution in Victorian Medicine*, London, Croom Helm.

Index